ON VOIDNESS

BUDDHIST TRADITION SERIES

Edited by

ALEX WAYMAN

VOLUME 23

ON VOIDNESS

A Study on Buddhist Nihilism

FERNANDO TOLA
CARMEN DRAGONETTI

MOTILAL BANARSIDASS PUBLISHERS
PRIVATE LIMITED • DELHI

First Edition: Delhi, 1995

ISBN: 81-208-1061-9

Also available at:

MOTILAL BANARSIDASS

41 U.A. Bungalow Road, Jawahar Nagar, Delhi 110 007
120 Royapettah High Road, Mylapore, Madras 600 004
16 St. Mark's Road, Bangalore 560 001
Ashok Rajpath, Patna 800 004
Chowk, Varanasi 221 001

PRINTED IN INDIA

BY JAINENDRA PRAKASH JAIN AT SHRI JAINENDRA PRESS,
A-45 NARAINA, PHASE I, NEW DELHI 110 028
AND PUBLISHED BY NARENDRA PRAKASH JAIN FOR
MOTILAL BANARSIDASS PUBLISHERS PRIVATE LIMITED,
BUNGALOW ROAD, DELHI 110 007

To the memory of
T.R.V. Murti,
The great Indian scholar,
whose book
The Central Philosophy of Buddhism
did so much to promote
the studies on Mādhyamika Philosophy

Foreword

The translation team of F. Tola and C. Dragonetti has treated the readers to a veritable feast to the eye of Mādhyamika treatises by the celebrated Nāgārjuna. While these treatises have previously been translated by other scholars, the importance of these works justifies this publication by a team that devotes intelligent and sensitive labor to these issues.

Doubtless Tola and Dragonetti are correct in treating Nāgārjuna's 'absolute' as voidness. But this is not a nihilistic position, since for Nāgārjuna illusions 'work'. And Nāgārjuna's voidness is an abundance.

The Buddhist Tradition Series proudly presents this pile of Nāgārjuna's gems.

ALEX WAYMAN

Contents

Preface

We present, in the four chapters of this book, four fundamental texts of the Mādhyamika school of Mahāyāna Buddhism, one of them in Sanskrit and three in Tibetan, together with their English translation. Each chapter also contains a study on each of these texts. In these studies we refer to the problem of authenticity of the texts, their contents, quotations from them in other texts, their principal editions and translations etc. In the first part of the Introduction we deal with the theory of Voidness (*Śūnyatā*) and in the four remaining parts we present a special analysis of the doctrines exposed in each of these texts in relation to the thesis of Voidness. We have accompanied our translations with numerous notes in order to facilitate the comprehension of the ideas that occur in these texts. We have included a Bibliography which contains the works quoted in the book.

In relation to the title of *Buddhist Nihilism* we must explain that, even if the Mādhyamika philosophy does not affirm nothingness, anyhow its conception of reality as 'void', the emphasis it lays on universal contingency, the affirmation of the unreality of all and the analytical-abolishing method in order to reach truth, have led us to the conclusion that the Mādhyamika philosophy represents the most radical degree of philosophical nihilism. Already in Ancient India the Mādhyamika philosophy was considered by its adversaries as the expression of *sarvāpavāda* or theory of absolute negation (Sthiramati, *ad Madhyāntavibhāga* I, 2).

Introduction

AN INDIAN PHILOSOPHY OF UNIVERSAL CONTINGENCY: NĀGĀRJUNA'S SCHOOL

The Normal Experience and the Philosophical Study of the Empirical Reality

The ordinary experience reveals to us a reality composed of beings and things which present themselves as existing *in se et per se*, as compact, continuous and unitary, as permanent and as real, i.e. as being such as we perceive them.

The Mādhyamika school of Buddhism, founded by Nāgārjuna at the beginning of our era, studies the reality we perceive and reaches a conclusion regarding that reality completely different from our ordinary experience. The empirical reality is composed of beings and things absolutely contingent. In this empirical reality, in which we live there is nothing existing *in se et per se*; nothing has a being that belongs to it by own right (*svabhāva*); in this reality everything is conditioned,[1] relative,[2] dependent, contingent. Moreover everything without exception is constituted of parts. No entity exists as a whole; there are only ensembles, conglomerates of parts,[3] elements, constituting factors.[4] Besides that nothing is permanent, inalterable; everything is in a process of change, submitted to an evolution which proceeds under the sign of decay and deterioration. And, as a consequence of what precedes, there is nothing which exists truly as it manifests itself before us (substantial, compact etc.). The empirical reality, as we perceive it, is only an appearance to which nothing real corresponds, something similar to a dream, to a mirage, to an illusion created by magic.

The conditionedness, the relativity, the dependence on another, the composedness, the impermanency, in a word, the *contingency* is the true nature, the true form of being of the empirical reality; and the form under which this reality appears to us is only an unreality, an illusion. So the ordinary experience is the opposite of the conclusion to which arrives the philosophical study of the perceptible world done by the Mādhyamika school.

Two Realities: The Reality of Concealment Saṃvṛtisatya), the True Reality (Paramārthasatya)

According to what precedes, for the Mādhyamika school there are two realities:[5] on one side, an apparent, phenomenic reality, the empirical reality as it appears before us (substantial, compact etc.), and on the other side, the true form of being of the apparent reality (unsubstantial, composed etc.), which is the true reality, in the same way as the serpent, under whose image we perceive the rope in the darkness, is the apparent reality, while the rope is the true reality.

The rope is a concealing reality, the threads that compose it are the true reality in regard to the rope; but at its own turn each thread is a concealing reality in regard to the filaments that compose it, and the filaments that compose it are the true reality in regard to the thread, and so on, without finding a last substantial reality.

Speaking in general modern terms, it could be said that the world as it appears to us is the concealing reality of the Mādhyamikas and that the atoms and energy which constitute the world are, in regard to it, the true nature of the world, the true reality. The Mādhyamika would add that the atoms and energy are, at their own turn, a concealing reality in regard to the elements which compose the atoms and energy and which are the true nature of the atoms and energy, the true reality, and so on, without finding a last substantial entity.

The apparent reality, the empirical reality as it manifests itself to us is called, by the Mādhyamika school, 'envelopment reality' or 'concealment reality' (*saṃvṛtisatya*). This is an appropriate term, because the appearance under which the empirical reality is perceived by us *envelops* or *conceals* its true form of being, which is the true reality (*paramārthasatya*).

Universal Contingency. 'Svabhāvaśūnyatā' and 'Pratītyasamutpāda' as Denominations of the True Reality

The true reality (*paramārthasatya*) can be designated with the words *svabhāvaśūnyatā* and *pratītyasamutpāda*.

Svabhāvaśūnyatā means 'emptiness (= absence) of an own being'.

Pratītyasamutpāda literally means 'dependent origination', but in the area of the Mādhyamika school it can be translated by 'Universal Relativity' as Stcherbatsky rightly does.[6] Both words designate the true nature, the true way of being (conditionality, relativity, etc.) of the empirical reality—true nature that is concealed under the false appearance of the empirical reality and which is the true reality. Both words express the basic and, from all points of view, important conception of the Mādhyamika school about the empirical reality: it is only *a totality of contingent beings and things,* in which there is nothing that exists *in se et per se.*

Many Western thinkers have deduced, from the contingency of the world, the existence of a non-contingent supreme principle, God. Cf. for example Copleston in 'The Existence of God: A Debate between Bertrand Russell and Father F.C. Copleston, S.J.,' in Bertrand Russell, *Why I am not a Christian, and other Essays on Religion and Related Subjects* (London: Unwin Books, 1967), p. 139:

> Well, for clarity's sake, I'll divide the argument (for contingency) in distinct stages. First of all, I should say, we know that there are at least some beings in the world which do not contain in themselves the reason for their existence. For example, I depend on my parents, and now on the air, and on food and so on. Now, secondly, the world is simply the real or imagined totality or aggregate of individual objects, none of which contain in themselves alone the reason for their existence. There isn't any world distinct from the objects which form it, any more than the human race is something apart from the members. Therefore, I should say, since objects or events exist, and since no object of experience contains within itself the reason of its existence, this reason, the totality of objects, must have a reason external to itself. That reason must be an existent being. Well, this being is either itself the reason for its own existence, or is not. If it is, well and good. If it is not, then we must proceed further. But if we proceed to infinity in that sense, then there's no explanation of existence at all. So, I should say, in order to explain existence, we must come to a being which contains within itself the reason for its own existence, that is to say, which cannot not-exist.

Nāgārjuna's school affirms also the contingency of everything, but from such a fact does not draw the conclusion that a non-contingent supreme principle, God, exists. For him the universal contingency has had no beginning, is *anādi*, and consequently it is irrelevant to ask when, how and why did it begin. The hypothesis of a beginningless contingency has the same function as the hypothesis of a beginningless god.

The Denial of the Empirical Reality

The Mādhyamika school does not stop within the limits of the two tenets we have already mentioned, i.e. the opposition between the phenomenic reality and the true reality (which is nothing else than the true nature of the phenomenic reality), and the universal contingency; it carries on its analysis of the reality and reaches a more radical position, a 'nihilistic' position. The school denies the true existence, the existence as it appears, of the empirical reality, of all its manifestations, of all the elements that constitute it, of all the categories that manifest themselves in it, of all the characteristics which are proper to it. For Nāgārjuna's school all beings and things, contingent by their own nature, which constitute the empirical reality, are unreal non-existent.

The great majority of the stanzas of the *Madhyamakakārikās* composed by Nāgārjuna is destined to deny the real existence of the principal manifestations and categories of the empirical reality: birth and destruction, causality, time, the sensorial activity, the elements that constitute man (*dharma*), passion and its subject, action and its agent, suffering, the consequence of actions (*karman*), the reincarnations cycle (*saṃsāra*), the ego (*ātman*), Buddha, the saving truths taught by Buddha, the liberation (*mokṣa*) from the reincarnation cycle, being and not being, etc. In the same way great part of the intellectual activity of Nāgārjuna's school has an identical aim.[7]

Fundamentation of the Mādhyamika Thesis

The Mādhyamika school has to establish and demonstrate its 'nihilistic' thesis against other philosophical and religious, Buddhist and non-Buddhist schools, which adopt realistic positions. This demonstration is carried on in different ways.

The school adduces, of course, the texts that contain Buddha's teaching (*āgama*), which duly interpreted can serve as a basis for its thesis. For Buddhist schools these texts contain the truth, but only for them, and consequently cannot be adduced against the thesis of non-Buddhist people.

Besides that, the school uses reasoning, logical argumentation (*yukti*). The arguments developed by the Mādhyamika thinkers to defend their own negative conceptions and to destroy contrary thesis are contained specially in the great commentaries that accompany the works of Nāgārjuna and of the other masters that followed him. Among those commentaries it is necessary to mention the most valuable commentary of Candrakīrti on Nāgārjuna's *Madhyamakakārikās*. This commentary reveals the parallel use of Buddha's word and logic. Generally the great masters of the Mādhyamika school, like Āryadeva, Buddhapālita, Candrakīrti, Śāntideva, Prajñākaramati, faithful to the school founder, adopt the *prāsaṅgika* or *reductio ad absurdum* method,[8] they do not adduce arguments of their own invention; they limit themselves to show the contradictory and absurd consequences that derive from the thesis and arguments of the rival schools. For instance, if one of these schools affirms the real origination of beings and things, the Mādhyamika will indicate that, in that case, origination should be either out of one self or out of another or out of one self and of another or without any cause, and will show that all these alternatives are logically impossible, employing for that aim, as basic principles of his own argumentation, the adversary's own principles.

Finally, the Mādhyamika school utilizes the analysis of the empirical reality in order to get results which destroy the rival doctrines and which found its own world conception. The treatises *Hastavālanāmaprakaraṇa* (stanzas and commentary),[9] give us an example of this procedure. The author investigates the empirical reality and finds that it is composed only of entities which, on being analyzed at their turn, happen to be mere appearances which cover or conceal other entities, which happen to be also mere appearances which cover or conceal other entities and so on. This analysis reaches the conclusion that it is impossible to find something substantial, permanent and irreducible, in which one could stop and establish oneself. The thesis of the real existence of the world becomes in this way untenable and the place becomes free for the Mādhyamika conception of the illusory character of the world.

The True Nature Comes Forth as a Result of the Abolition of the Empirical Reality. Śūnyatā as a Denomination of the True Reality

As a result of this abolishing and negative process we have referred to, we have the *impression* that, where the empirical reality previously existed, a huge 'voidness', 'emptiness' is being done, is coming forth, is remaining. That 'voidness', that the abolishing analysis *seems* to leave behind itself before us, is absolutely different from the empirical reality, since in it there exist no element, no manifestation, no category, that are proper of the empirical reality and which one by one have been eliminated by the abolishing Mādhyamika dialectic. That 'voidness' is the true reality, that has manifested itself after the elimination of the false appearance which constitutes the empirical reality.

On the basis of the experience that has been described, the word *śūnyatā* (voidness) serves also to designate, as a metaphor of course, the true nature of the empirical reality or, what is the same, the true reality. From all the terms that designate the true reality, *śūnyatā* is the most commonly used and it is the one we shall employ.

The 'Voidness' Exists Previously to the Abolitive Analysis

We have said that we have the *impression* that, as a consequence of the abolishing analysis, the 'voidness', i.e. the true reality, comes forth before us. This impression is caused by the fact that the abolishing analysis is realized by the discursive reason, which in its analysis and elimination of all the elements, factors, manifestations, categories, etc., of the empirical reality must proceed gradually; and so in our minds the idea is formed that the 'voidness', the true reality, *is being created* step by step. This impression does not correspond to the truth, because the 'voidness' *has been, is,* and *will be* always there, independently from our analysis, previously to it, although it has not been perceived.

Using the comparison of the modern conception of world already referred to, we could say that the atoms and energy exist previously to the experiment that reveals them.

The true reality, the 'voidness', extreme end to which the abolishing analysis cannot reach, can only be grasped *tota et simul*, in its total and absolute integrity, only in an act of intuitive yogic knowledge, which is reserved to the great *buddhas*. The contingency realized in its extreme point reveals to us the voidness in its extreme form.

The Doctrine of Universal Sameness (Samatā)

A well known stanza (*kārikā*) of Nāgārjuna (*Madhyamaka-kārikās* XXV, 19 and also 20) and its commentary, equally well known, by Candrakīrti, express that there is no difference between the *saṃsāra*, the empirical reality, and the *nirvāṇa*. Both effectively are only Voidness, *Sūnyatā*.

We have seen that in order to find the true nature of the *saṃsāra* it is necessary to eliminate through a rigorous abolishing analysis everything that manifests itself to us forming part of the *saṃsāra*.

We must act in a similar way to find the true nature of the *nirvāṇa*. The *nirvāṇa* is what is completely different from the empirical reality when this one is considered not in its true nature, the *śūnyatā*, but under the false appearance under which it presents itself before us. In order to discover what the *nirvāṇa* is we must also abolish everything that constitute the empirical reality, specially being and not being.[10] That abolishing process carried into its last consequences, total and absolute, will present to us the same *śūnyatā*, that we have found on applying to *saṃsāra* the same method.

Using the comparison of the modern conception of world again, we could say that all beings and things that form the world, are identical among themselves, since they all are, in their last essence, atoms and energy: the uniformity is so an universal attribute.

Primitive Buddhism is built on the opposition, on the insuperable difference between *saṃsāra* and *nirvāṇa*, *nirvāṇa* being considered as the full extinction of *saṃsāra*. For Nāgārjuna there is no difference: *saṃsāra* and *nirvāṇa* are the same, since both are Voidness.

We think that this is the only way to understand the idea of sameness between *nirvāṇa* and *saṃsāra*: that sameness has as its support the abolition of everything that is presented to us in the empirical level by our senses and our reason. It is impossible to understand that the sameness between both is based on the *saṃsāra* and *nirvāṇa* having as a common characteristic the *svabhāvaśūnyatā* and the *pratītyasamutpāda*, i.e. the total contingency, since *nirvāṇa* is precisely the unconditioned one, what is beyond contingency, beyond conditions and causes.

Empirical Reality, a Mere Mental Creation

We have said that for Nāgārjuna's school two realities are opposed: on one side, the true reality and on the other side the false one, which disappears with the abolishing analysis and which conceals or covers the first one. This second reality is a mere illusion in the common sense of the word, a mere mental creation, which is superimposed on the true reality, concealing it, in the same way as the illusory idea or image of a serpent which is superimposed on the rope seen in the darkness; in the same way as the illusory idea or image of a rope is superimposed on the conglomerate of threads which compose the rope, and the illusory idea or image of a thread is superimposed on the filaments that compose the thread and so on. The existence of the empirical reality as we normally see it is nothing else than the existence of an illusion, devoid of a true existence.

Using the same comparison as before, it is possible to say that, since the world is only atoms and energy without the empirical attributes of colour, taste, etc., the manifold variety of the world in terms of colours, taste, etc., is only a construction of our mind and senses, of our subjectivity and sensibility.

We find here the great function which the mind possesses in Nāgārjuna's school, as in all the Mahāyāna schools: the empirical reality is only a series or succession of illusions, of imaginations, of ideas, which our mind creates incessantly above the infinite abyss of universal Voidness. And this succession of mental creations has had no beginning, according to the *anāditva*'s postulate which is essential in Indian thought.[11] Of course it can come to an end through the method taught by Buddhism, and on that day, together with the cessation of the imaginary creations of the mind, the empirical reality will also disappear and there will remain only the universal emptiness, which it concealed and which constitutes the true way of being of everything.

Similarly, in relation to each man, we can say that when his mind ceases to work in a transitory or definitive way, the empirical reality ceases to exist with its variety and multiplicity, and, disconnected from the sensibility and subjectivity which produced its forthcoming, it remains in its amorphous state of atoms and energy.[12]

The great function, which the mind possesses in Nāgārjuna's school, must not induce us to be mistaken about its true nature: the mind which through its activity creates the illusory empirical reality, and which through the abolishing analysis gives us a glimpse of the absolute Voidness—the mind itself belongs also to the empirical reality and as such is also contingent, is also void.

In the terms of the comparison referred to, the mind and the senses themselves, constituted by atoms and energy, are not something apart from the world they create; they are nothing else than atoms and energy.

Irrelevant Questions

Questions that naturally come to mind are: why, when, and how the series of mental creations, which constitute the empirical reality, did begin? But these questions are irrelevant, because the series of mental creations has had no beginning and therefore nothing can be said about the cause, the moment and the manner in which that series began to flow, in the same way as these questions are irrelevant in references to *Brahman*, also beginningless.

Liberation

Empirical reality, according to what we have expressed, is just an illusion, a mental creation, and of the same nature are bondage to reincarnations and liberation from that bond. Consequently, the man who wishes to liberate himself from reincarnations (the supreme goal of all religious and philosophical systems in India) has not to destroy anything really existent, but to put an end to the series of mental creations which constitute the empirical reality and the series of reincarnations, that is to say he has only to stop mind functioning, which is the source of those illusory creations. This is the great goal to be reached.

This is not an easy task, because the essence of the mind is precisely the mental creativity. The destiny of man, while he is immersed in the empirical reality, in its infinite reincarnations, is to originate incessantly a series of mental creations. The overcoming of that destiny can only be obtained adopting the ethical and intellectual method that is fixed by Buddhism, with extraordinary effort, endeavour, and energy. When the mental creations cease, ceases *ipso facto* the empirical reality which they constitute, and the reincarnations which are a part of the empirical reality.[13]

Everything is Nirvanized ab aeterno

In Primitive Buddhism *nirvāṇa* was something completely different from the empirical reality, its abolition, its negation. The Mādhyamika school does not abandon this conception as it affirms that *nirvāṇa* is *śūnyatā*, Voidness, and consequently is the negation of all elements, manifestations, categories of the empirical reality.

To the *śūnyatā*, negation of all, the true reality, is opposed the empirical reality, which is a mere illusion, an erroneous mental creation. As a consequence of this *saṃsāra's* nature, there is not, there has never been and there will never be a *true* and *real* forthcoming of anything and therefore no real transmigration, no real destruction, nothing real. And this state of things that means a complete negation of everything, is precisely the universal Voidness or, what is the same: *nirvāṇa*. Therefore nothing has ever really abandoned the *śūnyatā* or *nirvāṇa* state.

Finally, in the terms of the general modern comparison we are using, since the atoms and the energy never transform themselves into the beings and things of the world we perceive, assuming the empirical attributes with which they appear before us; and since the world is only a creation of our mind and senses, we can say that nothing has really departed from its atoms and energy state, that it has always remained in that state, that is to say, that everything has been 'nirvanized' *ab aeterno* in Buddhist terminology.

If there was a *real* forthcoming, transmigration or destruction, there would be negation of *śūnyatā*, to which something *real* would be opposed. But as something *real* has never existed, does not exist and will never exist, the only thing that remains is the total *śūnyatā*.

It is not possible to argue that the uniqueness of *śūnyatā* is nullified by the illusory world which is opposed to it, because for Indian thought the uniqueness of a *true* reality that is postulated as unique, can only be destroyed by another *true* reality; the existence of an *illusory* reality, opposed to the true reality that is postulated as unique, does not eliminate the uniqueness of that true reality.

THE ḤASTAVĀLANĀMAPRAKARAṆA OF ĀRYADEVA AND VOIDNESS

As we have already said in the first part of this Introduction, this treatise is an example of the way in which the Mādhyamika school has recourse to the analysis of empirical reality in order to establish its thesis. This treatise does not adduce the authority of any canonical Buddhist text to found the thesis it develops. For that aim it makes use only of the analysis of reality. It does not go out of the limits of a philosophical reflection. And it accomplishes its task submitting itself to the exigencies of reason.

The present treatise does not mention the word *śūnyatā* and notwithstanding it constitutes an excellent introduction for the comprehension of the theory of Voidness sustained by the Mādhyamaka, as the analysis of reality it accomplishes ends in establishing, on one side, the universal contingency, the conditionedness, the non-existence of an own being, and, on the other side, the unreality of the world, its illusory character, its condition of a mere mental creation.

Besides that, this treatise provides us with an excellent example of how does the method (that we have called 'analytical abolishing') works: it disintegrates, so to say, the empirical reality, making it disappear before us, creating the impression of an abyss, an absence, a void.

Introduction

The treatise begins contrasting the normal knowledge of the empirical reality and its philosophical knowledge. The treatise, in its *kārikās* I and II and their respective commentary, makes us know, in a clear and succinct way, what are the normal knowledge and the philosophical knowledge and moreover the analytical abolishing method employed by the philosophical analysis.

Kārikā Ia-b and Its Commentary

First of all the treatise deals with normal knowledge. The error consists in taking one thing for another, in superimposing an illusory reality upon another to which the illusory representation does not correspond. Error is produced when determinate conditions are given, as for instance, in the case of the text, the penumbra, the perception of only certain attributes that are common to the real object (the rope) and to the illusory object (the serpent) as, for example, the thin and sinuous form of both. Error imposes itself on the mind, produces a conviction, a certainty which reveals itself in the emphatic enunciation: 'this is really such a thing'.

The disappearance of error is produced with the perception of the specific qualities of the rope (immobility, twisted form etc.) which distinguish it from the serpent. This second perception takes place due to some conditions which the treatise does not mention and which could be either a better illumination or an adaptation of the eye to obscurity or a reflection of the mind etc. Together with the disappearance of error, comes forth in the mind the certainty that the previous representation was only a fancy, something merely imagined, a false knowledge, because one discovers that that representation lacked a corresponding real object, that it was 'object-less', as the object proper to the illusion (the serpent) did not exist.

Kārikā Ic-d and Its Commentary

With the disappearance of error there remains the object (the rope), upon which the previous erroneous cognition (the serpent) was built, and the knowledge of that object. That object is considered as real and that knowledge is considered as valid in the domain of normal knowledge: the rope is known as a rope. And the previous certainty of the existence of the serpent has been replaced by a new certainty, apparently definitive: that of the existence of the rope. It is in this moment that the knowledge, that we have called philosophical, begins to function; it pretends to reach the true nature of things.

The philosophical knowledge applies to the object, that has remained, the analytical abolishing method. On analyzing the rope, it discovers that it is formed by parts, the threads, that the rope does not have an own being, that it does not exist in itself, independently from the threads that compose it, as something different from them. Consequently to the knowledge of the rope does not correspond a real object, 'rope', but another thing, a conglomerate of threads, which by convention is called 'rope'. The knowledge of the rope as a rope happens to be in this way so false as the knowledge of the rope as a serpent. The reason is the same:

the non-existence of a corresponding real object of the cognition. The certainty of the existence of the rope disappears for the benefit of the certainty of the existence of the threads.

The philosophical knowledge does not stop in the threads; it applies to them the same analytical abolishing method and discovers that at their own turn they are constituted by parts, the filaments, reaching in relation to the threads to the same conclusion which it has reached before in relation to the rope. It goes on applying the same method to 'the parts of the parts' and, on reaching in relation to them to the same conclusion to which it reached in relation to the rope, it finds that all of them depend on other, that no one of them has an own being, an autonomous existence and that therefore nothing real corresponds to the knowledge of the threads, the filaments etc. The knowledge of the parts of the rope is as false as the knowledge of the rope.

Here ends the analysis of the example of the rope which served to illustrate what are the erroneous knowledge, the normal knowledge and the philosophical knowledge and the passage from one to the other. Let us add that the erroneous knowledge comes forth exceptionally, when determinate conditions are given, and in determinate individuals, while normal knowledge is produced in general way in the great majority of individuals.

Kārikā IIa-d and Its Commentary

The present *kārikā* and its commentary apply to the empirical reality in its totality the results attained to in the previous *kārikā* and its commentary.

The normal knowledge presents to us an empirical reality that is unitary, compact, existing in itself, not depending on another entity for its existence. The normal knowledge is apparently a knowledge of really existent objects. The philosophical knowledge presents to us a reality totally different: divisible into infinite parts and therefore neither unitary nor compact, depending on these parts in order to be, impermanent, non-existing, unreal. The philosophical knowledge is perfectly aware that it deals with words, with conventional denominations, to which nothing really existing corresponds. Because of all what has been said, it is possible to conclude that the normal knowledge is an erroneous knowledge, because it presents to us a reality which does not exist as such, because it lacks a real object and because, lacking a real object, the object it makes known to us is a mere creation of our own imagination: an idea devoid of reality, a mere name.

Kārikā IIIa-b and Its Commentary

In the two *kārikās* that precede the author of the treatise has exposed his own theory. In *kārikā* III he will refute two objections that can be opposed to it, one (IIIa-b) from the point of view of atomism and the other (IIIc-d) from the point of view of idealism.

From the point of view of atomism the abolishing analysis carried on by the Mādhyamika must necessarily stop in the 'last part', i.e. the atom, which is without part and which for the atomists is really existent. Being without parts the atom is provided with an own being, which does not depend on something else for its existence. In this way the Mādhyamika theory of universal contingency is invalidated.

But the treatise's author does not admit the existence of the atom, that indivisible entity imagined by the atomists. The atom's existence is impugned by the Mādhyamika by reasons of logic nature. The atom for the Mādhyamika is like a garland of flowers born in the space or like the hare's horns, something unreal, that cannot be conceived.

The argument adduced by the Mādhyamika is that the atom as everything else is located in the space, and the space is divided into parts (north, south etc.) and consequently the atom participates in this division into parts, that is to say it does not exist as an *a-tom*, as something indivisible, as something really 'one'.

Kārikā IIIc-d and Its Commentary

As a consequence of the previous argumentation the treatise's author concludes in *kārikā* IIIc-d that the world is not a true reality, something having an own being, something unconditioned. The world is so only something imagined, a mere mental creation.

At this point the author presents an objection that can be made by a member of the idealist school: if it is true that it can be admitted that the objects of knowledge do not exist, that they lack an own being, that they are a mere illusion, anyhow the existence of the illusory thought that conceives those objects cannot be doubted. The mirage does not exist as something real, but the representation of the mirage is a real fact, something whose existence cannot be doubted. We must have in mind that, when the idealist sustains the existence of the illusory thought, it is necessary to understand that he is referring to an existence *in se et per se* and consequently real, since when the treatise's author refutes this objection, what he denies is the existence *in itself* of the illusory thought.

Kārikā IVa-d and Its Commentary

In this *kārikā* the author refutes the idealist objection. In the mind appear objects which do not exist, since they do not have an own being, an existence in themselves. These objects are therefore unreal. The rope, which we perceive does not exist as a rope, only as a conglomerate of threads. The same thing happens in the case of the mirage, which presents itself as an oasis (trees, water etc.), while the only thing that exists is sand. Up to here the Mādhyamika coincides with the idealist objector in relation to the unreality of the object of knowledge.

After the unreality of the object has been admitted, the author sustains that the knowledge, which is produced by that unreal object, cannot have an existence *in se*, a real existence.

The author founds his thesis in the observation of reality, in the quotidian experience: it has been never seen that something which does not exist in itself be able to produce something existing in itself.

Kārikā Va-d and Its Commentary

The present *kārikā* indicates the consequence that the knowledge of the true nature of things, i.e. that they are contingent, conditioned, dependent and therefore unreal, non-existent, mere names has for the man in regard to his attitude to life and his ethical behaviour. The wise man, who has found the true nature of things, frees himself from passions that enchain him to them and realizes in this way the ideal of serenity and impassability, which is one of the aims of Buddhist ethic. The same thing occurs with the man who being afraid because of the imaginary snake that he has perceived instead of the rope, is liberated from his fear as soon as he is aware of his false perception.

Kārikā VIa-d and Its Commentary

From all that has been said before comes forth the opposition between the two realities: one, apparent and provisory, the object of normal knowledge which is erroneous by its own nature, and the other true and unique, the object of philosophical knowledge, which reaches the true nature of things: the non-existence of an own being. Man is normally immersed in the apparent reality of the world, believes in the real existence of things and superimposes on them names established by convention. But, when he longs for liberation from passions in order to realize the Buddhist ideal of serenity, man must abstain from the usual form of viewing things and must thoroughly investigate the essence of reality, employing the method that is propounded by the treatise.

THE YUKTIṢAṢṬIKĀ OF NĀGĀRJUNA AND VOIDNESS

1. The fundamental thesis of the *Yuktiṣaṣṭikā* is that neither birth nor destruction really exist. Moreover, as birth and destruction are the means to come into existence and non-existence respectively, the treatise denies also the real existence and non-existence of everything. Cf. the invocation and *kārikās* 1, 2, 4, 7, 8, 10, 12-21, 23, 24, 26, 32, 39, 45, 48, 57 and their respective notes.

2. In order to demonstrate this thesis the treatise has recourse to the theory of universal conditionality: all is conditioned, all exists in dependence, nothing exists in and by itself. Cf. The invocation and *kārikās* 1, 12, 14, 18-20, 23-25, 27, 30, 39, 43-45, 48 and their respective notes.

3. And all that exists in dependence does not really exist, is a mere mental creation, a product of imagination, of ignorance, of erroneous knowledge. Cf. *Kārikās* 3, 7, 10, 15-17, 23-28, 34, 35, 37, 38, 39, 42, 44, 45, 49, 53, 54, 56 and their respective notes. The *Hastavālanāmaprakaraṇa*, a treatise included in this book, is a clear example of a Mādhyamika demonstration of the principle of the universal conditionality, of the universal contingency, of the character of simple illusion that belongs to everything, on the basis of the analysis of empirical reality.

4. And a true birth and a true destruction are not possible in relation to an illusion, to an unreal entity; only an illusory birth and an illusory destruction are possible. Cf. *kārikās* 7, 8, 14, 17-19. So, it is impossible to say, in relation to the oasis that appears in a

mirage, that it really came forth and really existed, that it was really destroyed and really ceased to be. In this case only an illusion, the illusion of the oasis, came forth, existed, was destroyed and ceased to be.

5. If the empirical reality *(saṃsāra)* is a mere mental creation, if all that constitutes it is to be found only in the mind, then, in order to destroy it, to make it cease, to be liberated from it, there is only one means: the cessation of the mental creation, of the illusion which produced the empirical reality. And this is to be got through the forthcoming of the knowledge which will 'show' us the only thing that 'is' there: Voidness. In order to eliminate the serpent, under whose form the rope appears in darkness, we cannot have recourse to a real destruction, through a blow for instance; the only way to eliminate it is to stop the error, that created the serpent, through the forthcoming of true knowledge, which will present to us what there really is, the rope. Cf. *kārikās* 2, 4-8, 10, 11, 17, 23, 34, 38, 55-57 and their respective notes.

The form of existence, the form of being of the mirage, of the illusion created by magic, of the Gandharva's city, of the serpent superimposed on the rope etc. (classical examples for unreal objects utilized by the Mādhyamika school) is the form of existence, the form of being of empirical reality in its totality. Thus, in the analysis made by the *Hastavālanāmaprakaraṇa*, the same status of the serpent, produced by an error-illusion, corresponds to the rope as a rope, to its parts, to its sub-parts etc., and to the entire empirical reality, when it is correctly examined.

6. In the treatise the author refers to a series of traditional Buddhist concepts. The principles are:

pratītyasamutpāda (The invocation and *kārikās* 1, 12, 14, 15, 18-20, 23, 37-39);
liberation (*kārikās* 4, 13, 23, 55, 56, 58, 59);
saṃsāra (*kārikās* 5, 6, 13, 14, 17, 18, 37, 42, 54, 56, 59);
nirvāṇa (*kārikās* 5, 6, 11, 20, 35, 56);
saṃskāras (*kārikās* 8, 18);
skandhas (*kārikā* 9)
skandhas, dhātus, āyatanas (*kārikā* 33);
gātis (*kārikās* 15, 26, 28, 32);
the Great Elements (*kārikā* 34).

The author explicitly attributes to all these concepts one or another of the characteristics dealt with before: conditionality, illusory nature, unreality, impossibility of a real birth and a real destruction, possibility of destruction only through an act of knowledge. But owing to the close relation of these characteristics among themselves, to attribute one of them means to attribute also the other ones.

As a consequence of what has been said, the traditional concepts enumerated above present themselves now with a content very different from that they had in the previous periods of Buddhism, i.e. in the early period and in the Hīnayāna period. In these two periods the possibility of a real birth and a real destruction was accepted and, although the conditionality of all was admitted, this did not lead to sustain the illusory character, the unreality of all. This change in these concepts manifests the passage from the realist position of the two first periods to the nihilistic-idealist position of Mahāyāna. It was unavoidable that this new position affected all the conceptions of Buddhist system, if one takes into account the logical rigour with which Indian thinkers carried to their ultimate consequences any principle they adopted.

7. Besides the subjects, which we have mentioned, the treatise deals with other ones, that are related to the theory of Voidness or that are examined from the point of view of that theory. They complement the subjects previously indicated. Thus we have:

The use of reasoning (*yukti*) as a means to reach the truth. Cf. the title and *kārikā* 2. This treatise, contrarily to the *Hastavālanāma-prakaraṇa*, does not have recourse to the analysis of reality; it keeps itself inside purely logical limits; reason starting from certain principles, draws out the consequences that derive from them in relation to several important traditional concepts that are examined from the point of view of the Mādhyamika school.

Value of mind. Cf. *kārikās* 17, 24, 34 and 36. By means of the mind man gets the knowledge of truth and is liberated from impurities and reincarnations; but man is also cheated by his own mind and thus is submitted to error and remains enchained to reincarnations. Moreover it is mind which creates the illusion of empirical reality and which can destroy it. On this last function of the mind see *kārikās* indicated in the points 3 and 5 above.

Suspension of judgement, *epoché*. Cf. *kārikās* 42, 47, 50-52 and 58. The conception of reality as Voidness induces the Mādhyamika to refrain from emitting a judgement which may imply the affirmation or negation of something in itself or of something in relation to another thing.

Ataraxia. Cf. *kārikās* 46, 49 and 58. If, on one side, suspension of judgement derives from a particular philosophical conception of reality, on the other side, it has as consequences the abstention from discussions and controversies and an attitude of serenity and imperturbability.

Moral effects that come forth respectively from ignorance and from the knowledge of truth: passions, impurities (desire, aversion, error), attachment and their absence. Cf. *kārikās* 49-58.

The sage and the ignorant. Cf. *kārikās* 1, 3-5, 7, 16, 18, 23-25, 29-31, 42-45 and 52-59. In these *kārikās* are confronted the sage and the ignorant. What distinguishes the former from the latter are the knowledge of the true reality, Voidness, and the intellectual and moral effects which originate from it. In these *kārikās* both are characterized according to these criteria.

Co-existence of the moral and the intellectual element in Buddha's teaching. Cf. *kārikā* 32.

Theory and practice. Cf. *kārikās* 31, 40 and 41. It is necessary to adequate moral action to philosophical theory.

Stages in the path of knowledge: passage from ingenuous realism to the 'knowledge of the true nature of things': their voidness of an own being. Cf. *kārikā* 30. There are three stages in the path that leads to true knowledge: ignorance and attachment, detachment without true knowledge and knowledge of voidness of an own being and consequent liberation: *nirvāṇa*.

Hermeneutic principle, *nītārtha* texts and *neyārtha* texts. Cf. *kārikās* 21 and 33. In the Buddhist texts we have several terms as 'production', 'destruction', *skandhas, dhātus, āyatanas,* which must not be understood in their direct, literal meaning, which tradition has attributed to them, but in an implied meaning which has to be established on the light of the theory of Voidness.

Sameness of *saṃsāra* and *nirvāṇa*. Cf. *kārikās* 6 and 11, since both are only Voidness, *śūnyatā*.

Transfer of merit. Cf. *kārikā* 60.

THE ŚŪNYATĀSAPTATI OF NĀGĀRJUNA AND VOIDNESS

The *Śūnyatāsaptati* differs from the *Hastāvalanāmaprakaraṇa* and the *Yuktiṣaṣṭikā* in the form in which it treats the central theme of Voidness. The first treatise starts from the analysis of a concrete and determined object (rope-serpent) of the empirical reality and applies the result it obtains to the whole of that reality. It establishes the universal conditionedness and contingency, the Voidness of all and, as a consequence, the illusory character of the empirical reality in its totality. We have in it the universalization of the principle of Voidness. The *Yuktiṣaṣṭikā* maintains itself in a theoretical and logical level, without doing an analysis of the material world concretely considered. It limits itself to the analysis of the categories which rule in the world (causality, time etc.) and focuses its interest in the specific categories of birth-being and destruction-non-being. The *Śūnyatāsaptati* like the *Yukti* maintains itself in a theoretical level, but differs from it in that it submits to analysis numerous categories of the empirical reality: birth, permanence, destruction, production, cause, existence, non-existence, time, action, perception, knowledge, object of knowledge, ignorance etc. The analysis throws as a result the conditionedness, the relativity, the absence of an own being as the essential characteristic of all those categories, and, as a consequence of that, the unreality, the logical impossibility and the illusory character of their existence.

From the examination of these particular cases it is deduced that the totality of existence is 'void' and unreal. Cf. *kārikās* 2, 3, 28, 30, 58.

The aim of these repeated analyses of the particular and diverse categories of the empirical reality is to gather the greatest number of cases in which the great principle of conditionedness reveals itself and which serve as a support for the universalization of that principle. It is not a meaningless procedure. We think that this form of acting pretends to accumulate as many proofs as it is possible for the thesis which the Mādhyamika has reached through deduction and which constitutes the great contribution of that school to Indian thought.

In the *Śūnyatāsaptati* we find a great number of references to themes and theories of Buddhism in general and of the Mādhyamika school in particular. Of course they are viewed from the central perspective of the Voidness theory which forms the central point of the treatise.

We have thus:

The conception of the two truths or realities. *Kārikās* 1, 69, 71.
The *nirvāṇa*. *Kārikās* 23-26.
The intentional formulations of Buddha. *Kārikā* 44.
The theory of perception. *Kārikās* 45-57.
Universal nirvanization *ab aeterno*. *Kārikā* 63.
Dependent origination: Voidness. *Kārikā* 68.
Obtention of *nirvāṇa*. *Kārikās* 72, 73.

THE CATUSTAVA OF NĀGĀRJUNA AND VOIDNESS

In these hymns we find the exposition of the fundamental theories of the Mādhyamika school in a succinct way, as is required by the nature of this kind of literature. All the formulations of its *kārikās* are in some relation with the essential thesis of Voidness, *Śūnyatā*: all is void, lacking an own being, insubstantial, a mere mental creation without a corresponding real object. As is seen by the scheme of exposition, that we give in the Introduction of the fourth chapter, elements, categories, manifestations of the empirical reality are enumerated one after the other in order to deny them existence, reality, substantiality owing to their character of conditioned.

The three first hymns, like the *Śūnyatāsaptati*, refer themselves to numerous elements, categories, etc., of the empirical reality in order to affirm their conditionedness and consequent unreality. The fourth hymn refers itself only to Buddha to declare that He, as anything else, is also 'void'.

The Mādhyamika theories exposed in these hymns are explicitly connected with Buddha. Specially in the *Lokātīta* and in the *Acintya* Buddha is presented as the Master who discovered and taught these theories. In the *Niraupamya* Buddha is described laying stress on His extraordinary physical and moral qualities, His discovery of truth, His spiritual attainments.

In the *Paramārtha* we find fundamentally the praise of Buddha, described from the point of view of supreme truth, in terms of Voidness, through negations. The Voidness of Buddha does not prevent the poet from expressing his intense devotion. Repeatedly the poet affirms his desire to praise Buddha, although he knows the non-existence of 'somebody' that can be praised and of 'somebody' that can praise, since all, including even Buddha, is 'void', unreal.

In these hymns we find references to the theory of the Three Bodies and devotion to Buddha is an important element in them. See notes 163 and 165 below.

NOTES

1. Everything comes forth through the cooperation of a series of causes (*hetu*) and conditions (*pratyaya*).
2. A thing is *high* in relation to another one that is *low* in regard to it; a person is a *father* in relation to his *son* and vice versa. In the same way as 'high', 'low', 'father', 'son' exist, so exists everything in the empirical reality.
3. A rope is composed by threads; each thread by filaments and so on. Man is only a conglomerate of material elements, which form the body, and of sensations, perception, volitions, acts of consciousness. In the same way as the rope and man are only conglomerates of parts, so is everything in the empirical reality.
4. One of the great thesis of Buddhism is that the whole as such does not exist, that only the parts exist, and the parts at their own turn can be analyzed into other parts and so on. Cf. Fernando Tola and Carmen Dragonetti 'Dignāga's Ālamabanaparīkṣāvṛtti', *Journal of Indian Philosophy*, vol. 10, no. 2, pp. 105-34, note 6 in p. 129.
5. The Mādhyamika school does not admit another reality besides the empirical illusory reality as it appears to us, and the true reality, which is the true nature of the former.
6. Th. Stcherbatsky, *The Conception of Buddhist Nirvāṇa, passim.*
7. For instance see Nāgārjuna's *Dvādaśadvāra* and Āryadeva's *Śataśāstra* and *Catuḥśataka*.
8. The Mādhyamika school was called skeptical by its rivals, because it refrained itself from emitting judgements. The suspension of judgement was a consequence of the conviction that the school has that any thesis, when it is duly analyzed, falls into contradiction and that the true reality cannot be reached by human reason.
9. See the text of *Hastavālanāmaprakaraṇavṛtti* in this volume.
10. This abolishing method corresponds to the method which the Hellenistic thinkers called *'aphâiresis'* (Albinos, *Didaskalikos* X, p. 165 ed. C.F. Hermann; Plotinus, *Enneades* VI, 7 (18), 36; Plutarchus, *Quaestiones Platonicae* 1001 E, who also uses *'périkopé*) or 'analysis' (Clemens Alexandrinus, *Stromata* V, 11, p. 374, 5 ed. O. Stählin; Kelsos *apud* Origenes, *Contra Celsum* 7, 42, P.G. II, col. 1481 (= p. 188 ed. R. Bader). Cf. John M. Whittaker, 'Neopythagorismus and Negative Theology', in *Symbolae Osloenses*, 44 (1969), pp. 109-25 (German translation in: *Der Mittelplatonismus,*

herausgegeben von Clemens Zintzen, Darmstadt: Wissenschaftliche Buchgesellschaft, 1981, pp. 169-86).

11. Cf. Fernando Tola and Carmen Dragonetti, '*Anāditva* or Beginninglessness in Indian Philosophy', in *Annals of the Bhandarkar Oriental Research Institute*.
12. Prakāśānanda, *Siddhāntamuktāvali*, commentary of stanza 10, expresses the idealistic thesis with the following words: '*ananubhūyamānaṃ dvaitaṃ nāsti*', (duality, when it is not perceived, does not exist), opposing it to the realistic thesis expressed in the following way: '*ajñatāsyāpi dvaitasya sattvam abhyupagacchanti*', ((realists) admit the existence of duality even when it is not perceived).
13. Death does not stop the series of mental creations; this series continues after death in the new following existences, without interruption, although with the oblivion of the past experiences, and in a new body.
14. The position assumed by the idealist objector in this treatise remembers us the position of Descartes: it may be that all that I think is false but it is necessary that I, who thinks, exist. Cf. *Discours de la Méthode, Quatrième partie*, p. 32 (édition Ch. Adam et P. Tannery VI). The accepted or hypothetical falsehood of the world brings both thinkers to the acceptance of the existence of thought, in the case of the idealist objector, of the thinking ego, in the case of Descartes. Each of them is thus coherent with his own tradition: the objector of this treatise with his phenomenist conception of man, which denies the existence of soul and Descartes with his substantial one. Moreover the idealist objector substantializes the thought, attributing to it an existence in and by itself. The extreme point of this philosophical trend is the theory of pure consciousness (*amalavijñāna*) sustained by Buddhist idealists, as for instance in the *Uttaratantra* and the *Śraddhotpāda*. Cf. Frauwallner, 'Amalavijñāna und Ālayavijñāna'. On his turn Descartes substantializes the thinking ego, transforming it into a *substantia cogitans*, a soul.

CHAPTER 1

The Hastavālanāmaprakaraṇavṛtti of Āryadeva

INTRODUCTION

The Text

1. In the Tibetan Buddhist Canon, *Bstan-ḥgyur*, there are two metrical translations of a small Sanskrit treatise. The first one: *Tōhoku* 3844 (*Sde-dge* edn.) = *Catalogue* 5244 (*Peking* edn.); the second one: Tōhoku 3848 = *Catalogue* 5248.

The first translation is composed of seven *kārikās*; the second one, of six.

In the same Canon we find two translations of a Sanskrit commentary (*vṛtti*) of these *kārikās*. The first one: *Tōhoku* 3845 = *Catalogue* 5245; the second one: *Tōhoku* 3849 = *Catalogue* 5249. These commentaries include seven and six *kārikās* respectively.

The colophons of these four translations attribute the original work (*kārikās* and *vṛtti*) to Āryadeva (in Tibetan Ḥphags-pa lha).

Translations 3844 and 3845 were done by Śraddhākaravarman and Rin-chen bzaṅ-po; translation 3849 was done by Dānaśīla, Dpal-ḥbyor sñiṅ-po and, as reviser, Dpal-brtsegs rakṣita. The translators of 3848 are not mentioned in the colophon of the translation. Probably they are the same translators as those of 3849.

These Tibetan translations have in their colophons the following titles for this treatise:

In Tibetan

3844: *Cha śas kyi yan lag ces bya baḥi rab tu byed pa* (*The treatise called 'The Parts of the Parts'*/),

5244: *Cha śas kyi yan lag ces bya baḥi rab tu byed pa* (*The treatise called 'The Parts of the Parts'*),

3848: *Rab tu byed pa lag paḥi tshad kyi tshig leḥur byas pa* (*Kārikās of the Treatise 'Hand-measure'*),
5248: *Rab tu byed pa lag paḥi tshad kyi thsig leḥur byas pa* (*Kārikās of the Treatise 'Hand-measure'*),
3845: *Cha śas kyi yan lag ces bya baḥi rab tu byed paḥi ḥgrel pa* (*Commentary upon the treatise called 'The Parts of the Parts'*),
5245: *Cha śas kyi yan lag ces bya baḥi rab tu byed paḥi ḥgrel pa* (*Commentary upon the treatise called 'The Parts of the Parts'*),
3849: *Lag paḥi tshad kyi ḥgrel pa* (*Commentary upon 'Hand-Measure'*),
5249: *Lag paḥi tshad kyi ḥgrel pa* (*Commentary upon 'Hand-measure'*).

In Sanskrit:

3844: *Hastavāsanāmaprakaraṇa* (*Treatise called 'Hand—?'*),
5244: *Hastavalanāmaprakaraṇa* (*Treatise called 'The Hair in the Hand'*),
3848: *Hastābhabaprakaraṇakārikā* (*Kārikās of the Treatise 'Hand—?'*),
5248: *Hastābhabaprakaraṇakārikā* (*Kārikās of the Treatise 'Hand—?'*),
3845: *Hastabāsanāmaprakaraṇabṛtti* (*Commentary upon the Treatise called 'Hand—?'*),
5245: *Hastabalanāmaprakāraṇabṛtti* (*Commentary upon the Treatise called 'The Hair in the Hand'*),
3849: *Hastābhababṛtti* (*Commentary of the 'Hand—?'*),
5249: *Hastābhababṛtti* (*Commentary of the 'Hand—?'*).

2. In the Chinese Buddhist Canon there are also two translations of a small Sanskrit work: *Taisho*, vol. XXXI, 1620 and 1621. (*Hōbōgirin, Répertoire*, p. 137).

Both translations have six *kārikās* each and the respective commentary.

Both translations attribute the work to Dignāga (in Chinese (T) Ch' en-na) (*c.* A.D. 480-540).

Translation 1620 was done by Paramārtha (in Chinese (T) Chen ti); translation 1621 was done by (Y) i-tsing.

The Chinese translations give for these works the following titles: 1620: *Kiai kiuan louen* and 1621: *Tchang tchong louen* (according to the *Répertoire*). The literal translation of the Chinese characters is in 1620: 'to loosen' or 'to explain'—'to roll up' or 'to grasp'—'treatise', and in 1621: 'the palm, of the hand'—'within'—'treatise'. It is difficult to establish the meaning of the first title; the second may mean: *The Treatise 'Within the Palm of the Hand'*.[1]

3. Besides the translations preserved in the Tibetan Buddhist Canon there are three manuscript copies of the Tibetan translations 3848 and 3849 = 5248 and 5249, two of them incomplete. They were found by Sir M.A. Stein in Tun-huang and were deposited in the India Office Library in London.[2] They are designated by Thomas and Ui with the letters a, *b*, *g* in Greek.

The colophons of these copies attribute the work to Āryadeva.

The comparison of the Tibetan and Chinese translations allows the conclusion that all these translations derive from the same Sanskrit text actually lost. The differences that we find must be attributed either to the translators or to the copyists.

Some Modern Editions and Translations of the Hastavālanāmaprakaraṇavṛtti

F.W. Thomas and H. Ui (1918), " 'The Hand Treatise', a work of Āryadeva", in *Journal of the Royal Asiatic Society*, vols. 1-2, pp. 267-310, published a Tibetan text of this work; it was eclectically constituted on the basis of the *Bstan-ḥgyur* translations and the Tun-huang copies. Besides that the work of Thomas and Ui contains the two Chinese translations, a conjectural reconstruction of the original Sanskrit text and an English translation of the Tibetan text, an introduction and notes.

J. Nagasawa (1955), 'Kanyaku nihon Taishō chibetto Yaku Shuryō Ron Chū Wayaku' ("The two Chinese versions compared, the Japanese translation of the Tibetan translation of the Commentary on the Treatise, 'The Measure of the Hand' "), in *Chizan Gakuho* No. 4, 19, pp. 46-56, edited both Chinese translations of the Treatise, and a Japanese version of the Tibetan translation 3849.

H. Ui (1958), *Jinna Chosaku no Kenkyū* ('Studies of the Works of Dignāga'), pp. 133-65, translated into Japanese the two Chinese translations.

E. Frauwallner (1959), 'Dignāga, sein Werk und seine Entwicklung', in *Wiener Zeitschrift*, pp. 83-164, (the text of the Treatise is to be found in pp. 152-56), published an eclectic Tibetan Text of the Treatise, taking into account for its constitution the *Sde dge*, Thomas and Ui's editions. This work is included also in his *Kleine Schriften*, 1982.

M. Hattori (1961), 'Dignāga ni okeru Kashō to Jitsuzai' ('Dignāga's opinion on *saṃvṛtisat* and *paramārthasat*'), in FAS no. 50 pp. 16-28, published a Japanese translation of the Tibetan version.

F. Tola and C. Dragonetti (1977, 1980, 1985), 'La doctrina del vacío en la escuela Madhyamaka y el Hastavālanāmaprakaraṇa', in *Revista Latinoamericana de Filosofía*, vol. 3, no. 2, Julio 1977, pp. 159-75 (=*El Budismo Mahāyāna*, 1980, pp. 75-101); '*The Hastavālanāmaprakaraṇavṛtti*', in *Journal of Religious Studies*, vol. VIII, Spring 1980, no. 1, pp. 18-31, and 'La Hastavālanāmaprakaraṇavṛtti de Āryadeva', in *Boletin de la Asociacion Española de Orientalistas*, 1985, pp. 137-55, published, respectively, a Spanish translation of the Tibetan text constituted by them (1977), and later on (1980) edited that text with an English translation, and finally re-edited it (1985) with a Spanish translation, introducing into the text and translation important changes.

Title of the Work

The colophons of the Tibetan and Chinese translations of the Treatise differ in relation to the Sanskrit title of the original work. We have adopted for the *kārikās* the title *Hastavālanāmaprakaraṇa*, given by the *Peking* edition (5244) and for the commentary the title *Hastavālanāmaprakaraṇavṛtti*, given by the *Peking* edition (5245). We think these were the titles of the original work, because all the Sanskrit, Tibetan and Chinese titles given in the respective colophons include the word 'hand' or 'palm of the hand', with the only exception of the Tibetan titles of *Tōhoku* 3844 and 3845 = *Catalogue* 5244 and 5245. Besides the *Hastavālanāmaprakaraṇavṛtti* belongs to a kind of titles quite common for a Sanskrit treatise.[3] The meaning of *Hastavālanāmaprakaraṇa* is "*Treatise named 'The Hair in the Hand'* ". With this title the author wanted to express that he explained the subject of this work as clearly as we can see a hair in the palm of our hand.

The Extension of the Treatise

With all probability the number of the *kārikās* was originally six, those that appear in the Tibetan translations 3848 (= 5248) and 3849 (= 5249), in the two Chinese translations and in the *a* and *g* copies found in Tun-huang, because the seventh *kārikā* appears only in the Tibetan translations 3844 (= 5244) and 3845 (= 5245) and in the *b* copy of Tun-huang; besides that, the treatise clearly ends with the sixth *kārikā* and the subject of the seventh *kārikā* refers to the *yoga* practices and has nothing to do with the subject of the other six *kārikās*.

Authorship of the Work

As we have said the four Tibetan translations and the Tun-huang copies attribute this work *kārikās* and *vṛtti* to Āryadeva, the disciple of Nāgārjuna who lived in third century A.D. Bu-ston, *History of Buddhism*, Part II, p. 131, also attributes it to Āryadeva. Among modern authors, A. Bareau, *Die Religionen Indiens III*, p. 137, and T.R.V. Murti, *The Central Philosophy of Buddhism*, p. 94, consider equally that Āryadeva is the *Hastavālanāmaprakaraṇa*'s author. F.W. Thomas, *quoted article*, p. 272; P.L. Vaidya, *Études sur Āryadeva*, p. 64, and M. Winternitz, *A History of Indian Literature*, II, p. 352, think that the *kārikās* may be written by Āryadeva and the commentary by Dignāga. On the contrary the two Chinese translations attribute the work to Dignāga. Among modern authors E. Frauwallner, 'Dignāga, sein Werk und seine Entwicklung', p. 127; M. Hattori, in his translation of the Treatise and in *Dignāga, On Perception*, p. 7 and note 41; K. Kunjunni Raja, the editor of the *New Catalogus Catalogorum*, vol. IX, p. 37; Karl H. Potter, *Bibliography of Indian Philosophies*, p. 95; D. Seyfort Ruegg, *The Literature*, p. 153 and note 151; H. Ui, *Jinna Chosaku* and A.K. Warder, *Indian Buddhism*, pp. 450-51 and 544, attribute it to Dignāga.

It is difficult to decide about the authorship of this work, because the elements for judgement are scarce, relative and contradictory. Anyhow we would be inclined to attribute it (*kārikās* and *vṛtti*) to Āryadeva taking into account the *kārikā* III and its commentary which seem to adopt a position opposed to the Yogācāra school to which we must reckon Dignāga, and considering also that there is not reason to separate the commentary from the *kārikās*.

The Present Work

We give the Tibetan text of the *Hastavālanāmaprakaraṇavṛtti* and its translation into English.

Our edition of the Tibetan text is based upon the *Sde-dge* edition 3845 (= Peking edition 5245). In some places that we indicate in note, for clearness sake we have left aside the *Sde-dge* reading and we have adopted some variant taken from the other recensions of the text already mentioned. We have not included in our edition *kārikā* 7 and its commentary for the reasons expressed in the section *The Extension of the Treatise.*

We have included this text in the present book, because we think it is a very valuable and interesting philosophical treatise and contributes very much to get a clear understanding of the Śūnyatā conception,[4] although this work does not appear either in the *kārikās* or in the commentary.

HASTAVĀLANĀMAPRAKARAṆAVṚTTI

Tibetan Text

rgya gar skad du / hastavālanāmaprakaraṇavṛtti[5] /
bod skad du / cha śas kyi yan lag ces bya baḥi rab tu byed paḥi ḥgrel pa /
ḥphags pa ḥjam dpal ye śes sems dpaḥ la phyag ḥtshal lo /

khams gsum paḥi tha sñad tsam la yaṅ dag paḥi don du kun du rtogs paḥi phyir / de kho na ñid kyi don khoṅ du ma chud paḥi sems can rnams la dṅos poḥi raṅ bźin rab tu dbye baḥi sgo nas / phyin ci ma log paḥi śes pa yaṅ dag par sgrub paḥi phyir ḥdi brtsams so /

thag pa la ni sbrul sñam ḥdzin /
thag par mthoṅ na don med do /

ḥdi na[6] yul ha caṅ gsal ba ma yin paḥi[7] ḥod tsam źig snaṅ ba źig na / thag paḥi gzugs spyiḥi[8] chos tsam[9] źig dmigs pas[10] ḥkhrul nas / ḥdi ni sbrul kho naḥo źes ṅes par ḥdzin paḥi ṅo boḥi[11] śes pa skye ste / khyad par gyi[12] raṅ gi ṅo bo khoṅ du ma chud paḥi phyir ro / deḥi khyad par ṅes par ḥdzin pa na / don ji lta ba ma yin par kun du rtog pas rab tu spros pa ñid kyi phyir / śes pa de yaṅ ḥkhrul paḥi śes pa don med pa kho nar ḥgyur ro /

de yi cha mthoṅ de la yaṅ/
sbrul bźin śes pa ḥkhrul pa yin//1//

thag pa de la yaṅ cha śas su phye nas brtag pa na/thag paḥi raṅ gi ṅo bo mi dmigs te/de ma dmigs na thag par dmigs pa yaṅ sbrul lo sñam paḥi blo bźin du ḥkhrul pa tsam ḥbaḥ źig tu zad do/yaṅ ji ltar thag paḥi śes pa[13] ḥkhrul pa yin pa[14] de bźin du/cha śas de yaṅ dum bu daṅ/ñag ma la sogs pa de dag la brtags na deḥi[15] raṅ gi ṅo bo ṅes par mi ḥdzin to/de ṅes par ma zin pas de la dmigs paḥi rnam pa can gyi blo yaṅ thag paḥi blo bźin du[16] ḥ khrul pa tsam kho naḥo/

btags paḥi[17] dṅos po thams cad la/
raṅ gi ṅo bo brtags pa na/
kun rdzob śes paḥi spyod yul ni/
ji sñed yod pa gźan las btags[18]//2//

ji ltar cha śas la sogs paḥi dbye bas tha dad paḥi thag pa la sogs pa la brtags pa na raṅ gi ṅo bo mi dmigs te/thag pa la sogs paḥi blo yaṅ sbrul lo sñam paḥi blo bźin du ḥkhrul pa yin pa de bźin du/ ṅos cha la sogs pa la ltos nas yod pa rdza ma daṅ phor bu la sogs tha sñad paḥi śes paḥi spyod yul ji sñed pa thams cad btags[19] yod pa kho na yin te/de dag mthar rab tu phye ba na/re źig bum pa la sogs pa ni tha sñad du btags pa[20] kho na yin no/gźan las[21] źes bya ba ni/don dam par ni ma yin no[22]/

cha med brtag par bya min phyir/
tha ma yaṅ ni med par mtshuṅs/

gaṅ yaṅ btags paḥi[23] dṅos po thams cad kyi tha ma rdul phra rab kyi rdzas cha med pa gcig pu de yaṅ/ brtag par bya ba ma yin paḥi raṅ gi ṅo bos dmigs par[24] mi ruṅ baḥi phyir/ nam mkhaḥi me tog gi phreṅ ba daṅ/ ri boṅ gi rwa la sogs pa daṅ mtshuṅs pas/de yaṅ dṅos po med pa ñid du ḥgrub bo/ci ste yaṅ ji ltar na brtag par bya ba ma yin paḥi mtshan ñid kyi[25] gtan tshigs des/rdul phra rab kyi rdzas yod pa ñid gcig pa ñid du med do źes śes par nus śe na/gaṅ gi phyir yod na ni phyogs cha tha dad paḥi phyir/dper na yod pa bum pa daṅ/snam bu daṅ śiṅ rta la sogs paḥi rdzas rnams ni/śar daṅ nub daṅ steṅ daṅ ḥog la sogs paḥi phyogs cha tha dad paḥi phyir/cha śas tha dad pa dag snaṅ ba ltar gal te rdul phra rab kyi rdzas kyaṅ yod par gyur na/gdon mi za bar phyogs cha tha dad paḥi phyir śar daṅ nub daṅ byaṅ daṅ steṅ la sogs paḥi cha śas khas blaṅ bar byaḥo/cha śas tha dad pa yin na ni rdul phra rab kyi rdzas gcig tu mi ḥgrub bo/rdzas kyi dbye ba maṅ po snaṅ baḥi phyir gcig pa ñid ni yod pa ma yin te/rdul phra rab mi dmigs pas rdul phra rab kyi rdzas su smra ba ḥdi thoṅ śig/

de phyir mkhas pas ḥkhrul pa tsam/
yaṅ dag don du min par brtag//3//

gaṅ gi phyir de ltar khams gsum la ḥkhrul pa tsam yin pa deḥi phyir/mkhas pa legs pa thob par ḥdod pas ḥdi la yaṅ dag paḥi don du brtag par mi byaḥo/gal te ḥdi sñam du bum pa la sogs pa phyi rol gyi dṅos po de dag ni/ṅo bo ñid mi rtogs paḥi[26] phyir med pa las kun brtags pa[27] yin pa bden no/de dag la dmigs paḥi rnam pa can gyi ḥkhrul paḥi śes pa ḥdi ni yod do[28]/dper na sgyu ma daṅ dri zaḥi groṅ khyer la sogs pa med kyaṅ/de dag la dmigs paḥi rnam pa can gyi śes pa lta buḥo źes bya bar ḥdod do źes/

ḥkhrul na de yaṅ ma dag phyir/
ji ltar snaṅ ba de ltar med/
don yod ma yin snaṅ ba ni
ji ltar de yi bdag ñid ḥgyur//4//

ḥkhrul pa de yaṅ rdzas kyi raṅ gi ṅo bo[29] śes pa yin na/rdzas de ni ṅo bo ñid de lta bur yod pa ma yin te/don de med na yaṅ raṅ gi ṅo bos ni nus pa med pas ma dag par ḥgyur ro/ma dag paḥi phyir ḥkhrul paḥi ṅo bo ñid de lta bur yod do źes bya bar ji lta bur śes/ ḥdi ltar[30] ḥjig rten na yaṅ sa bon la sogs pa skyed par byed pa med na/skyed par bya ba[31] myu gu la sogs pa yod do źes bya baḥi chos de lta bu yaṅ ma mthoṅ ṅo/de ñid kyi phyir sgyu maḥi dpe yaṅ ma grub par ṅas bśad do[32]/

gaṅ źig źib moḥi blo yis ni/
thams cad btags pa[33] kho nar śes/
blo ldan de yis chags la sogs/
bde bar sbrul gyis skrag bźin spoṅ//5//

ji skad bśad paḥi rnam pas[34] btags pa[35] tsam du yod paḥi khams gsum ḥdi la gaṅ źig bum pa la sogs pa rags paḥi blo bsal[36] te/źib moḥi blos rdzas med pa tha sñad tsam yin par ṅes par ḥdzin pa de ni/ji ltar thag pa la sbrul lo sñam paḥi śes pas kun nas bslaṅ baḥi ḥjigs pa deḥi khyad par rnam par dpyad nas thag par ṅes pa na/ deḥi sbrul gyis skrag pa med pa de bźin du/ḥdod chags la sogs pa de skyed par byed paḥi dṅos po dag la yoṅs su brtags pas[37] des kyaṅ/ḥdod chags la sogs pa ñon moṅs paḥi dra ba rnams bde bar dkaḥ ba med par riṅ por mi thogs pa kho nar spoṅ bar ḥgyur ro/

ḥjig rten pa yi don rtogs pas/
ḥjig rten bźin du bsgrub par bya/
kun nas ñon moṅs spoṅ ḥdod pas/
dam paḥi don gyis btsal bar bya[38]//6//

ji ltar ḥjig rten pa dag bum pa la sogs paḥi don la dṅos por rtog pas/ ḥdi bum paḥo/snam buḥo/śiṅ rtaḥo źes tha sñad ḥdogs pa de bźin du sṅon gyi bsgrub pas tha sñad du byaḥo/deḥi ḥog tu ḥdod chags la sogs pa ñon moṅs pa spoṅ bar ḥdod pa rnams kyis/ji skad bśad paḥi don dam paḥi mtshan ñid kyis dṅos po rnams yoṅs su btsal bar bya ste/de ltar dṅos po rnams yoṅs su tshol ba nas/deḥi ḥdod chags la sogs pa/ñon moṅs paḥi dra ba phyis mi skye bar ḥgyur ro/

cha śas kyi yan lag ces bya baḥi rab tu byed paḥi ḥgrel pa slob dpon ḥphags pa lhas mdzad pa rdzogs so/rgya gar gyi mkhan po Śraddhākaravarma daṅ bod kyi lotsāba Rin chen bzaṅ pos bsgyur paḥo/

COMMENTARY OF THE TREATISE NAMED THE HAIR IN THE HAND

Translation

In the language of India: *Hastavālanāmaprakaraṇavṛtti* (Commentary of the treatise named 'The Hair in the Hand'). In the language of Tibet: *Cha śas kyi yan lag ces bya baḥi rab tu byed paḥi ḥgrel pa* (Commentary of the treatise named 'The Parts of the Parts').

Homage to the noble Dhyānibodhisattva Mañjuśrī

This (treatise) has been composed in order that through the analysis of the nature of things, a non-erroneous knowledge be rightly produced in those persons who do not grasp the true meaning of reality,[39] because they consider as a true reality[40] the merely conventional denominations[41] which are the three worlds.[42]

1a-b *In front of a rope the idea of a snake is conceived;*[43] *when (the rope) is seen as a rope, (that idea) becomes without (a real corresponding) object.*[44]

In this matter (the treatise says:) (On seeing a rope) in some place lighted only by a not very clear light, through the error-illusion (produced) by the perception of only the attributes of the rope that in relation to form are common (to the rope and to the snake), there arises the cognition of a thing perceived with certainty, (cognition expressed in the following way:) 'This is indeed a snake', because the proper form of (its) specific properties has not been grasped.[45] When its specific properties are perceived with certainty, that cognition also becomes only an erroneous-illusory cognition without (a real corresponding) object, because of its being a vain fancy, owing to the knowledge that such an object (i.e. the snake) does not exist.

1c-d *When the parts of that (rope) are seen, also the cognition concerning that (rope) is erroneous-illusory, as (the cognition of) the snake.*

If one examines also that rope, dividing it into its parts, the existence in itself of the rope is not perceived. Since this (existence in itself of the rope) is not perceived, also the perception of the rope, like the idea of 'a snake', is only a mere error-illusion, nothing else. Moreover, just as the cognition of the rope is an error-illusion, in the same way, on examining also (at their turn) those parts and their (respective) fractions, particles etc., their existence in itself (i.e. the existence in itself of the parts of the rope) is not perceived. Since it (the existence in itself of the parts of the rope) is not perceived, also the idea which has the form of the perception of those (parts of the rope), like the idea of the rope, is only a mere error-illusion.[46]

2a-d *If the (alleged) existence in itself in all the dependent things is examined, whatever object there is of the empirical knowledge,*[47] *(this object) is dependent upon (something) other.*

In the same way as, when the rope etc., divided through the separation of their parts etc., are examined, their existence in itself is not perceived, and the idea also of the rope etc., like the idea of 'a snake', is an error-illusion, in the same way, when their parts etc.

are examined, whatever objects there are of the empirical knowledge,[48] pot, drinking cup etc., all are only dependent (upon something else).[49] And when they (all the things) are wholly divided up to the end, any thing, flask etc. is only dependent upon a convention.[50] '*(Dependent) upon (something) other*': 'Do not exist from the point of view of the absolute truth'.

3a-b *Since something without parts cannot be imagined, the (alleged) last (part) also is similar to (something) inexistent.*

That which is the last (part) of all conditioned things, the matter of the atom, the only one without parts,[51] that also is a non-existent thing,[52] because it is similar to a garland of sky-flowers and to a hare's horn[53] etc., since it cannot be perceived, because its existence in itself cannot be imagined.[54] But if it is asked whether it is possible to know how the matter of the atom, existing indeed, is not an unity, because a characteristic (of unity) cannot be imagined (for it), (the answer is:) because of the division into parts of the space—supposing that (that matter) exist. In the same way as for instance the existing matters of the flask, the cloth and the car etc., owing to the division into parts of the space: east, west, above and below etc., appear divided into parts, in the same way, if the matter of the atom also happens to exist, undoubtedly, owing to the division into parts of the space, the parts: east, west, north, above etc., must be admitted (as existing in the matter of the atom). Being divided into parts, the matter of the atom is not one. Since many divisions of the matter (of the atom) appear, (its) unity does not exist and, because the atom is not perceived,[55] let this affirmation (of unity) about the matter of the atom be abandoned.

3c-d *Therefore the wise man considers that the mere error-illusion (that are the three worlds) is not a true reality.*

Since thus in the three worlds there is only error-illusion, then the wise man who desires to obtain the *summum bonum* must not consider these (worlds) as a true reality. If so it is said: 'It is maintained that, (even if) it is true that those external things, the flask etc. are imagined out of nothing, since an existence in itself is not known (as belonging to them), (yet) this erroneous-illusory cognition, which has the form of the perception of those (things: the flask etc.), exists, in the same way as for instance, although the magic creation, the mirage etc. do not (really) exist, (yet) the cognition, which has the form of the perception of these (things: magic creation etc.), (exists)'[56], (we answer:)

4a-d *Those (things) also, since they are not real, are not such as they appear in the erroneous-illusory (cognition). As to the representation (in the mind) of an object which does not exist, how can it (i.e. the representation) have a real existence?*

Since that error-illusion is indeed (nothing else than) the cognition (of course erroneous) of the (presumed) existence in itself of the thing, since the thing is not (something possessing) such an existence in itself, and since also that object (of the erroneous-illusory cognition) does not exist, because it cannot (exist) with an existence in itself, (the object of the erroneous-illusory cognition) is unreal. Since (the object of the erroneous-illusory cognition) is not real, the existence in itself of the error-illusion is of the same class (i.e. unreal). How is this known? In this manner: in the world too, such a thing (as this) has (never) been seen, that even if the producer (the cause), like the seed etc., does not exist, (nevertheless) the produced (the effect), like the shoot etc., exists. Because of this we affirm that also the example of the magic creation (adduced by the opponent) is not valid.

5a-d *Whosoever with subtle mind knows that all the things are only dependent, that intelligent man easily throws out desire etc., as (the man who knows that there is no snake but only a rope, throws out) the fear (produced) by the snake.*

Whosoever, in these three worlds, which in consequence of what has been explained above are only conditioned, throws away the idea of the flask etc. being compact, and with subtle mind perceives with certainty that the things are non-existent, merely conventional denominations—in the same way as (for him)—the fear inspired by the thought that the rope is a serpent, when there is the certainty, through the examination of its characteristics (i.e. the characteristics of the rope), that it is (only) a rope, that fear of his (produced) by the serpent does not exist (anymore)—in the same way that (man) also, by having examined thoroughly the things that produce desire etc.,[57] eliminates the nets of the impurities,[58] desire etc., *easily* (that is to say:) 'without difficulty', 'only in short time'.[59]

6a-d *(The man) who perceives the things of the world should act as the worldly people in the established way; (the man) who wishes to eliminate the impurities must investigate according to the supreme reality.*

As worldly people, who consider things, a flask etc., as existing entities, impose[60] (on them) conventional denominations: 'this is a flask', 'this is a cloth', 'this is a car', in the same way one should act, in the formerly established way, according to conventions.[61] Afterwards those who wish to eliminate impurities, desire etc., must thoroughly investigate things according to the essence of the supreme reality as it has been explained, and, having thoroughly investigated things in that way, the nets of their impurities, desire etc. do not arise again.

(Here) ends the commentary of the treatise named "The Parts of the Parts" composed by the *ācārya* Āryadeva, translated by the Indian *pandit* Śhraddhākaravarman and the Tibetan *lotsāba* Rin chen bzaṅ po.

NOTES

1. For a discussion on the title see the article of F.W. Thomas and H. Ui, ' "The Hand Treatise", a work of Āryadeva', pp. 267, 272-73, and 310 note 1.
2. See F.W. Thomas and H. Ui, '"The Hand Treatise", a work of Āryadeva', p. 267.
3. Like Śaṅkara's *Hastāmalaka*, Bhavaviveka's *Karatalaratna*. See also *Vajrasūcika Upaniṣad* in *Sāmānya Vedānta Upaniṣads*, ed. A.M. Sastri, Adyar, 1921, Theosophical Society, p. 419; *Rāmāyaṇa* I, ed. G.H. Bhatt, Baroda, 1960, Oriental Institute, p. 29, critical apparatus 154 verse 7; Sarvajñātman, *Saṃkṣepaśārīraka* I, 262; Yāmuna, *Āgamaprāmaṇya*, introductory stanza.
4. This work constitutes an excellent example of the application of the method of abolishing analysis that is characteristic of the Mādhyamaka school of Buddhism.
5. hastavālanāmaprakaraṇavṛtti: 5245; 3845: hastabāsanāmaprakaraṇavṛtti.
6. ḥdi na: 3849; 3845: ḥdi ni.
7. gsal ba ma yin paḥi: our suggestion. Cf. Śaṅkara, *Bhāṣya* of Gauḍapāda's *Kārikās* II, 17; *rajjur mandāndhakāre*; 3845: skal ba ma yin pa.
8. spyiḥi: 3849; 3845: spyi.
9. chos tsam: 3849; 3845: chos can.

10. dmigs pas: 3849; 3845: dmigs pa la.
11. ṅo boḥi: 3849; 3845: ṅo bo.
12. khyad par gyi: 3849; 3845: khyad par.
13. thag paḥi śes pa: 3849; 3845: thag par śes la.
14. ḥkhrul pa yin pa: 3849; 3845: ḥkhrul pa.
15. brtags na deḥi: 3849; 3845: ltos pa ni.
16. blo yaṅ thag paḥi blo bźin du: 3849; 3845: blo bźin du.
17. btags paḥi: 5249; 3845: brtag paḥi.
18. kun rdzob śes paḥi spyod yul ni/ji sñed yod pa gźan las btags/: 5249; 3845: kun rdzob tu ni śes pa yis/spyod yul ji sñed brtags pa yin/.
19. btags: *a, g,* according to F.W. Thomas and H.Ui, p. 291; 3845: brtags pa.
20. btags pa: 5249; 3845: brtags pa.
21. gźan las: 5249; 3845: gźan du.
22. don dam par ni ma yin no/:5249; 3845: don dam pa ñid las so/.
23. btags paḥi: 5249; 3845: brtag paḥi.
24. dmigs par: 5245; 3845: dmigs pa.
25. mtshan ñid kyi: 5249; 3845: mtshan ñid.
26. rtogs paḥi: 3849; 3845: rtog paḥi.
27. brtags pa: 3849; 3845: brtags pas.
28. ḥkhrul paḥi śes pa ḥdi ni yod do: 5249; 3845: ḥkhrul pa tsam ḥdi yod de.
29. raṅ gi ṅo bo: our correction; 3845: raṅ gi ṅo bos.
30. ḥdi ltar: 3849; 3845: ji ltar.
31. bya ba: 3849; 3845: byed pa.
32. sgyu maḥi dpe yaṅ ma grub par ṅas bśad do: 3849 but suppressing: skyes buḥi after sgyu maḥi; 3845: sgyu ma lta bu ḥdod pa yaṅ ma grub par ṅes pa bśad pa yin no.
33. btags pa: 5249; 3845: brtags pa.
34. rnam pas: 3849; 3845: rnam par.
35. btags pa: 3849; 3845: brtags pa.
36. bsal: 5245; 3845: gsal.
37. brtags pas: 3849; 3845: brtags pa.
38. bya: 3849; 3845: byas.
39. Conditionality, relativity, dependence, composedness which constitute the authentic nature of everything.
40. A substance, something existing *in se et per se* or in other words 'with an own being (svabhāva)'.
41. A car, a cloth, a pot, etc., do not exist *in se et per se* as such; they are only a conglomerate of different pieces, threads, clay particles etc. The words 'car', 'cloth', 'pot', etc. designate by human convention those conglomerates, giving the erroneous impression that they are unitary entities really existing. The world is only a collection of those conglomerates designated by conventional denominations.
42. The three worlds: *kāmaloka, rūpaloka, arūpaloka.*
43. Classical simile in Indian philosophy: as somebody sees a rope in a dark place and thinks it is a serpent, so also people conceive the true reality (*Brahman, śūnyatā* etc.) as something which it is not, for instance as the empirical reality. V. Bhattacharya, *The Āgamaśāstra of Gauḍapāda,* p.

cxviii note 8, says that the simile rope-serpent is found probably for the first time in Gauḍapāda's work (eighth century A.D.); but as we see by this treatise this simile was employed in India at least three centuries before and in a Buddhist work. Probably its origin is Buddhist, taking into account that idealism, in which area this simile is utilized, arose in Buddhist schools. Other Buddhist authors which employ this simile: Candrakīrti, *Prasannapadā ad* XI, 1, XXV, 3; Sthiramati, *ṭīkā ad Madhyāntavibhāgaśāstra* I, 2 (ed. Pandeya, p. 12).

44. I.e. 'false'.

45. The text indicates the characteristics of error: one conceives as real something non-existent, and the error arises because the differences which distinguish one object from another are not grasped. Cf. Śaṅkara, *Bhāṣya* of the *Vedāntasūtras*, Introduction: *ke cit tu yatra yadadhyāsas tadvivekāgrahanibandhano bhrama iti.*

46. We can give an example in modern terms: we see a portion of skin and we think that the skin exists as such, as something real; if we examine the skin with a microscope, the skin disappears and instead of it we see the cells that compose it; an examination with a more powerful microscope will cause the cells to disappear and be replaced by the elements that constitute them and so on. According to the Mādhyamika school this analytical and abolishing process has no end. And because of this, although we cannot say that things are non-existent, nevertheless we can affirm that they are 'similar to (something) inexistent' (*kārikā* 3*a-b*).

47 The normal sensorial knowledge which does not penetrate unto the true nature of things and remains within the scope of the illusory appearance that our mind creates.

48. In the Tibetan text we have: *tha sñad paḥi śes pa(ḥi)* which literally refers to the 'conventional' knowledge, that is to say the knowledge that works with the conventional denominations superimposed upon things.

49. The present section establishes as a general principle the results obtained in the analysis of the rope.

50. No object exists really as such; objects are only, as already said, a conglomerate of different parts and elements, to which man imposes by convention a name, attributing them unconsciously unity and an independent being. See note 41.

51. What preçedes expresses the thesis of the Vaiśeṣikas, the Indian Atomists, which the author will refute. On the Vaiśeṣika school see the books or articles of B. Faddegon, H. Jacobi, A.B. Keith, H. Ui, M.K. Gangopadhyaya and P. Masson-Oursel.

52. In *kārikās* Ic-d and II the author maintains that everything can be divided into parts. Consequently it is not possible to attribute to it an existence in itself, an own being, substantiality. In this *kārikā* the author maintains that there is nothing which cannot be divided into parts, that even the smallest particle of anything, the atom, has parts. With this thesis the author opposes the Vaiśeṣika school which affirms the existence of the indivisible atom, real element, constitutive of everything. In the *Vaiśeṣikasūtras* (between 300 B.C. and A.D. 100), the oldest work of the school, we do not find arguments in

favour and against the existence of the atom, but in the *Nyāyasūtras* (third century A.D.) IV, 2, 14 etc. and in the subsequent works of the Nyāya school many arguments in favour and against the existence of the atom are recorded. In the Buddhist authors like Āryadeva, *Catuḥśataka* 215 (P.L. Vaidya, *Études sur Āryadeva*, pp. 80 and 137, and G. Tucci, 'Studi Mahāyānici I', p. 526); Candrakīrti, *Prasannapadā*, pp. 88-9 (ed. L. de la Vallée Poussin); Vasubandhu, *Viṃśatikā* 14; Śantideva, *Bodhicaryāvatāra* IX, 87, and Prajñākaramati, *Pañjikā ad locum* argumentation against the Atomic thesis is also found. The *Hastavālanāmaprakaraṇa* mentions only a part of this argumentation. Cf. O. Rosenberg, *Die Probleme der buddhistischen Philosophie*, Chapter 40; Y. Kajiyama, 'The Atomic Theory of Vasubandhu'.

53. Classical similes in the philosophy of India in order to indicate mere creations of the mind and therefore objects really non-existent. The atoms are said in *kārikā* 3a-b to be similar to (something) non-existent, i.e. they are in the same level as objects like 'skyflowers', 'hare's horns' etc.
54. It cannot be perceived not because of a deficiency or weakness of our senses—as an adversary could argue but because the logical analysis (Cf. *buddhyā vivecanāt, buddhyā vivecanam, Nyāyasūtra* IV, 2, 24-25 and *Bhāṣya ad locum*), as the one that follows in the text, forces us to conclude that it is not possible to accept an indivisible matter, independently of the capacity or incapacity of our senses to grasp it. Cf. Candrakīrti, *Prasannapadā* XVI, 4: *tatrāsau avijñeyasvarūpatvāt khapuṣpavan nāsty eveti.*
55. Cannot be established either by the senses or by reasoning.
56. The thesis now adduced maintains that it is possible to accept the unreality of the object and to consider it an illusion, but it is not possible to doubt the existence of the illusion itself, of the illusory thought. In the next section the author refutes the affirmation of the independent and real existence of the illusion as such. The author of the treatise does not affirm the total and absolute inexistence of the illusion, of the illusory thought; this illusion, this thought, exists from the point of view of the relative truth, as something 'void' of an own being, with the same *status* as its object. What the author of the treatise affirms is the non-existence of that illusion from the point of view of the absolute truth, as something existing *in se et per se*, as a substance. In order to establish his thesis the author of the treatise adduces the argument that, if the cause (the object in this case) is not really existent, the effect (the knowledge of the object) cannot really exist. Cf. Sthiramati, *Ṭīkā ad Madhyāntaṿibhāga* I, 2 (ed. R.N. Pandeya, p. 10): *na ca yad yasya kāraṇaṃ tadabhāve tasyotpattir yujyate;* and the celebrated aphorism of the Mādhyamaka school: *śūnyebhya eva śūnyā dharmāḥ prabhavanti dharmebhyaḥ* (*Pratītyasamutpādahṛdayakārikā* 4). The thesis presented in this section by the opponent is similar to the one maintained by the Yogācāra school. This school accepted the sole existence of consciousness which, under the power of error, creates the illusion of an external world. On the Yogācāra school of Buddhism see A.K. Chaterjee, S. Dasgupta, P.T. Raju, J. Masuda, J. Kitayama indicated in the Bibliography.
57. He analyses the things that produce desire etc. in the same way in which he

analyses the rope etc. and finds that they have not an own existence, that they are unreal and that consequently he must not make them an object of desire etc. in the same way as a wise person does not make an object of desire things that he sees in a dream. Cf. Śāntideva, *Bodhicaryāvatāra* IX, 88, and Prajñākaramati, *Pañjikā ad locum.*

58. Desire, hatred, error.
59. As it is seen by this section and the following one, in order to be able to transform in a reality the moral ideal of the elimination of passions, it is necessary previously to grasp the true nature (conditionedness etc.) of things. The adequate conception of the world is so necessary as the moral discipline in order to obtain the desired aim.
60. The word 'impose' (*adhyāropa, adhyāsa*) designates the process by which the mind, deceived by error, attributes to the true reality a nature that does not belong to it.
61. In the sphere of normal life one has to act according to the net of conventions that have been established by human mind, employing the conventional names given to beings and things, even if this implicates the attribution to them of an own existence and unity.

CHAPTER 2

The Yuktiṣaṣṭikākārikā of Nāgārjuna

INTRODUCTION

Yuktiṣaṣṭikā's Authorship

In general terms tradition considers that the *Yuktiṣaṣṭikā* was written by Nāgārjuna (second century A.D.), the founder of the philosophical school Mādhyamaka of Mahāyāna Buddhism.

Candrakīrti, *Prasannapadā*, p. 3, 1.15, ed. P.L. Vaidya (p. 9, 1.4, ed. L. de la Vallée Poussin) attributes expressly a *pāda*, that he quotes, to Nāgārjuna, and this *pāda* corresponds to a part of *kārikā* 19 of the *Yuktiṣaṣṭikā*, and in the same commentary, p. 3, 1.22, ed. P.L. Vaidya (p. 10, 1.4, ed. L. de la Vallée Poussin) he quotes again the same *pāda*, attributing it to the *ācārya*, by which word we must understand Nāgārjuna.

In the *Subhāṣitasaṃgraha* 28 *kārikā* 19 of the *Yuktiṣaṣṭikā* is quoted and expressly attributed to Nāgārjuna.

The *Madhyamakaśāstrastuti* of Candrakīrti, whose original Sanskrit text was discovered by G. Tucci and published by J.W. de Jong in *Oriens Extremus* IX, pp. 47-56, includes the *Yuktiṣaṣṭikā* among the eight works which it attributes to Nāgārjuna. The Tibetan translation of the *Madhyamakaśāstrastuti* was known before Tucci's discovery. It is included at the end of the Tibetan translation of Candrakīrti's *Prasannapadā*, but it is not found in any of the Sanskrit manuscripts of this commentary.

Bu-ston, *History of Buddhism* Part I, pp. 50-51, considers the *Yuktiṣaṣṭikā* as one of the six principal treatises of Nāgārjuna.

The colophons of the Tibetan translation of the *Yuktiṣaṣṭikā*, in *Sde-dge* and *Peking* editions, and the colophon of the Chinese translation of this work, attribute it to Nāgārjuna.

Modern authors generally attribute the *Yuktiṣaṣṭikā* to

Nāgārjuna. Cf. A. Bareau, *Die Religionen Indiens* III, p. 136; T.R.V. Murti, *The Central Philosophy of Buddhism*, pp. 88-89 (who follows Bu-ston's opinion); Phil. Schäffer, *Yuktiṣaṣṭikā*, pp. 2-3; P.L. Vaidya, *Études sur Āryadeva*, pp. 48-49; K.V. Ramanan, *Nāgārjuna's Philosophy*, p. 35; A.K. Warder, *Indian Buddhism*, p. 375; M. Winternitz, *A History of Indian Literature*, vol. II, p. 346; D. Seyfort Ruegg, *The Literature of the Mādhyamaka School*, pp. 19-20; Uriūtsu Ryūshin, *A Study of Nāgārjuna.*

Editions and Translations of the Yuktiṣaṣṭikā, kārikās and Commentary

The *Yuktiṣaṣṭikā* has, as its name indicates, 60 *kārikās*. This treatise was commented by Nāgārjuna himself and also by Candrakīrti—Nāgārjuna's commentator.

The kārikās' text. The Sanskrit text has not been preserved. Only some Sanskrit *kārikās* from it have come to us, quoted in Sanskrit works like Candrakīrti's *Prasannapadā*, Prajñākaramati's *Pañjikā, Subhāṣitasaṃgraha*.

We know this work thanks to its Tibetan and Chinese translations.

Tibetan translation of the kārikās. Tōhoku 3825 = *Catalogue* 5225. It was done by Mutitaśrī and Pa-tshab Ñi-ma grags.

Chinese translation of the kārikās. Taisho 1575. Nanjio 1307. It was done by Dānapāla (?).

The commentaries' text. Nāgārjuna's commentary of the *Yuktiṣaṣikākārikās* has not been preserved either in its Sanskrit original text or in any translation.[1] Candrakīrti's commentary has come to us only in its Tibetan translation: *Tōhoku* 3864 = *Catalogue* 5265. This translation was made by Jinamitra, Dānaśīla, Śīlendrabodhi and Ye-śes sde.

Now we indicate some modern editions and translations:

German translation of the Chinese translation of the kārikās. Phil. Schäffer, *Yuktiṣaṣṭikā, Die 60 Sätze des Negativismus*, 1923, pp. 7-21. At the end of his translation, Schäffer adds the text of the Tibetan (Peking edn.) and of the Chinese (Tokyo edn.) translations.

Japanese translations of the Tibetan translation of the kārikās and of Candrakīrti's commentary. Susumu Yamaguchi, in *Otani Gakuhō* (Otani Bulletin), vol. 7, No. 3, 1925, pp. 66-119 and in *Chūgan Bukkyō Ronkō* (Studies on Madhyamaka Buddhism), 1944, reprint. 1965, pp. 29-109. In both publications Yamaguchi includes the text of the Tibetan translation of the *kārikās*, the text of the Chinese translation of the same and the Japanese translation of the *kārikās* from the Tibetan version.

Uriūtsu Ryūshin, in an article 'Nāgārjuna Kenkyū (1)' ('Studies on Nāgārjuna, 1'), published in *Meiō Daigaku Jimbun Kiyō* (Bulletin of Humanities of Meijo College), no. 14, 1973, pp. 23-40, translates into Japanese the invocation and *kārikās* 1-3 and gives also a reconstruction into Sanskrit of these four stanzas. His translation and reconstruction is from the Tibetan version.

Uriūtsu Ryūshin, in his article 'Nāgārjuna Kenkyū (2)', published in *Kyōto Joshi Daigaku Jimbun Ronsō* (Collection of Treatises on Humanities of the Women's University of Kyōto), no. 23, 1974, pp. 134-60, presents a Japanese translation and a Sanskrit reconstruction of *kārikās* 4-12 from the Tibetan text.

Uriūtsu Ryūshin, in *Daijo Butten* ('Literature of Mahāyāna Buddhism') 14, 1974, pp. 5-88, presents the Japanese translation of the *kārikās* and commentary from the Tibetan version.

Uriūtsu Ryūshin, in *Nāgārjuna Kenkyū* ('A Study of Nāgārjuna'), 1985, pp. 67-206, gives the Tibetan version, a Sanskrit reconstruction and the Japanese translation from the Tibetan text, and finally an exegesis of the text with reference to Candrakīrti's commentary.

English Translations of the Tibetan Translation of the Kārikās

Chr. Lindtner, in *Nagarjuniana*, 1985, pp. 100-19, published the Tibetan version with the Sanskrit quotations, and an English translation.

F. Tola and C. Dragonetti, in an article 'The *Yuktiṣaṣṭikākārikā* of Nāgārjuna', published in *The Journal of the International Association of Buddhist Studies*, 6, 2, 1983, pp. 94-123, present the Tibetan text and an English translation. Cf. in the same journal, vol. 8, no. 1, 1985, pp. 116-17.

Spanish Translation of the Tibetan Translation of the Kārikās

F. Tola and C. Dragonetti, in their article, 'Yuktiṣaṣṭikākārikā. Las sesenta estrofas de la argumentación de Nāgārjuna', published in *Boletín de la Asociación Española de Orientalistas*, 1983, pp. 5-38, give the Tibetan version of the text together with its Spanish translation.

Kārikās Quoted in Other Sanskrit Texts

The *Kārikās* 1, 5, 6, 19, 30, 33, 34, 39, 46, 47, 48 and 55 of the *Yuktiṣaṣṭikā* have been preserved in other Buddhist Sanskrit texts.

Kārikā 1 Kālacakra (Dus kyi ḥkhor lo), *Sekoddeśaṭīkā*, p. 48, ed. M.E. Carelli, Baroda, 1941:

astināstivyatikrāntā buddhir yeṣāṃ nirāśrayā/
gambhīras tair nirālambaḥ pratyayārtho vibhāvyate/

Kārikā 5 Āryadeva, *Cittaviśuddhiprakaraṇa*, 24, ed. Patel:

saṃsāraṃ caiva nirvāṇaṃ manyante 'tattvadarśinaḥ/
na saṃsāraṃ na nirvāṇam manyante tattvadarśinaḥ//

Kārikā 6 Ratnakīrti, *Nibandhāvalī*, p. 139, ed. A. Thakur, 1975 (with *eva* for *etan* in b):

nirvāṇaṃ ca bhavaś caiva dvayam etan na vidyate/
parijñānaṃ bhavasyaiva nirvāṇaṃ iti kathyate//

Kārikā 19 Candrakīrti, *Prasannapadā ad* I, 1 p. 3, I.16, ed. P.L. Vaidya = p. 9, 1.5, ed. L. de la Vallée Poussin:

tat tat prāpya yad utpannaṃ notpannaṃ tatsvabhāvataḥ/

Subhāṣitasaṃgraha 28, p. 395, ll. 19-20, ed. C. Bendall:

tat tat prāpya yad utpannam notpannaṃ tat-svābhavataḥ/
svabhāvena yad utpannaṃ anutpannanāma tat kathaṃ//

Kārikā 30 *Subhāṣitasaṃgraha*, p. 385, ll. 10-11, ed. C. Bendall:

sarvam astīti vaktavyam ādau tattvagaveṣiṇā/
paścād avagatārthasya niḥsaṅgasya viviktatā//

Kārikā 33 Prajñākaramati, *Pañjikā ad* IX,7, p. 181, ll. 25-26, ed. P.L. Vaidya = p. 376, ed. L. de la Vallée Poussin:

mamety aham iti proktaṃ yathā kāryavaśāj jinaiḥ/
tathā kāryavaśāt proktāḥ skandhāyatanadhātavaḥ//

Kārikā 34 [2] Jñānaśrimitra, *Sākārasaṃgrahasūtra* 3.27, p. 545, ed. Anantalal Thakkur:

mahābhūtādi vijñāne proktaṃ samavarudhyate/
tajjñāne vigamaṃ yāti nanu mithyā vikalpitam//

Kārikā 39 [3] Prajñākaramati, *Pañjikā ad* IX, 85, p. 234, ll. 20-21, ed. P.L. Vaidya = p. 500, ed. L. de la Vallée Poussin:

hetutaḥ saṃbhavo yasya sthitir na pratyayair vinā/
vigamaḥ pratyayābhāvāt so 'stīty avagataḥ katham//

Kārikās 46-48 Haribhadra, *Āloka*, p. 161, ed. Wogihara, 1932-35 = pp. 343-44 ed. P.L. Vaidya, 1960:

rāgadveṣodbhavas tīvraduṣṭadṛṣṭiparigrahaḥ/
vivādās tatsamutthāś ca bhāvābhyupagame sati//

sa hetuḥ sarvadṛṣṭīnāṃ kleśotpattir na taṃ vinā/
tasmāt tasmin parijñāte dṛṣṭikleśaparikṣayaḥ//

parijñā tasya keneti pratītyotpādadarśanāt/
pratītya jātaṃ cājātam āha tattvavidāṃ varaḥ//

Kārikā 55 Āryadeva, *Cittaviśuddhiprakaraṇa*, 20, ed. Patel:

bālā rajyanti rūpeṣu vairāgyaṃ yānti madhyamāḥ/
svabhāvajñā vimucyante rūpasyottamabuddhayaḥ//

Sanskrit Restoration of Some Kārikās of the Yuktiṣaṣṭikā

As we have said, Uriūtsu Ryūshin published the restoration of the Sanskrit text of the invocation and of the first twelve *kārikās* in 1973 and 1974 and of the whole text in 1985.

Let us indicate also that *kārikā* 6 of the *Pratītyasamutpādahṛdayakārikā* (in Tibetan *Rten-ciṅ-ḥbrel-bar-ḥbyuṅ-baḥi sñiṅpoḥi tshig-leḥur-byas-pa*, in Chinese *Yin yuan sin louen song*) is identical with *kārikā* 12 of the *Yuktiṣaṣṭikākārikā*, being the only difference that in the second *pāda* the *Pratītyasamutpādahṛdayakārikā* speaks of cessation (*chad-pa* in Tibetan) while the *Yuktiṣaṣṭikākārikā* refers to birth (*skye-ba* in Tibetan).

V.V. Gokhale in his article '*Encore: the* Pratītyasamutpādahṛdayākārikā *of* Nāgārjuna', p. 67, gives the reconstruction of *kārikā* 6 of the *Pratītyasamutpādahṛdayakārikā* into Sanskrit (from Tibetan), which reads as follows:

bhāvasyā 'py atisūkṣmasya yenocchedo vikalpitaḥ/
tenā 'vipaścitā 'dṛṣṭā pratyayotpattir arthataḥ//

Scheme of the Exposition

According to Uriūtu, *Daijō Butten* 14, the distribution of the subject-matter of this treatise is the following one:

Preface: Standpoint of the treatise.

1. *Kārikā* 1: The meaning of Dependent Origination (I): Its profoundity.
2. *Kārikās* 2-3: The meaning of Dependent Origination (II): It is beyond being and non-being.
3. *Kārikās* 4-5: *Saṃsāra* and *nirvāṇa* do not exist either as being or as non-being.
4. *Kārikās* 6-9: If *saṃsāra* is known, that is *nirvāṇa.*
5. *Kārikās* 10-11a-b: Meaning of Dependent Origination (III): Neither birth nor cessation.
6. *Kārikās* 11c-d-12: Dependent Origination and *Nirvāṇa.*
7. *Kārikās* 13-19: There is not production (beginning) in what is produced in dependence: falsehood of existence.
8. *Kārikā* 20: There is not cessation in what is produced in dependence.
9. *Kārikās* 21-23: Explanation of production and cessation as a method of salvation.
10. *Kārikās* 24-29: The knowledge of the falsehood of existence.
11. *Kārikās* 30-35: For what purpose it is said that all things exist.
12. *Kārikās* 36-37: Establishment of the world as an illusion.
13. *Kārikās* 38-39: When the illusion ceases, the world does not exist anymore.
14. *Kārikās* 40-44: Criticism of the different opinion of Buddhist and non-Buddhist who say that substance exists.
15. *Kārikās* 45-49: Right understanding and lack of understanding of Dependent Origination.
16. *Kārikās* 50-51: The saints do not discuss sustaining the existence.
17. *Kārikās* 52-56: The standpoint of wise men and the attachment of fools.
18. *Kārikās* 57-59: The *Nirvāṇa* of the saints.
19. *Kārikā* 60: Conclusion: Transference of merit through this book.

We give now our own distribution:

Invocation, kārikās 1-2: Theme of the treatise: true meaning of

Dependent Origination, elimination of birth=being and destruction=non-being.

Kārikā 3: Why liberation cannot be obtained through non-being?

Kārikā 4: The sole means to obtain liberation.

Kārikā 5: Effect of the perception of truth.

Kārikā 6: What really is *nirvāṇa*.

Kārikās 7-10: Production and cessation. Their cause. Their unreality.

Kārikā 11: No diversity as a consequence of true knowledge.

Kārikās 12-23: Negation of production (beginning) and cessation (end). Condemnation of theories that affirm them. True meaning of Dependent Origination.

Kārikās 24-28: Insubstantiality, impermanence, unreality of the empirical world.

Kārikā 29: The ignorant and the sage.

Kārikā 30: Gradual comprehension of Voidness.

Kārikā 31: Consequences of the non-full comprehension of Voidness.

Kārikā 32: The true teaching of Buddha.

Kārikā 33: Propedeutic use of language by the Buddhas.

Kārikās 34-35: Falsehood of the Great Elements and of everything except *Nirvāṇa*.

Kārikā 36: Mind as the source of good and evil.

Kārikās 37-39: Unreality of the world because of being caused by ignorance.

Kārikās 40-41: Coherent behaviour of realists and blamable behaviour of some Buddhists who do not act according to the Teaching.

Kārikās 42-47: The evil consequences of the acceptance of substantiality.

Kārikā 48: The great principle: Universal Relativity.

Kārikā 49: Evil consequences of error.

Kārikās 50-52: The consequences of the non-acceptance and of the acceptance of dogmas.

Kārikās 53-54: Relation of the ignorant and the sage to objects.

Kārikās 55-56: Categories of men and stages in the path of liberation.

Kārikās 57-59: The knowledge of the true nature of things, the destruction of any dogma and the realization of *śūnyatā* mean liberation.

Kārikā 60: Transference of merit.

Importance of the Yuktiṣaṣṭikā

This small treatise in verse, of 60 *kārikās*, develops some themes characteristic of the Madhyamaka school of Buddhism, specially the fundamental one of birth-being and destruction-non-being. All of them are examined from the central point of view of *śūnyatā* in beautiful verses of logical and clear exposition. The *Yukti* can be considered one of the most important treatises of Nāgārjuna.

The Present Work

We offer in this chapter the Tibetan text of the *Yuktiṣaṣṭikākārikā* and its English translation, with some notes.

We have adopted the text of the *Sde-dge* edition of the Tibetan Buddhist Canon: *Bstan-ḥgyur, Dbu-ma,* Tsa. $20b^1$-$22b^6$ (*Tōhoku* 3825), comparing it with the text as given in the Peking edition: *Bstan-ḥgyur* vol. 95, *Mdo-ḥgrel* (*Dbu-ma*) XVII, 11-2-2 ($22b^2$-$25a^7$) (*Catalogue* 5225), and with the text of the *Yuktiṣaṣṭikākārikās* included in Candrakīrti's commentary, in its *Sde-dge* edition: *Bstan-ḥgyur, Dbu-ma,* Ya. $1b^1$-$30b^6$ (*Tōhoku* 3864). In some places, which we indicate in note, we have left aside the reading of *Sde-dge* edition to adopt the reading of the *Peking* edition of the *kārikās* and/or the reading of the *Sde-dge* edition of the *kārikās* included in the commentary of Candrakīrti.

From *kārikā* 48 we have followed the verse distribution of the Peking edition and of Candrakīrti's commentary, because in *Sde-dge* edition there is an extra verse which appears at the beginning of *kārikā* 48 and renders difficult the following distribution of the *kārikās*.[4]

The Tibetan title of this work is *Rigs-pa drug-cu-paḥi tshig-leḥur-byas-pa-shes-bya-ba*, which corresponds to the Sanskrit *Yuktiṣaṣṭikākārikānāma*.

RIGS PA DRUG CU PAḤI TSHIG LEḤUR BYAS PA
(*Yuktiṣaṣṭikākārikā*)

Tibetan Text

rgya gar skad du/ yuktiṣaṣṭikākārikānāma/
bod skad du/
rigs pa drug cu paḥi tshig leḥur byas pa źes bya ba/
ḥjam dpal gźon nur gyur pa la phyag ḥtshal lo/

(Invocation)

gaṅ gis[5] skye daṅ ḥjig pa dag/
tshul ḥdi yis ni spaṅs gyur pa/
rten ciṅ ḥbyuṅ ba gsuṅs pa yi/
thub dbaṅ de la phyag ḥtshal lo//

1 gaṅ dag gi blo[6] yod med las/
rnam par ḥdas śiṅ mi gnas pa/
de dag gis ni rkyen gyi don/
zab mo dmigs med rnam par rtogs//

2 re źig ñes kun ḥbyuṅ baḥi gnas/
med ñid rnam par bzlog zin gyis/
rigs pa[7] gaṅ gis yod ñid yaṅ[8]/
bzlog par ḥgyur ba mñan par gyis//

3 ji ltar byis pas rnam brtags bźin/
dṅos po gal te bden ḥgyur na/
de dṅos med pas rnam thar du/
gaṅ gis mi ḥdod rgyu ci źig//

4 yod pas rnam par mi grol te/
med pas srid pa ḥdi las min/
dṅos daṅ dṅos med yoṅs śes pas/
bdag ñid chen po rnam par grol//

5 de ñid ma mthoṅ ḥjig rten daṅ/
mya ṅan ḥdas par rlom sems te/
de ñid gzigs rnams ḥjig rten daṅ/
mya ṅan ḥdas par rlom sems med//

6 srid pa daṅ ni mya ṅan ḥdas/
gñis po ḥdi ni yod ma yin/
srid pa yoṅs su śes pa ñid/
mya ṅan ḥdas śes bya bar brjod//

7 dṅos po byuṅ ba źig pa la/
ji ltar ḥgog par brtags pa bźin/
de bźin dam pa rnams kyis kyaṅ/
sgyu ma byas paḥi[9] ḥgog pa bźed //

8 rnam par ḥjig pas ḥgog ḥgyur gyi/
ḥdus byas yoṅs su śes pas min/
de ni su la mṅon sum ḥgyur/
źig śes pa der ji ltar ḥgyur//

9 gal te phuṅ po ma ḥgags na/
ñon moṅs zad kyaṅ ḥdas mi ḥgyur/
gaṅ tshe ḥdir ni ḥgags gyur pa/
de yi tshe na grol bar ḥgyur//

10 ma rig rkyen gyis byuṅ ba la/
yaṅ dag ye śes kyis gzigs nas/
skye ba daṅ ni ḥgags paḥaṅ ruṅ/
ḥgaḥ yaṅ dmigs par mi ḥgyur ro//

11 de ñid mthoṅ chos mya ṅan las[10]/
ḥdas śiṅ bya ba byas paḥaṅ yin/
gal te chos śes mjug thogs su/
ḥdi la bye brag yod na ni//

12 dṅos po śin tu phra ba la ḥaṅ/
gaṅ gis skye bar rnam brtags pa/
rnam par mi mkhas de yis[11] ni/
rkyen las byuṅ baḥi don ma mthoṅ//

13 ñon moṅs zad paḥi dge sloṅ gi/
gal te ḥkhor ba rnam ldog na/
ci phyir rdsogs saṅs rgyas rnams kyis/
de yi rtsom pa rnam mi bśad//

14 rtsom pa yod na ṅes par yaṅ/
lta bar ḥgyur ba yoṅs su ḥdzin/

rten ciṅ ḥbrel par ḥbyuṅ ba gaṅ/
de la sṅon daṅ tha ma ci//

15 sṅon skyes pa ni ji ltar na/
phyi nas slar yaṅ bzlog par ḥgyur/
sṅon daṅ phyi maḥi mthaḥ bral ba/
ḥgro ba sgyu ma bźin du snaṅ//

16 gaṅ tshe sgyu ma ḥbyuṅ źe ḥam/
gaṅ tshe ḥjig par ḥgyur sñam du/
sgyu ma śes pa der mi rmoṅs/
sgyu ma mi śes yoṅs su sred//

17 srid pa smig rgyu sgyu ḥdra bar/
blo yis mthoṅ bar gyur na ni[12]/
sṅon gyi mthaḥ ḥam phyi maḥi mthaḥ/
lta bas yoṅs su slad mi ḥgyur//

18 gaṅ dag gis ni ḥdus byas la/
skye daṅ ḥjig pa rnam brtags pa/
de dag rten ḥbyuṅ ḥkhor lo yis/
ḥgro ba rnam par mi śes so[13]//

19 de daṅ de brten gaṅ ḥbyuṅ de/
raṅ gi dṅos por skyes ma yin/
raṅ gi dṅos por[14] gaṅ ma skyes/
de ni skye źes ji ltar bya//

20 rgyu zad ñid las źi ba ni/
zad ces bya bar mṅon pa[15] ste/
raṅ bźin gyis ni gaṅ ma zad/
de la zad ces ji ltar brjod//

21 de ltar ci yaṅ skye ba med/
ci yaṅ ḥgag par mi ḥgyur ro/
skye ba daṅ ni ḥjig paḥi las/
dgos paḥi don du bstan paḥo//

22 skye ba śes pas ḥjig pa śes/
ḥjig pa śes pas mi rtag śes/
mi rtag ñid la ḥjug śes pas/
dam paḥi chos kyaṅ rtogs par[16] ḥgyur//

23 gaṅ dag rten ciṅ ḥbrel ḥbyuṅ ba/
skye daṅ ḥjig pa rnam spaṅs par/
śes par gyur pa de dag ni/
lta gyur[17] srid paḥi rgya mtsho brgal//

24 so soḥi skye bo dṅos bdag can/
yod daṅ med par phyin ci log/
ñes pas ñon moṅs dbaṅ gyur rnams/
raṅ gi sems kyis bslus par ḥgyur//

25 dṅos la mkhas pa rnams kyis ni/
dṅos po mi rtag bslu baḥi chos/
gsog daṅ stoṅ pa bdag med pa/
rnam par dben źes bya bar mthoṅ//

26 gnas med dmigs pa yod ma yin/
rtsa ba med ciṅ gnas pa med/
ma rig rgyu las śin tu byuṅ/
thog ma dbus mthaḥ rnam par spaṅs//

27 chu śiṅ bźin du sñiṅ po med/
dri zaḥi groṅ khyer ḥdra ba ste/
rmoṅs paḥi groṅ khyer mi bzad paḥi/
ḥgro ba sgyu ma bźin du snaṅ//

28 tshaṅs sogs ḥjig rten ḥdi la ni/
bden par rab tu gaṅ snaṅ ba/
de ni ḥphags la brdsun źes gsuṅs/
ḥdi las gźan lta ci źig lus//

29 ḥjig rten ma rig ldoṅs gyur pa/
sred pa rgyun gyi[18] rjes ḥbraṅ daṅ/
mkhas pa sred pa daṅ bral ba/
dge ba rnams lta ga la mñam//

30 de ñid tshol la thog mar ni/
thams cad yod ces brjod par bya/
don rnams rtogs śiṅ chags med la/
phyis ni rnam par dben paḥo[19]//

31 rnam par dben don mi śes la/
thos pa tsam la ḥjug byed ciṅ/
gaṅ dag bsod nams mi byed pa/

skyes bu tha śal de dag brlag//

32 las rnams ḥbras bu bcas ñid daṅ/
ḥgro ba dag kyaṅ yaṅ dag bśad/
de yi raṅ bźin yoṅs śes daṅ/
skye ba med pa dag kyaṅ bstan//

33 dgos paḥi dbaṅ gis rgyal ba rnams/
ṅa daṅ ṅa yi źes gsuṅs ltar/
phuṅ po khams daṅ skye mched rnams/
de bźin dgos paḥi dbaṅ gis gsuṅs//

34 ḥbyuṅ ba che la sogs bśad pa/
rnam par śes su yaṅ dag ḥdu/
de śes pas ni ḥbral ḥgyur na/
log par rnam brtags ma yin nam//

35 mya ṅan ḥdas pa bden gcig pur/
rgyal ba rnams kyis gaṅ gsuṅs pa/
de tshe lhag ma log min źes/
mkhas pa su źig rtog par byed//

36 ji srid yid kyi rnam gyo ba/
de srid bdud kyi spyod yul de/
de lta yin na ḥdi la ni/
ñes pa med par cis mi ḥthad//

37 ḥjig rten ma rig rkyen can du/
gaṅ phyir saṅs rgyas rnams gsuṅs pa/
ḥdi yi phyir na ḥjig rten ḥdi/
rnam rtog yin źes cis mi ḥthad//

38 ma rig ḥgags par gyur pa na/
gaṅ źig ḥgag pa ḥgyur ba de/
mi śes pa las kun brtags par/
ji lta bur na gsal mi ḥgyur//

39 rgyu yod pa las gaṅ byuṅ źin[20]/
rkyen med par ni gnas pa med/
rkyen med phyir yaṅ ḥjig ḥgyur ba/
de ni yod ces ji ltar rtogs//

40 gal te yod par smra ba rnams/

dṅos la źen par[21] gnas pa ni/
lam de ñid la gnas pa ste/
de la ṅo mtshar cuṅ zad med//

41 saṅs rgyas lam la brten nas ni/
kun la mi rtag smra ba rnams/
rtsod pa yis ni dṅos po la[22]/
chags gnas[23] gaṅ yin de smad do//

42 ḥdi ḥam deḥo źes gaṅ du/
rnam par dpyad nas mi dmigs na/
rtsod pa ḥdi ḥam de bden źes/
mkhas pa su źig smra bar ḥgyur//

43 gaṅ dag gis[24] ni ma brten par/
bdag gam ḥjig rten mṅon źen pa/
de dag kye ma rtag mi rtag/
la sogs lta bas ḥphrogs pa yin//

44 gaṅ dag brten nas dṅos po rnams/
de ñid du ni grub ḥdod pa/
de dag la yaṅ rtag[25] stsogs skyon/
de dag ji ltar ḥbyuṅ mi ḥgyur//

45 gaṅ dag brten nas dṅos po rnams/
chu yi zla ba lta bur ni/
yaṅ dag ma yin log min par/
ḥdod pa de dag ltas mi ḥphrogs//

46 dṅos por khas len yod na ni/
ḥdod chags źe sdaṅ ḥbyuṅ ba yi/
lta ba mi bzad ma ruṅs ḥbyuṅ/
de las byuṅ baḥi rtsod par[26] ḥgyur//

47 de ni lta ba kun gyi rgyu/
de med ñon moṅs mi skye ste/
de phyir de ni yoṅs śes na/
lta daṅ ñon moṅs yoṅs su ḥbyaṅ//

48[27] gaṅ gis de śes ḥgyur źe na[28]/
brten nas ḥbyuṅ ba mthoṅ ba ste[29]/
brten nas skye ba ma skyes śes[30]/
de ñid mkhyen pa mchog gis gsuṅs//

49 log paḥi śes pas[31] zil gnon pa/
bden pa min la bden ḥdsin paḥi[32]/
yoṅs su ḥdsin daṅ rtsod stsogs kyi/
rim pa chags las ḥbyuṅ bar ḥgyur//

50 che baḥi bdag ñid can de dag/
rnams la phyogs med rtsod pa med/
gaṅ rnams la ni phyogs med pa/
de la gźan phyogs ga la yod//

51 gaṅ yaṅ ruṅ baḥi gnas rñed nas/
ñon moṅs sbrul gdug gyo can gyis/
zin par ḥgyur te gaṅ gi sems/
gnas med de dag zin mi ḥgyur//

52 gnas bcas sems daṅ ldan rnams la/
ñon moṅs dug chen cis mi ḥgyur/
gaṅ tshe tha mal ḥdug pa yaṅ[33]/
ñon moṅs sbrul gyis zin par ḥgyur//

53 byis pa bden par ḥdu śes pas/
gzugs brñan la ni chags pa bźin/
de ltar ḥjig rten rmoṅs paḥi phyir/
yul gyi gzeb la thogs par ḥgyur//

54 bdag ñid che rnams dṅos po dag/
gzugs brñan lta bur ye śes kyi/
mig gis mthoṅ nas yul źes ni/
bya baḥi ḥdam la mi thogs so//

55 byis pa rnams ni gzugs la chags/
bar ma dag ni chags bral ḥgyur/
gzugs kyi raṅ bźin śes pa yi/
blo mchog ldan pa rnam par grol//

56 sdug sñam pa las chags par ḥgyur/
de las bzlog pas ḥdod chags bral/
sgyu maḥi skyes bu ltar dben par/
mthoṅ nas mya ṅan ḥdaḥ bar ḥgyur//

57 log paḥi śes pas mṅon gdun baḥi/
ñon moṅs skyon rnams gaṅ yin de/
dṅos daṅ dṅos med rnam rtog pa/

don śes ḥgyur la mi ḥbyuṅ ṅo//

58 gnas yod na ni ḥdod chags daṅ/
ḥdod chags bral bar ḥgyur źig na/
gnas med bdag ñid chen po rnams/
chags pa med ciṅ chags bral min//

59 gaṅ dag rnam par dben sñam du/
gyo baḥi yid kyaṅ mi gyo ba/
ñon moṅs sbrul gyis dkrugs gyur pa/
mi zad srid paḥi rgya mtsho brgal//

60 dge ba ḥdi yis skye bo kun/
bsod nams ye śes tshogs bsags te/
bsod nams ye śes las byuṅ baḥi/
dam pa gñis ni thob par śog//

Rigs pa drug cu paḥi tshig leḥur byas pa źes bya ba slob dpon ḥphags pa Klu sgrub kyi źal sṅa ṅas mdzad pa rdzogs so// rgya gar gyi mkhan po Mutitaśrīḥi źal sṅa ṅas daṅ bod kyi lotsāba Pa-tshab Ñi-ma grags kyis bcos te gtan la phab paḥo//

THE SIXTY STANZAS OF REASONING

Translation

In the language of India: *Yuktiṣaṣṭikākārikānāma* (The *kārikās* named 'The sixty stanzas of Reasoning').

In the language of Tibet: *Rigs pa drug cu paḥi tshig leḥur byas pa źes bya ba* (The *kārikās* named 'The sixty stanzas of Reasoning').

Homage to the young Mañjuśrī

(Invocation)

Homage to the Lord of *munis*, who taught the Dependent Origination[34] and by whom, through this method,[35] birth and destruction have been eliminated.[36]

1[37] Those (men) whose mind, having gone beyond being and non-being,[38] does not cling (to anything),[39] (those men) understand the profound and supportless meaning of 'condition'.[40]

2 Now listen through which reasoning being[41] also is eliminated by those who have already eliminated non-being, the source of all evils.[42]

3 If, as is thought by the ignorant, things are real, then which is the reason why liberation by means of non-being is not admitted?[43]

4 Through being there is no liberation, through non-being there is no (liberation) from this existence;[44] only through the full knowledge of existence and non-existence[45] are great beings liberated.[46]

5[47] Those men who do not see the truth believe in the world and in the *nirvāṇa*;[48] those who perceive the truth do not believe in the world and in the *nirvāṇa*.

6[49] Existence and *nirvāṇa*—both do not exist. It has been taught that the perfect knowledge of existence is *nirvāṇa*.[50]

7 In the same way as the superior men consider the cessation of a thing that has been born, when it is destroyed, in the same way they consider the cessation of something created by magic.[51]

8 (If) cessation of conglomerates occurred through destruction and not through their perfect knowledge, where would that (cessation) be perceived? How could (the notion of) destruction occur in relation to those (conglomerates)?[52]

9 If the *skandhas* do not cease, one is not nirvanized even with the destruction of the impurities.[53] In the moment in which they (the *skandhas*) cease, in that moment one is liberated.[54]

10 When it is seen through correct knowledge that production is by cause of ignorance, (then) neither birth nor cessation are perceived at all.[55]

11 Having obtained *nirvāṇa* in this world, one has done

what has to be done[56]—if, after knowing the Doctrine, there were still here diversity.[57]

12 The extremely ignorant person who imagines production even in the utmost subtle things[59] does not perceive the meaning of the Dependent Origination.[60]

13 If the *saṃsāra* of the monk, whose impurities have been destroyed, comes (really) to an end, why did the perfect *buddhas* deny its beginning?[61]

14 If there were a beginning (for things) then certainly it would be perceived, it would be grasped.[62] But how can there be a beginning and an end for something that is produced depending on causes?[63]

15 How could something, that was formerly produced, cease afterwards?[64] The states of existence, devoid of the extremes of beginning and end, appear as a magical illusion.

16 When it is imagined that a magical illusion arises or it is destroyed, those persons who know (what is) the magical illusion, are not deceived with regard to it; those persons who do not know (what is) the magical illusion, ardently desire it.[65]

17 When one perceives with his mind that existence is similar to a mirage, to a magical illusion, one is not (anymore) corrupted by the views of a beginning or an end.[66]

18 Those persons who imagine that there is birth and destruction in the things that are composed, those persons do not know the world as (what it really is:) the wheel of Dependent Origination.[67]

19[68] What arises depending on this or that, that is not produced as a thing with an own being. Whatever is not produced as a thing with an own being, how can it be called 'produced'?[69]

20 It is evident that, in relation to somebody who has come

to an end through the cessation of the causes,[70] it can be said 'he ceased'.[71] In relation to somebody who has not ceased *in se et per se*, how can it be said 'he ceased'?

21 Thus nothing is produced, nothing ceases. (The Masters) have spoken about the processes of production and destruction (only) by reason of necessity.[72]

22 By knowing (what) production (is), destruction is known; (by) knowing (what) destruction (is), impermanence is known; through the knowledge which penetrates into impermanence, the Supreme Truth is understood.[73]

23 These persons who know that Dependent Origination is deprived of production and destruction,[74] those persons have crossed the ocean of existence,[75] created by the false views.[76]

24 Common people, who believe that things possess substantiality, who are mistaken about being and non-being, dominated by evil and impurities, are deceived by their own mind.[77]

25 Those persons who know the reality,[78] perceive that things are impermanent, that their characteristic is fraud,[79] that they are vain and void, insubstantial, lacking an own being.

26 The intolerable states of existence,[80] which have not a fundament, which are not support-point (of any cognition), which have not a root, which do not maintain (anything),[81] which have come forth from ignorance as their cause,[82] and are deprived of beginning, middle and end,[83]

27 which have no core, like the plantain trunk,[84] similar to the city of the *Gandharvas*,[85] domain of error, appear as magical illusions.

28 They, that in the worlds of Brahmā etc.,[86] appear as true, are declared to the Āryas (by Buddha) to be false. Which other thing remains there different from them?[87]

29 The views of worldly people, blinded by ignorance,

persisting in the stream of desire, and (those) of wise men, free from desire, and virtuous, in what respect are they similar?[88]

30[89] By the person who seeks the truth it must be said at the beginning (of his search): 'all things exist'; afterwards, when he knows the (nature of) things and is liberated from desire, (for him there is) separatedness.[90]

31 Those wicked persons, who having not grasped the meaning of Voidness, and having come up to a mere hearing (of the Doctrine),[91] do not accomplish meritorious deeds,[92] are destroyed.

32 The concomitancy of actions and their 'fruits' and also the diverse states of existence have been correctly explained; the knowledge of their true nature and also the non-existence of their birth have been taught.[93]

33[94] In the same way as by the Victorious,[95] by force of necessity, 'I', 'mine' have been said,[96] in the same way, by force of necessity, *'skandhas'*, *'dhātus'*, *'āyatanas'*[97] have been said (by them).[98]

34[99] The so called Great Elements[100] etc. are contained in consciousness; since, by knowing this,[101] they are dissolved, are they (all) not false mental creations?[102]

35 If the Victorious ones have said that *nirvāṇa* is the only true thing,[103] then which man could think that the rest is not false?[104]

36 So long as there is agitation of the mind, (mind) is the domain of Māra,[105] if that is so, why is not admitted that faultlessness is there?[106]

37 Since the Buddhas have said that the world has ignorance as its cause, then why is not admitted that this world is (only) a mental creation?[107]

38 How could a thing, which ceases when ignorance ceases, not reveal itself as a mental creation (coming forth) from ignorance?[108]

39[109] How is it possible to understand that a thing (really) exists, which having come forth owing to a cause, does not endure when its cause does not exist, and which disappears with the non-existence of the cause?[110]

40 If realists,[111] persist in their attachment to objects, (while) persisting in that very path (of realism), there is nothing surprising in it.[112]

41 Those persons who, because of adhering to Buddha's path, affirm that all is impermanent and who nevertheless through their discussions persist in their attachment to objects,[113] those persons really are blamable![114]

42 Which wise man will say, while discussing, that 'this' or 'that' is true, since, after investigation, he does not perceive anywhere either a 'this' or a 'that'?[115]

43 (Those persons) who are attached to the self or the world as unconditioned, those persons alas! are captivated by the false theories of permanence, impermanence etc.[116]

44 For those persons, who affirm that dependent things are established as really existing, for those persons how can the evils of (the belief in) permanence etc. not be produced?[117]

45 (Those persons) who affirm that dependent things, like the reflection of the moon in the water, are not existent, are not non-existent,[118] those persons are not captivated by (wrong) theories.[119]

46[120] When there is acceptance of things (as really existing), the intolerable, pernicious theories, arisen from attachment and hatred, arise, and discussions arising from them occur.[121]

47[122] That (acceptance) is the cause of all (false) theories; when it is absent, impurities are not born; therefore, when one understands this perfectly, theories and impurities are completely cleansed.

48[123] If it is asked how this[124] is known, (we answer:) the

Supreme Knower of reality perceived Dependent Origination, and therefore said: 'What is born dependently, is not born (in reality)'.[125]

49 (In the man) overcome by erroneous knowledge,[126] the (following) series is produced from passion: perception of reality in what is not real, acceptance (of that false reality as true), controversies etc.[127]

50 The great beings[128] hold no thesis; they do not debate. For those persons who hold no thesis, how can there be a contrary thesis?[129]

51 When one assumes any standpoint,[130] one is captured by the cunning poisonous serpent of the impurities.[131] Those persons whose mind lacks any standpoint, are not captured.

52 How will not the great poison of impurities originate in those persons who have a mind possessing standpoints, since, living like common people,[132] they are (easily) captured by the serpent of impurities?

53 In the same way as the ignorant man, believing that a reflected image is (something) real, becomes passionately fond of it, in the same way people, because of error, get imprisoned in the net of the objects.

54 The great beings, seeing with the eye of knowledge, that things are as a reflected image, are not captured in the swamp that are the objects.

55[133] Ignorant persons are attached to forms;[134] those in the middle[135] become detached; those who possess a lofty mind, who know the true nature of forms, become liberated.

56 Through the idea (that something is) 'agreeable', (the ignorant persons) become attached (to it); separating themselves from that (idea), (those in the middle) are free from attachment; when (the lofty-minded) see (that everything), as the man created by magic, is devoid of an own being,[136] they attain *nirvāṇa*.[137]

57 Those faults, the impurities, which belong to the persons afflicted by the erroneous knowledge, do not arise when the (true) meaning of being and non-being[138] (after they have been) well investigated, is known.

58 If a standpoint[139] exists, passion (exists); and if (the standpoint) is destroyed, freedom from passion occurs; (but) for the great beings who have no standpoint there is neither passion nor freedom from passion.[140]

59 Those persons whose mind, although unsteady (by nature), becomes steady as they consider that (everything) lacks an own being,[141] those persons will cross the ocean of the intolerable existence, agitated by the serpent of the impurities.

60 Through the virtue (of this treatise), may all beings, having accumulated the stores of merit and knowledge, obtain the two excellences,[142] which come forth from merit and knowledge![143]

(Here) ends the *kārikās* named 'The sixty stanzas of reasoning' composed by the venerable *ācārya* Nāgārjuna, revised and fixed in their definitive form by the Indian *pandit* Mutitaśrī and the Tibetan *lotsāba* Pa-tshab Ñi-ma grags.

NOTES

1. P.L. Vaidya, *Études sur Āryadeva*, p. 49, affirms that Nāgārjuna's commentary has been preserved only in a Tibetan translation and gives as a reference the *Tibetan Canon Mdo* XVII, 7, Cordier III, p. 292. Cf. Lalou, *Répertoire*, p. 122, where the title of this work is found: *Rigs pa drug cu paḥi* (*raṅ ḥgrel*). It is a mistake of Vaidya, since Nāgārjuna's commentary to his own treatise has not been preserved either in Sanskrit or in Tibetan. The work mentioned by Vaidya has not been found and its title has been reconstructed with the help of the Index, where it is attributed to Nāgārjuna, without indicating who is its translator, according to *Catalogue of Kanjur and Tanjur*, p. 350.
2. Cf. D.S. Ruegg, *The Literature of the Madhyamaka School of Philosophy in India*, p. 20, note 44. Ruegg changes *yāti* into *yadi*.
3. The Sanskrit text of this *kārikā* quoted by Candrakīrti and Prajñākaramati corresponds *exactly* to the Tibetan translation of *kārikā* 4 of *Lokātītastava*,

not so to the Tibetan translation of *kārikā* 39 of the *Yuktiṣaṣṭikā*, even if it expresses a similar idea. Nevertheless Vaidya and L. de la Vallée Poussin, in their editions of the *Pañjikā* consider that it is a quotation of the *Yuktiṣaṣṭikā*.

4. See note 27.
5. gaṅ gis: *Peking*. *Sde-dge*: gaṅ gi.
6. gaṅ dag gi blo: *Peking*. *Sde-dge*: gaṅ gis blo gros.
7. rigs pa: *Peking* and *Vṛtti*. *Sde-dge*: rigs paḥi.
8. yaṅ: *Vṛtti*. *Sde-dge*: daṅ.
9. byas paḥi: *Peking*. *Sde-dge*: byas ltaḥi.
10. mya ṅan las: *Peking*. *Sde-dge*: mya ṅan ḥdas.
11. de yis: *Peking* and *Vṛtti*. *Sde-dge*: de yi.
12. gyur na ni: *Vṛtti*. *Sde-dge*: gyur pa ni.
13. ḥgro ba rnam par mi śes so: *Peking*. *Sde-dge*: ḥkhor loḥi ḥgro ba rnam mi rtog.
14. dṅos por: *Peking*. *Sde-dge*: dṅos po.
15. mṅon pa: *Vṛtti*. *Sde-dge*: rtog pa.
16. rtogs par: *Peking* and *Vṛtti*. *Sde-dge*: rtog par.
17. lta gyur: *Vṛtti*. *Sde-dge*: ltar gyur.
18. rgyun gyi: *Peking* and *Vṛtti*. *Sde-dge*: rgyun gyis.
19. dben paḥo: *Peking*. *Sde-dge*: dban paḥo.
20. rgyu yod pa las gaṅ byuṅ źin: *Vṛtti*. *Sde-dge*: gaṅ źig rgyu daṅ bcas ḥbyuṅ źiṅ.
21. dṅos la źen par: *Vṛtti*. *Sde-dge*: dṅos mchog źen nas.
22. rtsod pa yis ni dṅos po la: *Vṛtti*. *Sde-dge*: rtsod pas dṅos rnams mchog bzuṅ bas.
23. chags gnas: *Vṛtti*. *Sde-dge*: gnas pa.
24. gaṅ dag gis: *Vṛtti*. *Sde-dge*: de dag gis.
25. rtag: *Vṛtti*. *Sde-dge*: rtags.
26. rtsod par: *Peking*. *Sde-dge*: spyod par.
27. We suppress the line *dṅos por khas len yod na ni* which appears in the *Sde-dge* edition of the *kārikās* and does not appear either in the Peking edition of the *kārikās* or in the *Sde-dge* edition of the *Vṛtti* of Candrakīrti and which is identical to the first line of *kārikā* 46.
28. źe na: *Vṛtti*. *Sde-dge*: sñam na.
29. ste: *Vṛtti*. *Sde-dge*: de.
30. śes: *Vṛtti*. *Sde-dge* : pas.
31. śes pas: *Vṛtti*. *Sde-dge*: śes pa.
32. ḥdsin paḥi: *Peking* and *Vṛtti*. *Sde-dge*: rdsun paḥi.
33. This line is not found in the *Sde-dge* edition. We take it from the *Sde-dge* edition of Candrakīrti's commentary.
34. In the Madhyamaka school the word *pratītyasamutpāda* (Tibetan: rten ciṅ ḥbyuṅ ba) designates principally the universal relativity and, as a consequence, the non-substantiality of every thing. The presence of the term Dependent Origination in the invocation of the treatise and its presentation as the teaching per excellence of Buddha indicate the great importance attributed to it by the Madhyamaka school.

35. The method developed in this treatise, which is the analytical-abolishing method of the Madhyamaka school. Cf. F. Tola and C. Dragonetti, 'Nāgārjuna's conception of 'voidness' (*śūnyatā*)'.
36. Birth and destruction, which were eliminated by Buddha by application of the principle of *pratītyasamutpāda* or universal relativity, constitute also the theme of the present treatise. Cf. note 41.
37. See Introduction, *Kārikās quoted* . . .
38. That is to say: established in the Middle Way which denies equally being, existence, and non-being, non-existence, and affirms only 'Voidness' which is neither something nor nothing. Existence or being and non-existence or non-being are only creations of our minds and nothing real corresponds to them.
39. Neither emotionally nor intellectually.
40. The real meaning of 'condition' is *profound*, because it can be grasped only by a mind well trained in the Mādhyamika dialectic, and is *supportless*, because to the notion of 'condition' nothing real corresponds, since from the *paramārtha* point of view even causality is abolished.
41 This *kārikā* indicates which will be the theme of the treatise: the negation of being and non-being. But what the treatise will eliminate in reality are, on one side, *birth, production, origination* and, on the other side, *destruction*, as being illusory products of our mind: nothing is truly born, nothing is truly destroyed; birth and destruction are not really produced. This change in the treatise's subject is comprehensible, since in our empirical reality birth is the necessary condition of existence and destruction the necessary condition of non-existence. If we eliminate birth and destruction as being nothing else than illusions, we eliminate at the same time existence and non-existence, their effects.

    The title of the treatise and this *kārikā* show the importance of reasoning (*yukti, rigs pa*) to attain the truth and avoid the evil consequences of wrong beliefs.
42. Not only the belief in non-being or destruction is the source of all evils, but also the belief in being or birth has the same consequence. To believe that things are really born, that they really exist, creates attachment to them; to believe that they are really destroyed, that they really come into non-existence provokes fear and sorrow. And these feelings give rise to actions which require new incarnations in order that they receive their adequate moral retribution.
43. If the *saṃsāra*, which contains the totality of things including the reincarnations, man, human mind, etc., is really existent, i.e. has an own being, exists *in se et per se*, then it can never be destroyed, since something that has an own being can never lose it. This is the answer to the question of the *kārikā*, answer given afterwards by *kārikā* 15. See note 64.
44. Nobody can hope to be liberated either by means of birth and existence or by means of destruction and non-existence, since they are unreal, mere creations of our mind, and nobody can be liberated through something non-existent *in se*.
45. In the second part of the *kārikā* we have the true doctrine about the means

of liberation. Things have only an illusory existence, produced by an erroneous act of our mind. Therefore the only way 'to destroy' them is to put an end to the erroneous act of our mind that creates them and this is the correct knowledge of their true nature, the knowledge that they are only illusion. If we see a rope and think it is a serpent, we cannot destroy the serpent by killing it; the only way to 'destroy' the serpent is to put an end to our mistake and to see what we really have before us: a rope.

46. Only the knowledge of the true nature of things allows man to adopt a behaviour which does not provoke actions which enchain to *saṃsāra*, and which permits liberation.

47. See Introduction: *Kārikās quoted* . . .

48. The world and the *nirvāṇa* are neither existent nor non-existent, they are void, Voidness, beyond being and non-being. The wise man, who has reached to the knowledge that all is void, has no more erroneous ideas regarding them, does not think that they exist, and consequently cannot make them an object of his desires, as a woman seen in a dream cannot be loved by a wise man.

49. See Introduction. *Kārikās quoted* . . .

50. There is no existence, or, what is the same, there is no *saṃsāra* and there is no *nirvāṇa*, since existence (as non-existence) is wholly denied by Nāgārjuna. The knowledge of the universal Voidness is liberation, is *nirvāṇa*. The man, who realizes that all is void, who realizes *śūnyatā*, has thereby stopped the creation of illusions by his mind, has destroyed the empirical reality (*saṃsāra*), which is nothing else that one of these illusions created by his mind. The destruction in this way of *saṃsāra* is liberation.

The assertion that *saṃsāra* and *nirvāṇa* do not exist, does not imply the affirmation of their nothingness, since both extremes of being and non-being are equally denied by Nāgārjuna.

51. The destruction of things, that belong to our empirical reality, that we consider as really existent and that *seem* to have come forth in some moment, is not different from the destruction of something created by magic. In both cases we have only an illusory destruction, not a real one.

52. The conglomerates are illusory, non-existent, because they are only a collection of parts, and the parts at their own turn are illusory because they are also only a collection of sub-parts, and so on without the possibility to find, in this abolishing analysis, anything that could not be analyzed into parts and that would constitute something real, existing *in se et per se* (Cf. F. Tola and C. Dragonetti, 'Ālambanaparīkṣā', p. 103, note 20, and the treatise *Hastavālanāmaprakaraṇa*, included in this book). If somebody affirms that the conglomerate ceases to be through destruction one may ask him the two questions that contains the *kārikā*: (1) how could a destruction take place in something that does not really exist, and (2) how could the idea of destruction occur in our minds in relation to something, the conglomerate, that does not exist, how could we relate the idea of destruction to something non-existent?

These difficulties do not occur when, knowing that the conglomerate does not really exist, we consider that its cessation takes place through true knowledge, which presents to us the true nature of the conglomerate (non-existent since there is before us only a collection of parts) and consequently makes it disappear.

53. The *kleśas*, impurities, depravities, afflictions, are simple adherences to that psycho-physic unity, constituted by the *skandhas*, that is the man, something adventitious and secondary; their destruction does not produce the *skandhas'* destruction. See note 97.

54. The opinion expressed in this *kārikā* is of a person who believes in the real existence of the *skandhas* and that only the destruction of these *skandhas* can produce liberation. The true doctrine according to Nāgārjuna is expounded in *kārikā* 10.

55. When it is said that the *skandhas*, the impurities, or the *saṃsāra* (*kārikā* 13) are produced, cease or are destroyed, we must understand that there is not a true production, cessation or destruction, that there is only the appearance or the disappearance of the illusory creations that constitute the *skandhas*, the impurities, and the *saṃsāra*, since the *skandhas*, the impurities, and the *saṃsāra* have no true existence, are mere creations of our minds, and as such they cannot be really produced or destroyed. Only the true knowledge of the illusory nature of the *skandhas*, impurities, and *saṃsāra*, produced by the abolishing analysis which is a characteristic feature of the Madhyamaka school, can eliminate the illusory mental creation of 'birth' and 'destruction' of the *skandhas* etc. and give us the certainty of their non-existence.

56. He is one who has reached his aim; nothing remains for him to be done in tnis world.

57. When a man, following the Buddhist discipline, has obtained the intellectual knowledge of the Doctrine, has got its yogic or mystical knowledge, and has realized *śūnyatā*, then he has reached *nirvāṇa*. Then it is said that 'he has done what he had to do'. This is a wrong way of speaking because as soon as one has got the intellectual and yogic knowledge of the Doctrine and has realized *śūnyatā* and reached *nirvāṇa*, all diversity, that characterizes the empirical reality in which he was included, has disappeared for him. It is not possible to say any more that 'he has done what he had to do', since this expression implicates a set of diversities. If diversity subsisted for him after realizing *śūnyatā*, that expression would be correct.

58. Cf. *Pratītyasamutpādahṛdayakārikā*, attributed to Nāgārjuna, *kārikā* 6, whose reconstruction into Sanskrit by Gokhale has been given in the Introduction of the present article. The fact that this *kārikā* 12 appears in the *Pratītyasamutpādahṛdayakārikā* 6, complete and independent, induces to consider that this *kārikā* 12 has in itself its own complete meaning and that there is no need to unite to it the two last *pādas* of *kārikā* 11, as it is usually done.

59. The expression 'the utmost subtle things' designates the atoms.

60. The conglomerates do not arise, are not born or produced, since they are non-existent, unreal. The same thing happens with their parts and sub-parts including the most subtle ones; they do not arise, because they do not exist really, as they also are composed things. Even the atom is something

that can be divided into parts (cf. *Viṃśatikā* and *Hastavālanāmaprakaraṇa* this last in this book) and therefore does not exist in truth, and therefore cannot either arise or be destroyed. If it is necessary to say that the atom does not arise, it is not because it is eternal as the atomists say, but because it is unreal, and for an unreal thing there is no birth.

61. If the *saṃsāra* can be destroyed, it must have had a beginning. We cannot admit that a thing can be destroyed, if previously it did not come into existence, i.e. if it did not have a beginning. Therefore the question arises why did the Buddhas, on one side, teach that an end can be put to the *saṃsāra*, and, on the other, declare that the *saṃsāra* has no beginning. The answer to this question is that for the Buddhas the *saṃsāra* is an illusion and consequently, if they said that an end can be put to it, it must be understood that that end for them consisted in destroying that illusion by stopping the activity of the mind which creates that illusion; and when the Buddhas said that the *saṃsāra* has no beginning their idea was that the *saṃsāra*, as a mere illusion, can have no real beginning.

62. If things had a beginning, it would be perceived by our senses or established by our reason. But things depending on causes have neither beginning nor end, since they are unreal and as such have neither beginning nor end, that could be perceived.

63. A contingent thing, which has not an own being and which depends on causes and conditions for its production, existence and disappearance, is not a thing really existing. This is a fundamental principle of Nāgārjuna's philosophy. A rope does not really exist, since it depends for its existence on the threads that compose it. *Kārikā* 39 expresses the same idea enlarging it.

64. If something did come forth with an own being, it could not lose it and therefore it could not end. See Candrakīrti, *Prasannapadā ad* XXI, 17; Nāgārjuna, *Madhyamakaśāstra* XXIII, 24 and commentary of Candrakīrti; *Śūnyatāsaptati* 16 in this book. This is also a principle admitted by Hindu, thinkers. Cf. Gaudapāda, *Āgamaśāstra* IV, 7, 9 and 29; and commentary of Śaṅkara *ad locum*; Sūreśvara, *Saṃbandhavārtika* 56; Saṅkara, *Upadeśaśahasrī*, *Gadyaprabandha* II, 2, 45 (*svabhāvasyāvarjanīyatvat*). Maṇdana Miśra, *Brahmasiddhi*, p. 20, ll. 2-3.

65. The persons who do not know what magic is, desire the woman magically created, they enjoy seeing her, they suffer when the magical creation comes to an end. In the same way those who do not know the true nature of the empirical reality can love the beings and things that belong to it and can suffer with their destruction. It does not happen so with the persons who know that everything is unreal, illusory.

66. If existence, i.e. the *saṃsāra*, is unreal, it cannot have a real beginning or a real end. When one has grasped this truth, one does not fall any more in the affirmation either that things have a birth, a beginning and consequently exist or that they are destroyed, that they have an end and consequently become non-existent.

67. They do not perceive that the world is only a process, an eternal chain of causes and effects, and consequently is only an illusion, a creation of our minds.

68. See Introduction, *kārikās quoted* . . . The last two *pādas* of the Sanskrit quotation of the *Subhāṣitasaṃgraha* express an idea different from that of the Tibetan version.
69. What arises in dependence is devoid of an own being. Consequently it is unreal, non-existent and, as being unreal and non-existent, it is not possible to say, in relation to it, that it has *really* arisen. Its origination is as unreal as its existence.
70. The causes, whose cessation produces *nirvāṇa*, the liberation, are the ignorance of the true nature of oneself and of the world, the attachment to beings and things, the actions inspired by that ignorance, and the creative mental activity which gives rise to the illusory empirical reality.
71. He obtained *nirvāṇa*, is liberated.
72. To be able to communicate with other beings.
73. When one knows that production does not really exist, that its essence is mere illusion, one knows also that destruction too does not exist, that it also is an illusion, since it is necessary that a thing be first really produced in order to be afterwards really destroyed. When one knows that destruction does not exist, one knows also that impermanence too does not exist, because in order that a thing be impermanent, it is necessary that it be destroyed. But since production does not exist, one has to know that permanence too does not exist, since a thing that is not born cannot be permanent. The knowledge of the non-existence of birth, destruction, permanence and impermanence allows one to understand the Supreme Truth, i.e. the universal Voidness.
74. Dependent Origination (*Pratītyasamutpāda*) is *Śūnyatā*. *Śūnyatā* is reached when, through the abolishing analysis, all categories, elements, manifestations of the empirical reality, including production and destruction are eliminated. So Dependent Origination, which is reached through that abolition, is deprived of everything, is absolutely 'void'.
75. When *śūnyatā* is realized, one has conquered liberation from the empirical reality—the ocean of existence.
76. The false views consist in the belief that things are substantial, that they are really produced and really destroyed.
77. Mind, well or badly directed, is the source of all good or evil.
78. *Śūnyatā* which constitutes the Supreme Reality or Truth.
79. As having no true existence, as being mere illusory creations of our minds and notwithstanding presenting themselves, fraudulently, as real and true.
80. The different forms under which beings can be reborn.
81. These attributes indicate the insubstantial character of the states of existence, which consequently cannot constitute the fundament of anything or have anything as their fundament.
82. The ignorance of the true nature of reality gives birth to the false ideas regarding it, to the illusion of worlds with beings and things.
83. Beings are not really born, do not really exist and do not really cease.
84. The trunk of the plantain tree (*kadalī* in Sanskrit) is formed only by several sheaths or membranes. When these sheaths or membranes are taken out,

nothing is found inside.

85. A frequent metaphor in Nāgārjuna to express unreality.
86. The different worlds in which beings are born.
87. Besides the True Reality, i.e. the *śūnyatā*, mentioned in *kārikā* 25, and the empirical reality, referred to in *kārikās* 26-28, there is nothing else, and the True Reality, i.e. *śūnyatā*, is only the true nature, the true way of being of the empirical reality.
88. The adherence to desire of worldly people has its root in ignorance; wise men are free form desire precisely through their wisdom.
89. See Introduction: *Kārikās quoted* . . .
90. The first reaction of a person is to believe in the true existence of the world in which he lives and acts; only after submitting himself to the Buddha's intellectual and moral disciplines he will reach the true knowledge which presents him all things as void, i.e. unreal. We understand *rnam par dben pa* of the text (*viviktatā* in the Sanskrit quotation) as the state of being separated from or devoid of an own being, i.e. as *śūnyatā*. We do not think that in the present case this word indicates the state of isolation from the world gained by the wise man.
91. The idea is that they have not gone beyond the 'letter' of the Doctrine, they have only 'heard' the words, but they did not either grasp its meaning or act according to its precepts.
92. Do not follow Buddha's moral precepts.
93. Buddha, in his teaching, has not limited himself to teach only that actions are always accompanied by consequences and the different forms of reincarnations, in which actions receive their corresponding moral retribution; he has also taught the true nature (void, unreal, non-existent) of actions, of their consequences and of reincarnations and that they are not really produced. His moral teaching was accompanied by a metaphysical one.
94. See Introduction: *Kārikās quoted* . . .
95. The Buddhas who defeated ignorance, attachment, sensuality etc.
96. For Buddhism there is not a permanent and autonomous 'ego'; man is only a current of consciousnesses. Therefore it is not possible to say 'mine'.
97. The *skandhas, dhātus* and *āyatanas* are the elements or factors of existence, grouped in diverse combinations.
98. When the Buddhas use the words 'I', 'mine', '*skandhas*' etc., they do so knowing perfectly that there is no true 'I' etc. provided with an own being. They were obliged to employ these words in order to be able to communicate their teaching to other persons.
99. See Introduction, *Kārikās quoted* . . .
100. The Great Elements are: ether, air, fire, water, earth.
101. By knowing the true nature of the Great Elements etc. This true nature is *śūnyatā*, the absence of every thing that belongs to the empirical reality, which is reached through the abolishing analysis.
102. If the Great Elements etc. cease to appear as things really existing, when the abolishing analysis is applied to them, that is to say: only through a mental process, and not through any physical act, we may conclude that

they are only mental creations, since only a mental creation can be destroyed by means of a mental act. Cf. notes 107 and 108. And moreover they are *false* mental creations since nothing real corresponds to them. This *kārikā* establishes important characteristics of the Great Elements, falsely considered as the basis of the empirical reality as a whole: they are in consciousness, they are only ideas; they cease to be as soon as their true nature is known, and lastly they are false creations.

103. Everything is unreal and consequently deceiving and illusory. *Nirvāṇa* is the supreme reality, Voidness, and as such the only thing that *in our language* can be called true. Cf. Candrakīrti, *Prasannapadā ad* XIII, 1.
104. As being a false creation of the mind, to which nothing real corresponds and which is superimposed as a concealing veil upon the true reality.
105. An *agitated* mind is a mind full of attachments and aversions provoked by the ignorance of the true nature of beings and things. In this state the mind is under the power of Māra, the personification of evil: ignorance, desire and hatred. Man liberates himself from Māra, when his mind becomes calm and serene, because of the destruction of passions that agitate him.
106. As the faults of man, i.e. ignorance and passions, are to be found in his mind, so also faultlessness, i.e. absence of ignorance and passions is to be found in his mind. In the mind reside man's perdition and salvation.
107. Ignorance is only a mental act, therefore, it can give rise only to a mental creation.
108. Whatever ceases by an act of a mere mental nature must itself be also something of mental nature.
109. See Introduction: *Kārikās quoted* . . .
110. See note 63.
111. In Tibetan *yod par smra ba rnams* = *āstivādins* in Sanskrit, i.e. those who maintain that everything exists (*āsti*), who affirm the reality of things and do not accept their illusory character.
112. One must not get surprised when one sees that the realists feel affection for themselves and for the other beings and things, because for them everything has a real existence. They act logically.
113. To discuss means two things: (1) that one admits that "'*this' or 'that' is true*" (as the following *kārikā* says) or wrong and (2) that one feels attachment to something (what one defends) or aversion for something (what one refutes). But Buddha has taught that things are impermanent, that they constantly change, that they are evanescent and consequently devoid of an own being, that nothing really exists and has condemned attachment and aversion as having their source in the belief of the real existence of things and as being the cause of all evils. Discussion is so contrary to Buddha's teaching.
114. Because there is contradition between what they openly sustain (the impermanence of all etc.) and their behaviour and their discussions, which reveal that they admit the permanent existence of things and are attached to them.
115. Since all is illusory, lacking a true existence.
116. Only when one admits the existence of a real self or world, it is possible to

discuss whether that self or that world are eternal or not, and to adhere to either one of these points of view. When one is convinced that nothing is really born and consequently nothing really exists or is really destroyed, then the discussion about permanence or impermanence and the adherence to any of these two extreme points of view is impossible. The next *kārikā* expresses a similar idea. The position criticized in this *kārikā* is that of a non-Buddhist substantialist.

117. This *kārikā* refers to the Buddhist who belongs to Hīnayāna and affirms the Dependent Origination of things and also their real existence.

118. The reflection of the moon in the water, the mirage, the magical illusion, the serpent superimposed on the rope are not *really* existent but it cannot be said that they are completely, absolutely non-existent. They exist with the existence of unreal things. And such is the status of the total empirical reality. The position expressed in this *kārikā* is that of the Mādhyamikas who affirm the illusory character of everything.

119. By any wrong theory that presupposes the reality of things, like those theories that affirm real birth and existence or real destruction and non-existence.

120. See Introduction: *Kārikās quoted* . . .

121. When one attributes reality to beings and things, then the feelings of attachment and aversion for them or against them arise; by the force of these feelings the wrong theories about permanence or impermanence are developed and one gets involved in discussions defending or attacking these theories.

122. See Introduction: *Kārikās quoted* . . .

123. See Introduction: *Kārikās quoted* . . . As we have said in note 27 we suppress the first line of this *kārikā* which appears in the *Sde-dge* edition. We add as a fourth line of this *kārikā* the fourth line which appears in *Peking* edition (*de ñid mkhyen pa mchog gis gsuṅs*).

124. How is it known that the belief that things have an own being is the source of the evils indicated in *kārikās* 46 and 47? This is known, because Buddha discovered the Universal Relativity (*pratītyasamutpāda*) and founded on it (according to the Mādhyamika school) his principle that things, because of being produced by causes, are not really born. And as long as this true nature of things is not grasped, one remains entangled in empirical reality and submitted to passions and error.

125. See note 63 and *kārikā* 39.

126. Erroneous knowledge: the attribution to things of an own being, of a true existence.

127. Passion, false perception, adhesion to an apparent truth, discussions etc. are the pernicious consequences of a wrong view on the nature of things.

128. The great beings, *che baḥi bdag ñid can* in Tibetan, *mahātman* in Sanskrit, are in this case those who have reached the knowledge that all is unreal, void.

129. See *kārikā* 42. Not to sustain any thesis is the philosophical position of the Mādhyamika school, based on its conception of Voidness. By this philosophical position and through the avoidance of discussions it provokes, a

moral aim is attained: calm, serenity, the ideal of *ataraxia* so much appreciated in Indian spirituality.

130. *Standpoint*: basis, fundament, principle upon which a theory is built. For instance, a dogma as substantiality, real birth and destruction of things etc.
131. Cf. note 53.
132. People who have not realized the true nature of things and therefore are submerged in all the evils (passions, discussions etc.) that only the realization of that true nature eliminates.
133. See Introduction: *Kārikās quoted* . . .
134. 'Form' (in Tibetan *gzugs*, in Sanskrit *rūpa*) indicates the visible form, the object of the sight, but the other sense objects in general are also understood.
135. Those who have gone half the way in the path of spiritual progress. From the moral point of view they are well directed towards the goal, but they are still lacking the philosophical insight which allows seeing the true nature of things. This philosophical insight is possessed by the third category of men, mentioned in this *kārikā*.
136. Cf. note 90.
137. The categories of persons mentioned in this *kārikā* correspond to those referred to in the previous *kārikā*.
138. The true meaning of being and non-being (as of birth and destruction), is that they are only mental creations to which nothing really existing corresponds.
139. As the belief in the real existence of beings and things. Cf. note 130.
140. From the point of view of relative truth it can be said that, with the existence or disappearance of the standpoint, passion and freedom from passion take place. But from the point of view of supreme truth, for the *mahātmans* who are established in it and are beyond any standpoint, there is neither passion nor dispassion.
141. When man realizes *śūnyatā* his mind becomes free from passions and therefore possesses calm and serenity. Cf. *kārikā* 36 and notes 105 and 106.
142. They obtain the spiritual superiority which derives from accumulation of merits and the intellectual superiority which derives from knowledge.
143. We have in this *kārikā* an example of transference of merit.

CHAPTER 3

The *Śūnyatāsaptatikārikā* of Nāgārjuna

INTRODUCTION

The Śūnyatāsaptati

In the Tibetan Canon, *Bstan-ḥgyur, Sde-dge* edition, *Tōhoku* 3827, and *Peking* edition, *Catalogue* 5227, there is a small treatise in verse, which receives in Tibetan the title of *Stoṅ-pa-ñid bdun-cu-paḥi tshig-leḥur byas-pa źes-bya-ba* and in Sanskrit that of *Śūnyatāsaptatikārikānāma*.

Both editions attribute this treatise to Klu-sgrub=Nāgārjuna.

The Tibetan translation of this treatise was made by Gźon-nu-mchog (=Kumāravara?[1]), Gñan Dar-ma grags (=Dharmakīrti III?[1]) and Khu,[2] according to *Tōhoku*; and by Gźon-nu mchog and Dharma grags according to *Catalogue*. These translators lived at the end of the eleventh century.[3]

The treatise is composed of seventy-three *kārikās*, stanzas, contrarily to what its name indicates. So it can supposed that three of its *kārikās* are interpolations, which were added after the treatise was written. It is not easy to decide which were the three interpolated *kārikās*.

The Sanskrit text of the treatise has not been preserved. There is no Chinese translation of it.

The *kārikās*, which constitute the *Śūnyatāsaptati*, are included also in two of the three commentaries which exist of the treatise (*Tōhoku* 3831=*Catalogue* 5231 and *Tōhoku* 3867=*Catalogue* 5268), to which we shall refer later on. So we have three recensions of the text of this work. These three recensions present differences among themselves. The recension of the commentary *Tōhoku* 3867=*Catalogue* 5268 is nearer to the recension of the *kārikās* contained in *Tōhoku* 3827=*Catalogue* 5227, which we have mentioned, than to the recension of the other commentary, *Tōhoku* 3831=*Catalogue* 5231.

The Author

References. The colophon of the Tibetan translation of this treatise, done at the end of the eleventh century, in the *Sde-dge* edition 3827 and in the *Peking* edition 5227, attribute it to Nāgārjuna.

Candrakīrti (*c*. 600-650), *Madhyamakaśāstrastuti*, stanza 10, includes the *Śūnyatāsaptati* among the works of Nāgārjuna, that he had studied.

Bhavya[4] (?), *Madhyamakaratnapradīpa*, ed. *Sde-dge* 3854, 264 b 5-6, mentions the *Śūnyatāsaptati* together with other works of Nāgārjuna: *Mūlamadhyamakakārikā*, *Vigrahavyāvartanī*, *Yuktiṣaṣṭikā* and *Vaidalyaprakaraṇa*, expressing that they maintain that things do not come forth. He does not mention the author of these works.

Śāntarakṣita (eighth century) and Kamalaśīla (*c*. 740-795). Śāntarakṣita, *Madhyamakālaṃkāravṛtti*, ed. *Sde-dge* 3885, 74a[1]-74a[4], quotes some *subhāṣita* (*legs par gsuṅs pa*) which he attributes to Blo gros bzaṅ po. The third one of these *subhāṣita* happens to be *kārikā* 58 of the *Śūnyatāsaptati*. Kamalaśīla, *Madhyamakālaṃkārapañjikā*, ed. *Sde-dge* 3886, 121a[3]-121b[1], makes clear that these *subhāṣitas* are of Nāgārjuna and he indicates the works of Nāgārjuna from which they are taken; for the third *subhāṣita* he gives rightly as its source the *Śūnyatāsaptati*, without indicating the number of the *kārikā*.

Atiśa (eleventh century), *Bodhipathapradīpa* 205, p. 130 ed. Eimer, refers to the *Śūnyatāsaptati* together with the *Yukti* (*ṣaṣṭikā*) and the *Mūlamadhyamaka* (*kārikā*), without indicating the author's name, and expressing that in all of them the theory of Voidness of an own being is expounded.

Buston (fourteenth century), *History of Buddhism*, I, pp. 50-51 (Obermiller's translation), includes this work, which, according to him, expounds 'the theory of the Relativity of all elements of existence, devoid of the extremities of causality (*rten-ḥbrel=pratītyasamutpāda*) and pluralism (*spros-pa, prapañca*)'—among the six main treatises of Nāgārjuna.

Tāranātha (end of the sixteenth century, beginning of the seventeenth) in his *History of Buddhism in India*, p. 57, ll. 3-4, Schiefner's edition (= p. 71 Schiefner's translation) refers to the 'five treatises on Nyāya' (*rigs paḥi tshogs lṅa, yukti-corpus*, Ruegg, *The Literature*, p. 8). According to Schiefner, p. 302 of his translation of Tarānātha, with that Tibetan expression the following works are referred to: *Mūlamadhyamakakārikā, Yuktiṣaṣṭikā, Śūnyatāsaptati, Vigraha-vyāvartaṇī* and *Vaidalya*.

It is possible to consider that the testimonies, we have mentioned, are testimonies in favour of the *Śūnyatāsaptati's* authenticity. Anyhow it is necessary to take into account the fact that the distance that separate these references from Nāgārjuna can weaken their strength.

Commentaries. As we have already said, there exist three commentaries of the *Śūnyatāsaptati*, to which we shall refer later on with more detail. One of them is attributed to the same Nāgārjuna, another to Candrakīrti, the great commentator of the *Mūlamadhyamakakārikās*, the basic and undoubted work of Nāgārjuna, and the third one to Parahita (bhadra). Parahita is one of the most important Indian masters who worked in Kashmir and in Tibet at the end of the eleventh century and beginning of the twelfth.[5]

The fact that Candrakīrti, who can be considered as the 'official' commentator of Nāgārjuna, and Parahita, an important author, have written commentaries related to the *Śūnyatāsaptati* can be taken as another argument in favour of the authenticity of this treatise.

Quotations. Some *kārikās* of the *Śūnyatāsaptati* appear in other works. They are indicated by Lindtner, in his notes to his translation, *Nagarjuniana*, pp. 31-69. They are:

Kārikā 5 in *Dvādaśadvāraka* 26, *Taisho* XXX, 1568, p. 167a, ll. 23-24, without indication of author and of the work from which it comes.

Kārikā 8 ibid., p. 160a, ll. 22-23. The text indicates that the *kārikā* belongs to the *Śūnyatāsaptati*, but does not indicate the name of its author.

Kārikā 19 ibid., p. 164b, ll. 27-28, without indication either of its author or of its source.

Kārikās 19-21 in *Akutobhayā ad* XXI, 6. The text indicates that the *kārikās* come from the *Śūnyatāsaptati*, but without the author's name.

Kārikā 21 in *Madhyamakālaṃkāravṛtti, Sde-dge* edition 3885, 76a[4]-76a[5], without indication either of its author or of its source.

Kārikā 58 in *Madhyamakālaṃkāravṛtti, Sde-dge* edition 3885, 74a[3]. We have referred to this quotation in relation to Śāntarakṣita and Kamalaśīla.

With the exception of *kārikā* 58, the quotations of *kārikās* that precede do not contribute anything to determine who is the author of the *Śūnyatāsaptati*, since these quotations are done without author's indication.

Ideas. Method. Style. Quality. The ideas expressed in this treatise are characteristic of Nāgārjuna's system, perhaps with two exceptions:

Kārikās 40-42. In these *kārikās* we may have a reference to the *nirmāṇakāya*. But the conception of *nirmāṇakāya* is later than Nāgārjuna.[6]

Kārikā 60. The argument expounded in this *kārikā* in order to demonstrate the existence of 'only mind' is one of the classic arguments of the *Vijñānavāda*.[7]

The *Mūlamadhyamakakārikās* present to us the characteristic method of Nāgārjuna: on one side, we have that his fundamental aim is to prove the universal 'Voidness', that everything is relative, conditioned, composed and that, therefore, the empirical reality, when it is rigorously analyzed, gradually disappears before us and comes to be only a creation of our minds, submerged by its own nature in error; and, on the other side, we have that Nāgārjuna, in order to establish this thesis, takes one by one the different aspects, elements, categories, manifestations of the empirical reality, demonstrating that they are 'void', non-existent, illusory. This aim and the form to reach it belong also to the *Śūnyatāptati*.

In the *Mūlamadhyamakakārikās* and in the *Śūnyatāsaptati* we find a similar style: the density of thought, the novelty and subtlety of ideas, the conciseness of expression.

In relation to quality, the *Śūnyatāsaptati* is a most valuable work, worthy of Nāgārjuna, because of its rich content and its strict form of expression, although it does not possess the clear distribution of the themes that is possessed by the *Mūlamadhyamakakārikās*.

The preceding considerations can be taken as indications for the work's authenticity. Anyhow their value is reduced owing to the content of *kārikās* 40-42 and 60 and by the fact that the ideas exposed in this treatise and the method it applies, although they are characteristic of Nāgārjuna, they are also characteristic of Nāgārjuna's disciples.

Modern authors. Modern authors in general accept the authenticity of this treatise. Cf. Winternitz, *A History of Indian Literature* II, p. 346; Vaidya, *Études sur Āryadeva*, p. 49; Venkata Ramanan,

Nāgārjuna's Philosophy, p. 36; Ruegg, *The Literature of the Madhyamaka School of Philosophy in India*, pp. 20-21; Lindtner, *Nagarjuniana*, pp. 11 and 31, and *Nagarjunas Filosofiske Vaerker*, *passim*; Chatterjee, *The Philosophy of Nāgārjuna*, p. 19; Murti, *The Central Philosophy of Buddhism*, p. 89; and Yamaguchi and Uriūtsu Ryūshin in their respective editions and translations.

Conclusion. In our opinion, after weighing the circumstances we have referred to, the *Śūnyatāsaptati* can be considered as an authentic work of Nāgārjuna.

Commentaries

There are three commentaries of the *Śūnyatāsaptati*. Their Sanskrit text has not been preserved, and there is not a Chinese version of these. We know these only through their Tibetan translations.

1. *Stoṅ-pa-ñid bdun-cu-paḥi ḥgrel-pa, Śūnyatāsaptativṛtti* (*Svavṛtti*) *Tōhoku* 3831=*Catalogue* 5231. *Sde-dge* and *Peking* editions attributes this commentary to Nāgārjuna. The Tibetan translation was made by Jinamitra and Ye-śes-sde (Jñānasena), according to *Sde-dge* edition; *Peking* edition does not indicate who were the translators. The translation was done in the beginning of the ninth century, which is the epoch in which the two named translators lived.[8]

Ruegg, *The Literature*, p. 20 and p. 21 note 45, does not say anything about the authenticity of this commentary; he limits himself to express that it is attributed to Nāgārjuna. Lindtner, *Nagarjuniana*, p. 31, considers that there is not a good reason to doubt its authenticity.

Anyhow, we think that the following consideration can be adduced against the attribution of this commentary to Nāgārjuna: Nāgārjuna wrote his 'Treatise in 70 *kārikās*'; we must understand that this work contained as its name indicates, only 70 *kārikās* and that therefore three of the 73 *kārikās*, which the treatise contains, were added *a posteriori*, that they are apocryphal *kārikās*. Why did Nāgārjuna, if he really was the author of this commentary, comment 72 *kārikās* (the last *kārikā* of the treatise has not been commented), that is, to say two *kārikās* more, that he had not written?; of course it can be said either that, although Nāgārjuna named his treatise 'in 70 *kārikās*', he did not limit himself to that number and wrote in reality 73 *kārikās* and so there is nothing surprising in the fact that he commented 72 of them; or that some other author added to the treatise three *kārikās* and the commentary of two of them.

2. *Stoṅ-ñid bdun-cu-paḥi ḥgrel-pa, Śūnyatāsaptativṛtti, Tōhoku* 3867=*Catalogue* 5268. Both editions attribute this commentary to Zla-ba grags-pa=Candrakīrti. The translation into the Tibetan was made by Abhayākara and D(h)arma-grags (=Dharmakīrti III), according to both editions. The translators lived at the end of the eleventh century.[9]

Ruegg, *The Literature*, p. 81, and Lindtner, 'Candrakīrti's Pañcaskandhaprakaraṇa', p. 88, consider this commentary to be authentic.

3. *Stoṅ-pa-ñid bdun-cu-paḥi rnam-par-bśad-pa, Śūnyatāsaptativṛtti, Tōhoku* 3868=*Catalogue* 5269. Both editions attribute this subcommentary to Gźan-la phan-pa=Parahita (bhadra). The Tibetan version was done by the same Parahita and Gźon-nu mchog, who, as we have already indicated, lived at the end of the eleventh century and beginning of the twelfth.

Ruegg, *The Literature*, p. 116, and Naudou, *Les Bouddhistes Kaśmīriens*, p. 182, consider that this commentary was written by Parahita.[10]

Scheme of the Exposition

As we have already expressed the distribution of the *kārikās*, according to the themes that are developed in the treatise, is not very clear.

According to Lindtner, *Nāgārjuniana*, p. 33, the themes treated in the *Śūnyatāsaptati* are distributed in the following order:

1. *Kārikās* 1-6: The *dharmas* (elements of existence) exist only according to relative truth (*saṃvṛti*), since logic (*yukti*) demonstrates that according to absolute truth (*paramārtha*) nothing comes forth.
2. *Kārikās* 7-26: Everything is *pratītyasamutpanna*, produced in dependence, or *śūnya*, void. So *nirvāṇa* is simply *anutpāda*, non-origination.
3. *Kārikās* 27-32: Several aspects of *bhāva*, existence, refuted as relative.
4. *Kārikās* 33-44: According to orthodox Buddhism *karman* is also *śūnya*, void.
5. *Kārikās* 45-57: Refutation of the five *skandhas* (constituent elements of man), specially of *rūpa* (material element).

6. *Kārikās* 58-66: The ignorance, *avidyā*, disappears when it is understood that nothing exists really.
7. *Kārikās* 67-73: So *paramārtha*, the supreme truth, is simply *śūnyatā*, Voidness, *anutpāda*, non-origination etc. Anyhow since generally the supreme truth (*paramārtha*) is not grasped, in order to reach it one has to recur to relative truth (*saṃvṛti*) with faith (*śraddhā*).

Uriūtsu Ryūshin, in his translation in *Daijo Butten*, distributes the subject of this treatise in the following way:

Kārikās 1-4:	Meaning of voidness: all things are insubstantial.
Kārikās 5-6:	Composed things (*saṃskṛta*) do not come forth.
Kārikā 7:	What exists, numbers, etc., are in dependent relation.
Kārikās 8-14:	The twelve members of the *pratītyasamutpāda* do not arise.
Kārikās 15-22:	The grasping of an own being, of birth and destruction (of things) are not to be admitted.
Kārikās 23-26:	What is arising, what is cessation?
Kārikās 27-28:	The subject and the object of knowledge are established in mutual dependence.
Kārikā 29:	Time does not exist with an own being.
Kārikās 30-32:	The conditioned things (*saṃskṛta*) etc. do not exist.
Kārikās 33-44:	Action does not exist with an own being.
Kārikās 45-51:	Material objects do not exist with an own being.
Kārikās 52-57:	The sense-organs, their object and the sensation do not exist with an own being.
Kārikās 58-61:	Impermanent things etc. do not exist.
Kārikās 62-66:	Perception of what is false and of what it true.
Kārikās 67-73:	The terms 'conditioned arising' and 'voidness'.

We give now our own distribution of the subject matter of the *Śūnyatāsaptati*:

Kārikā 1:	The two truths.
Kārikās 2-3:	Universal voidness.
Kārikā 4:	Impossibility of birth, permanence and destruction.
Kārikā 5:	Impossibility of being produced.
Kārikā 6:	Impossibility of the cause.
Kārikā 7:	'One' and 'multiple' are relative notions. Denial of

	the essential characteristics.
Kārikās 8-14:	Denial of Dependent Origination.
Kārikās 15-18:	Impossibility of the existence of an own being.
Kārikās 19-22:	Impossibility of existence and non-existence.
Kārikās 23-26:	*Nirvāṇa.*
Kārikā 27:	Inexistence *in se et per se* of characteristic and characterized.
Kārikā 28:	Application of what precedes to other cases.
Kārikā 29:	Non-existence of the three times.
Kārikā 30:	Non-existence of everything.
Kārikā 31:	Non-existence of destruction, permanence and birth.
Kārikā 32:	Conditioned and non-conditioned.
Kārikā 33-43:	Non-existence of action, the agent, and the retribution.
Kārikā 44:	Intentional formulations of Buddha.
Kārikās 45-46:	Impossibility of the object of visual knowledge.
Kārikās 47-52:	Impossibility of perception or visual knowledge.
Kārikās 53-54:	Voidness of the *āyatanas*.
Kārikā 55:	Non-existence of consciousness, of the object and of the subject of knowledge.
Kārikā 56:	Unreality of consciousness.
Kārikā 57:	Non-existence of consciousness, of the object and of the subject of knowledge.
Kārikā 58:	Everything is impermanent; nothing exists.
Kārikās 59-61:	Unreality of the *kleśas* and of the imagination that produces them.
Kārikā 62:	Neither ignorance nor the other members of the Dependent Origination exist.
Kārikā 63:	Everything is calm; everything is nirvanized.
Kārikās 64-65:	The ignorance and the twelve members.
Kārikā 66:	Unreality of the *saṃskāras*.
Kārikā 67:	Non-existence of things and no-things.
Kārikā 68:	Dependent Origination=Voidness.
Kārikās 69-71:	Supreme truth=Dependent Origination. Value of relative truth.
Kārikās 72-73:	Means to reach *nirvāṇa*.

Doctrinary Content

After having given the distribution of the *kārikās* according to their subject-matter, as established by Lindtner, Uriūtsu and ourselves, it does not seem necessary to give an exposition of the ideas exposed in this treatise. As for Nāgārjuna's doctrine in its general lines, we refer to our article[11] on this matter and to the 'Introduction' of the present work.

Modern Editions and Translations

S. Yamaguchi, in *Bukkyō Kenkyū* (Studies on Buddhism), 1923-24, vol. V, nos. 1, 3, 4; vol. VI, no. 1, re-edited in *Bukkyō Gaku Bunshū* (Collection of Studies on Buddhism), 1972, vol. I, p. 5-117. In this article Yamaguchi includes a critical edition of the Tibetan text of the *kārikās* according to the *svavṛtti* (*Peking* 5231) together with the different readings of the *kārikās* alone (*Peking* 5227) and of the *kārikās* contained in the commentary of Candrakīrti (*Peking* 5268). He accompanies his translation with a Japanese translation of the *kārikās* of the *svavṛtti* and with many notes containing extracts from the three commentaries.

Ch. Lindtner in *Nagarjuniana*, 1982, pp. 34-69, edits the Tibetan text of the *kārikās* (*Peking* 5227) and of the *kārikās* contained in the *Svavṛtti* (*Peking* 5231). His edition is accompanied by an English translation of *kārikās* 5227, and also by numerous notes indicating parallel passages of other works. Moreover Lindtner edited the complete Tibetan text of the *Svavṛtti* (*kārikās* and commentary), taking into account the *Sde-dge, Narthang* and *Peking* editions ('*Editio minor sine apparatu critico-Derge-Narthang-Peking*'), in *Nagarjunas Filosofiske Vaerker*, 1982, pp. 219-44. In this same book he offers a complete Danish translation of the said *Svavṛtti*, pp. 136-64.

Uriūtsu Ryūshin, published a Japanese translation of the *Svavṛtti*, on the basis of its Tibetan version (*Peking* 5231), in vol. 14 of the Series *Daijō Butten* (Buddhist Scriptures), 1975, pp. 89-132.

Sempa Dorje published the Tibetan text of the commentary attributed to Nāgārjuna with a reconstruction of it into Sanskrit and a Hindi translation of all: *Śūnyatāsaptati*, 1985.

Finally, according to *Buddhist Text Information*, no. 13 (Dec. 1977), p. 12 and specially no. 18 (Dec. 1978), p. 9, Felix Erb is preparing a critical edition of the *Svavṛtti* together with its German translation and extracts from Candrakīrti's commentary (*Peking* 5268).

The Present Work

We present in this book the Tibetan text of the *Śūnyatāsaptati* and its English translation with notes. The text we edit is that of the *kārikās* as contained in the commentary denominated *Svavṛtti, Sde-dge* 3831, *Dbu-ma,* Tsa, $110a^4$-$121a^4$. We have elected this recension of the *kārikās,* because it seems to us that its text is the clearest and more comprehensible one and besides that, because it is accompanied by the commentary attributed to Nāgārjuna, the treatise's author. Only in some places, that we have indicated in notes, we have adopted a reading different from that of 3831, indicating the provenance of the adopted reading and the discarded reading. The majority of the adopted reading come from the same *Svavṛtti.*

In the Seminar of Japanese of our institution we have read, compared and commented with Prof. Roberto Oest, the translations into Japanese of the *Śūnyatāsaptati* done by S. Yamaguchi and R. Uriūtsu.

STOṄ PA ÑID BDUN CU PAḤI ḤGREL PA
(ŚŪNYATĀSAPTATIVṚTTI)

Tibetan Text

1 gnas paḥam skye ḥjig yod med dam/
dman paḥam mñam paḥam khyad par can/
saṅs rgyas ḥjig rten sñad[12] dbaṅ gis/
gsuṅ gi yaṅ dag dbaṅ gis min//

2 bdag med bdag med min bdag daṅ/
bdag med min pas brjod ḥgaḥḥaṅ med/
brjod par bya baḥi chos rnams kun/
mya ṅan ḥdas mtshuṅs raṅ bźin stoṅ//

3 gaṅ phyir dṅos po thams cad kyi/
raṅ bźin rgyu rkyen tshogs pa ḥam/
so so rnams laḥam thams cad la/
yod min de phyir stoṅ pa yin//

4 yod pa yod phyir skye ma yin/
med pa med paḥi phyir ma yin/
chos mi mthun phyir yod med min/
skye ba med phyir gnas ḥgag med//

5 skyes pa bskyed par bya ba min/
ma skyes pa yaṅ bskyed bya min/
skye baḥi tshe yaṅ bskyed bya min/
skyes[13] daṅ ma skyes pa yi phyir//

6 ḥbras yod ḥbras daṅ ldan paḥi rgyu/
de med na ni rgyu min mtshuṅs/
yod min med pa min[14] na ḥgal/
dus gsum rnams su ḥthad ma yin//

7 gcig med par ni maṅ po daṅ/
maṅ po med par gcig mi ḥjug/
de phyir brten nas dṅos po rnams/
ḥbyuṅ ba mtshan ma med pa yin//

8 rten ḥbyuṅ yan lag bcu gñis gaṅ/
sdug bsṅal ḥbras can de ma skyes/
sems gcig la yaṅ mi ḥthad la/
du ma la yaṅ mi ḥthad do//

9 mi rtag rtag min bdag med pa/
bdag min mi gtsaṅ gtsaṅ ma yin/
sdug bsṅal bde ba ma yin te/
de phyir phyin ci log rnams med//

10 de med na ni phyin ci log/
bźi las skyes paḥi ma rig med/
de med na ni ḥdu byed rnams/
mi ḥbyuṅ lhag mahaṅ de bźin no//

11 ma rig ḥdu byed med mi[15] ḥbyuṅ/
de med ḥdu byed mi ḥbyuṅ bas/
de gñis phan tshun rgyu phyir yaṅ/
raṅ bźin gyis ni ma grub yin[16]//

12 gaṅ źig bdag ñid raṅ bźin gyis/
ma grub des gźan[17] ji ltar bskyed/
de lta bas na pha rol po/
ma grub rkyen gźan skyed pa min//

13 pha bu ma yin bu pha min/
de gñis phan tshun med min la/
de gñis cig car yaṅ min ltar/
yan lag bcu gñis de bźin no//

14 rmi lam yul brten bde sdug daṅ/
yul dehaṅ med ltar brten nas gaṅ/
ḥbyuṅ ba de yaṅ de bźin med/
brten nas gaṅ yin de yaṅ med//

15 gal te dṅos rnams raṅ bźin gyis/
med na dman mñam khyad ḥphags ñid/
yod min sna tshogs ñid mi ḥgrub/
rgyu las mṅon par grub pa med//

16 raṅ bźin grub brten dṅos mi[18] ḥgyur/
ma brten par yaṅ ga la yod/
raṅ bźin med ñid mi ḥgyur źiṅ/
raṅ bźin yod pa mi ḥjig go//

17 med la raṅ gi dṅos po ḥam/
gźan dṅos ḥjig par ga la ḥgyur/
de phyir gźan dṅos dṅos med daṅ/
dṅos daṅ raṅ dṅos log pa yin//

18 gal te dṅos po stoṅ yin na/
ḥgag par mi ḥgyur skye mi ḥgyur/
ṅo bo ñid kyis stoṅ pa la/
gaṅ la ḥgag ciṅ gaṅ la skye//

19 dṅos daṅ dṅos med cig car med/
dṅos med med par dṅos po med/
rtag tu dṅos daṅ dṅos med ḥgyur/
dṅos med dṅos po med mi ḥbyuṅ//

20 dṅos po med par dṅos med med/
bdag las ma yin gźan las min/
de lta bas na dṅos po med/
de med na ni dṅos med med//

21 dṅos po yod pa ñid na rtag/
med na ṅes par chad pa yin/
dṅos po yod na de gñis min/
de phyir dṅos po khas blaṅs min//

22 rgyun gyi phyir na de med de/
rgyu byin nas ni dṅos po ḥgag/
sṅa ma bźin du ḥdi ma grub/
rgyun chad pa yi ñes paḥaṅ yod//

23 skye ḥjig gzigs pas mya ṅan ḥdas/
lam bstan stoṅ ñid phyir ma yin/
ḥdi dag phan tshun bzlog phyir daṅ/
log paḥi phyir na mthoṅ ba yin//

24 gal te skye daṅ ḥgag med na/
gaṅ źig ḥgag phyir mya ṅan ḥdas/
gaṅ źig raṅ bźin skye med ciṅ/
ḥgag med de thar ma yin nam//

25 gal te myaṅ ḥdas ḥgog na chad[19]/
gal te ćig śos ltar na rtag[20]/
de phyir dṅos daṅ dṅos med min/
skye med ḥgag paḥaṅ med pa yin//

26 gal te ḥgog pa ḥgaḥ gnas yod/
dṅos med par yaṅ der ḥgyur ro/
dṅos med par yaṅ de med de/
dṅos med med par yaṅ de med//

27 mtshan gźi las mtshan grub mtshan las/
mtshan gźi grub ste raṅ ma grub/
gcig las gcig kyaṅ ma grub ste/
ma grub ma grub sgrub byed min//

28 ḥdis ni rgyu daṅ ḥbras bu daṅ/
tshor bcas tshor ba po sogs daṅ/
lta po blta bya sogs ciḥaṅ ruṅ/
de kun ma lus bśad pa yin//

29 mi gnas phan tshun grub phyir daṅ/
ḥtshol phyir bdag ñid ma grub phyir/
dṅos po med phyir dus gsum ni/
yod pa ma yin rtog pa tsam//

30 gaṅ phyir skye daṅ gnas daṅ ḥjig/
ḥdus byas mtshan ñid ḥdi gsum med/
de phyir ḥdus byas ḥdus ma byas/
ci yaṅ yod pa ma yin no//

31 ma źig mi ḥjig źig paḥaṅ min/
gnas pa gnas pa ma yin te/
mi gnas pa yaṅ gnas ma yin/
skyes pa mi skye ma skyes min//

32 ḥdus byas daṅ ni ḥdus ma byas/
du ma ma yin gcig ma yin/
yod min med min yod med min/
mtshams ḥdir rnam pa ḥdi kun ḥdus//

33 las gnas pa ni bcom ldan gsuṅs/
bla ma las bdag ḥbras bu daṅ/
sems can las bdag bya ba daṅ/
las rnams chud za min par gsuṅs//

34 gaṅ phyir raṅ bźin med bstan pa/
de phyir de ma skyes pa las/
mi ḥjig bdag ḥdzin de las skye/
de skyed ḥdzin deḥaṅ rnam rtog las//

35 gal te las ni raṅ bźin ḥgyur/
de las skyes lus rtag par ḥgyur/
sdug bsṅal rnam smin can mi ḥgyur/
de phyir las kyaṅ bdag tu ḥgyur//

36 las ni rkyen skyes ci yaṅ med/
rkyen min skye baḥaṅ yod min te/
ḥdu byed rnams ni sgyu ma daṅ/
dri zaḥi groṅ khyer smig rgyu ḥdra//

37 las ni ñon moṅs rgyu mtshan can/
ḥdu byed ñon moṅs las bdag ñid/
lus ni las kyi rgyu mtshan can/
gsum kaḥaṅ ṅo bo ñid kyis stoṅ//

38 las med na ni byed pa med/
de gñis med par ḥbras bu med/
de med phyir na za ba po/
med pa yin pas dben pa ni//

39 yaṅ dag mthoṅ phyir las stoṅ par/
legs par rnam par śes na ni/
las mi ḥbyuṅ ste las med na/
las las gaṅ byuṅ mi ḥbyuṅ ṅo//

40 ji ltar bcom ldan de bźin gśegs/
de ni rdzu ḥphrul gyis sprul pa/
sprul pa mdzad la sprul des kyaṅ/
sprul pa gźan źig sprul par byed//

41 de las de bźin gśegs sprul stoṅ/
sprul pas sprul pa smos ci dgos/
rtog pa tsam gaṅ ci yaṅ ruṅ/
de dag gñi ga yod pa yin//

42 de bźin byed po sprul par mtshuṅs/
las ni sprul pas sprul daṅ mtshuṅs/
raṅ bźin gyis ni stoṅ pa yin/
rtog tsam gaṅ ciḥaṅ ruṅ bar yod//

43 gal te raṅ bźin gyis las yod/
mya ṅan ḥdas las byed po med/
gal te med na las skyed paḥi/
ḥbras bu sdug daṅ mi sdug med//

44 yod ces pa yod med ces paḥaṅ/
yod de yod med ces deḥaṅ yod/
saṅs rgyas rnams kyis dgoṅs na ni/
gsuṅs pa rtogs par sla ma yin//

45 gal te gzugs ḥbyuṅ las byuṅ na/
yaṅ dag min las gzugs ḥbyuṅ ḥgyur/
raṅ gi ṅo bo las ma yin/
de med phyir na gźan las min//

46 gcig laḥaṅ[21] bźi ni yod min źiṅ/
bźi laḥaṅ gcig ni yod min na/
ḥbyuṅ ba che bźi med brten nas/
gzugs ni ji ltar ḥgrub par ḥgyur//

47 śin tu mi ḥdzin phyir gal te/
rtags las śe na rtags de med/
rgyu daṅ rkyen las byed phyir ro/
yod naḥaṅ rtags med rigs ma yin//

48 gal te gzugs ni ḥdzin ḥgyur na/
bdag gi raṅ bźin ñid ḥdzin ḥgyur/
med pa[22] rkyen las skyes paḥi blos/
gzugs med ji ltar ḥdzin par ḥgyur//

49 gaṅ tshe blo ḥbyuṅ skad cig pas/
gzugs skyes skad cig mi ḥdzin na/
de yis ḥdas daṅ ma ḥoṅs paḥi/
gzugs ni ji ltar rtogs par ḥgyur//

50 gaṅ tshe nam yaṅ kha dog dbyibs/
tha dad ñid ni yod ma yin/
tha dad gcig tu ḥdzin pa med/
de gñis gzugs su grags phyir ro//

51 mig blo mig la yod min te/
gzugs la yod min bar naḥaṅ med/
mig daṅ gzugs la brten nas de/
yoṅs su rtog pa log pa yin//

52 gal te mig bdag mi mthoṅ na/
de gzugs mthoṅ bar ji ltar ḥgyur/
de phyir mig daṅ gzugs bdag med/
skye mched lhag maḥaṅ de daṅ ḥdra//

53 mig de raṅ bdag ñid kyis stoṅ/
de ni gźan bdag ñid kyis stoṅ/
gzugs kyaṅ de bźin stoṅ pa ste/
skye mched lhag maḥaṅ de bźin stoṅ//

54 gal te gcig reg lhan cig ḥgyur/
de tshe gźan rnams stoṅ pa yin/
stoṅ paḥaṅ mi stoṅ mi sten[23] te/
mi stoṅ pa yaṅ stoṅ pa min//

55 gsum po yod min mi gnas paḥi/
raṅ bźin ḥdu ba yod min pas/
de bdag ñid kyis reg pa med/
de phyir tshor ba yod ma yin//

56 naṅ daṅ phyi yi skye mched la/
brten nas rnam par śes pa ḥbyuṅ/
de lta bas na rnam śes med/
smig rgyu sgyu ma bźin du stoṅ//

57 rnam śes rnam śes bya brten nas/
ḥbyuṅ bas yod min śes pa daṅ/
rnam śes bya med phyir deḥi phyir/
rnam śes byed pa med pa ñid//

58 thams cad mi rtag mi rtag paḥam/
yaṅ na rtag pa ci yaṅ med/
dṅos yod rtag daṅ mi rtag ñid/
yin na de ltar ga la yod//

59 sdug daṅ mi sdug phyin ci log/
rkyen skyes chags sdaṅ gti mug rnams/
ḥbyuṅ ste de phyir raṅ bźin gyis/
ḥdod chags źe sdaṅ gti mug med//

60 gaṅ phyir der chags der sdaṅ der/
rmoṅs pa de phyir de dag ni/
rnam rtog gis bskyed rnam rtog kyaṅ/
yaṅ dag ñid du yod ma yin//

61 rnam brtag bya gaṅ de yod min/
brtag bya med rtog ga la yod/
de phyir rkyen las skyes paḥi phyir/
brtag bya rnam par rtog pa stoṅ//

62 yaṅ dag mthoṅ phyir phyin ci log/
bźi las skyes paḥi ma rig med/
de med phyir na ḥdu byed rnams/
mi ḥbyuṅ lhag maḥaṅ de bźin no//

63 gaṅ brten gaṅ skyes de de las/
skyes de de med mi ḥbyuṅ ṅo/
dṅos daṅ dṅos med ḥdus byas daṅ/
ḥdus ma byas źi [24] mya ṅan ḥdas//

64 rgyu daṅ rkyen las skyes dṅos rnams/
yaṅ dag par ni rtog pa gaṅ/
de ni ston pas ma rig gsuṅs/
de las yan lag bcu gñis ḥbyuṅ//

65 yaṅ dag mthoṅ phyir dṅos stoṅ par/
legs śes ma rig mi ḥbyuṅ ba/
de ni ma rig ḥgog pa yin/
de phyir yan lag bcu gñis ḥgag//

66 ḥdu byed dri zaḥi groṅ khyer daṅ/
sgyu ma smig rgyu chu bur daṅ/
chu yi dbu ba mtshuṅs pa ste/
rmi lam mgal meḥi ḥkhor lo ḥdra//

67 raṅ bźin gyis ni dṅos ḥgaḥ[25] med
ḥdi la dṅos po med paḥaṅ med/
rgyu daṅ rkyen las skyes pa yi/
dṅos daṅ dṅos med stoṅ pa yin//

68 dṅos po thams cad raṅ bźin gyis/
stoṅ pa yin pas dṅos rnams kyi[26]/
rten ḥbyuṅ de ni de bźin gśegs/
mtshuṅs pa med par ñe bar bstan//

69 dam paḥi don ni der zad do/
saṅs rgyas bcom ldan ḥdas kyis ni/
ḥjig rten tha sñad brten nas su/
sna tshogs thams cad yaṅ dag brtag[27]//

70 ḥjig rten pa yi bstan mi ḥjig/
yaṅ dag chos bstan ci yaṅ med/
de bźin gśegs bśad ma rtogs nas/
de phyir sgrub rtog med ḥdir skrag//

71 ḥdi brten ḥdi ḥbyuṅ źes bya ba ni/
ḥjig rten sgrub ḥdi ḥgog mi mdzad/
rten ḥbyuṅ gaṅ de raṅ bźin med/
ji ltar de yod yaṅ dag ṅes//

72 dad ldan yaṅ dag tshol lhur len/
chos bstan gaṅ laḥaṅ mi brten gaṅ/
sgrub ḥdir rigs pas rjes gñer te/
dṅos daṅ dṅos med spaṅs nas źi //

73 rkyen ñid ḥdi pa ḥdi śes nas/
lta ṅan dra baḥi rtog pa ldog/
chags rmoṅs khoṅ khro spaṅ phyir te/
ma gos mya ṅan ḥdas ñer ḥgro//

THE SEVENTY STANZAS ON VOIDNESS

Translation

The Two Truths

1 Although the Buddhas, according to the world's convention, speak of permanence, birth and destruction, of existence and non-existence, of inferiority, sameness and superiority, according to the true reality, nothing (of that) exists.[28]

Voidness of All (2-3)

2 Substance does not exist,[29] non-substance does not exist;[30] since substance and non-substance do not exist, nothing that is to be designated by words exists at all.[31] All the things, that are to be designated by words, similar to *nirvāṇa,*[32] are void of an own being.[33]

3 Since the own being of all things is nowhere, neither in the conglomerate of causes and conditions nor in each of them[34]—because of this, (all things) are void (of own being).[35]

Impossibility of Birth, Permanence and Destruction

4 (Something) existent cannot be born, since it is (already) existent;[36] (something) non-existent (can) not (be born), since it is non-existent;[37] (something) existent and non-existent (at the same time) (can) not (be born), since (both concepts) are contradictory between themselves.[38] Because birth does not exist, neither permanence nor destruction exist.[39]

Impossibility of Being Produced

5 What has been (already) born cannot be produced; what has been (not yet) born cannot be produced either; what is being born cannot be produced either, since it is (at the same time, already) born and not (yet) born.[40]

Impossibility of the Cause

6 If the effect existed,[41] (there would be) a cause provided (already) with its effect;[42] if that effect does not exist, the cause is similar to (something) non-existent;[43] and it is contradictory that (the effect) be not existent and be not non-existent (at the same time than the cause).[44] (Therefore) the cause is not logically possible in any of the three times.[45]

One and Multiple are Relative Notions. Denial of the Essential Characteristics

7 Without the one, the multiple does not exist; without the multiple, the one does not exist; for this reason things arisen in dependence, are devoid of essential characteristics.[46]

Denial of Dependent Origination (8-14)

8 Those twelve members[47] of Dependent Origination,[48] which have suffering[49] as their effect, are not born, since they are not logically possible in one (single) consciousness, nor are they possible in several (consciousnesses).[50]

9 Impermanence, permanence do not exist; non-substance, substance do not exist; impurity, purity do not exist; suffering, happiness do not exist.[51] Because of this, the (four) errors[52] do not exist.[53]

10 Since these[54] do not exist, ignorance, which arises out of the four errors, do not exist; since it does not exist, the *saṃskāras*[55] do not arise, nor the remaining (members).[56]

11 Since ignorance does not arise without *saṃskāras*, and without it the *saṃskāras* do not arise,[57] both, because they are (reciprocally) cause of each other, cannot be admitted as having an own being.

12 By a thing, which is not admitted with the nature of a substance, how could another thing be produced?[58] Therefore conditions,[59] which are not admitted (as having an own being), cannot produce other ones.

13 As the father is not the son, (and) the son is not the father[60] (and) both cannot be the one without the other[61] (and) both do not exist simultaneously,[62] so are the twelve members.[63]

14 As happiness and suffering, which depend on an object (seen) in dreams, do not exist nor (does) that object (exist),[64] so a thing which has arisen in dependence does not exist, nor does exist that, depending on what that thing has arisen.[65]

Impossibility of the Existence of an Own Being (15-18)

15 If things did not exist with an own being, inferiority, sameness and superiority would not exist, diversity would not be

admissible, origination out of cause would not exist.[66]

16[67] (If things were) admitted with an own being, they could not become things in dependence.[68] If they are not things in dependence, what happens?[69] Since an own being cannot become non-existent, whatever happened to exist with an own being, could not perish (ever).[70]

17 Since (an own being) does not exist, how could (things) be 'a thing in itself', or 'another thing' or perish.[71] Therefore, 'another thing', 'no thing',[72] 'thing', 'thing in itself' are errors.[73]

18 If things are void (of an own being),[74] they are not destroyed,[75] they are not born.[76] In relation to (something) devoid of an own being, where destruction could be produced? Where birth could be produced?[77]

Impossibility of Existence and Inexistence (19-22)

19 A thing existing and not existing at the same time is not (possible)[78] without the not existing thing, the existing thing is not (possible);[79] the existing thing and the not existing thing would be eternal;[80] without the existing thing, the not existing thing does not arise.[81]

20 Without the existing thing there is not the not existing thing;[82] (a thing) does not exist out of itself;[83] does not exist out of another one;[84] so things do not exist;[85] if these[86] do not exist, (these same) things are not (possible) (as) not existing.[87]

21 If there were existence in itself of things, there would be eternalism;[88] if there were non-existence in itself, there would be nihilism;[89] if things existed, both (would be), (and this) is not (possible);[90] therefore[91] things are not admitted.

22 Because of the series (of birth and destruction), they (eternalism and nihilism) are not produced; if there is a cause, things cease.[92] As (we have said) before, this is not admissible;[93] moreover the logical defect of the destruction of the series would be produced.[94]

The Nirvāṇa (23-26)

23 (Although Buddha), considering birth and destruction, has taught the path to *nirvāṇa*,[95] (yet) owing to Voidness they do

not exist,[96] since they are contradictory between themselves[97] and are perceived (only) because of error.[98]

24 If birth and cessation do not exist, through the cessation of what would *nirvāṇa* be produced?[99] Not being born and not ceasing *in se et per se*, is that not liberation?[100]

25 If *nirvāṇa* is cessation, there is nihilism;[101] if it is the other (alternative), there is eternalism;[102] therefore it is neither an existing thing nor a non-existing thing; it is without birth and cessation.[103]

26 If a cessation did subsist, then it would have to be without the existence of the thing;[104] (but) it cannot be without the existence of the thing;[105] nor can it be without the non-existence of the thing.[106]

The Characteristic and the Characterized (Thing)

27 It is admitted that the characteristic is on account of the characterized (thing); and it is admitted that the characterized (thing) is on account of the characteristic;[107] therefore it is not admitted that they exist *in se et per se*;[108] nor can it be admitted that both (exist) one on account of the other,[109] since what is not admitted cannot make another thing—that itself is not admitted—to be admitted.[110]

Application of What Precedes to Other Cases

28 With this[111] it has been completely explained all that can exist: cause and effect, sensation together with the object of sensation etc., who sees and the visible (thing) etc.

Inexistence of the Three Times

29 Because they do not remain,[112] because they are admitted one in relation to the other one,[113] because they are inferred,[114] because they cannot be admitted as a substance,[115] because things do not exist,[116] the three times do not exist, they are only an idea.

Inexistence of All

30 Since birth, permanence and destruction, these three characteristics of the conditioned (things) do not exist,[117] because of this, what is conditioned[118] and what is not-conditioned[119]—nothing exists.

Non-existence of Destruction, Permanence and Birth

31 Destruction does not exist for what has not (yet) been destroyed[120] nor does it exist for what has (already) been destroyed;[121] permanence does not exist for what has (already) endured;[122] permanence does not exist either for what does not yet endure;[123] birth does not exist for what has (already) been born,[124] nor does it exist for what has not (yet) been born.[125]

Conditioned and Non-conditioned Things

32 What is conditioned and what is non-conditioned are not multiplicity nor unity; they are not being, they are not non-being; they are not being and non-being; inside these extremes are completely comprehended these (two) aspects.[126]

Inexistence of Action, the Agent, and the Retribution (33-43)

33[127] The *Bhagvant* has said that the action subsists;[128] the Master has said that the actions have their own fruit,[129] that the actions belong to each living being[130] and that the actions do not perish.[131]

34 Since it has been taught that (action) has not an own being,[132] therefore, because it does not arise, it does not perish;[133] it arises out of the conception of an ego,[134] and also that conception, which makes it to arise, arises (at its own turn) out of a (mere) idea.[135]

35 If action were with an own being, the body, which arises out of it, would be eternal;[136] it could not be provided with the ripening that is suffering;[137] because of this, action would be also a substance.[138]

36 No action, arisen out of conditions, does exist;[139] nor does exist (any action) arisen out of non-conditions;[140] *saṃskāras* are similar to a magical illusion, to the *gandharvas'* city, to a mirage.[141]

37 Action has as its cause the impurities;[142] the *saṃskāras* are constituted by impurities and action;[143] the body has action as its cause;[144] the three[145] are void of an own being.[146]

38 Since action does not exist, the doer of the action does not

exist;[147] since both do not exist, the fruit of the action does not exist;[148] since the experiencer (of the fruit) does not exist, owing to the non-existence of that (fruit),[149] (all) is devoid (of an own being).[150]

39 If, because of having seen reality,[151] one understands well that action is empty of an own being, action does not (really) arise;[152] since action does not exist, that, which (apparently) has arisen out of action, does not (really) arise.[153]

40 In the same way as the *Bhagavant*, the *Tathāgata*, through his extraordinary powers[154] creates (for himself) apparently (a body),[155] and after having produced this apparent creation, through this same apparent creation creates apparently (other) apparent creation,[156]

41 —there the apparent creation[157] of the *Tathāgata* is void;[158] still more (are void) the apparent creations (apparently created) by the apparent creation;[159] both[160] are only ideas—

42 in the same way,[161] who acts, similar to the apparent creation,[162] and the action (which he performs), similar to the apparent creation (apparently created) by the apparent creation,[163] are void of an own being,[164] they exist as something which is only an idea.[165]

43 If action existed with an own being, *nirvāṇa* would not exist[166] not the doer of the action;[167] if (action) does not exist (with an own being), the fruit produced by action—suffering and non-suffering—do not exist.[168]

Intentional Formulations of the Buddhas

44 (In the *sūtras*) it is said: 'Exists'; it is said: 'Does not exist'; it is also said: 'Exists and does not exist.'[169] It is not easy to understand what has been intentionally[170] said by the Buddhas.

Impossibility of the Object of Visual Knowledge (45-46)

45 If the visible (thing)[171] arose from the material elements,[172] the visible (thing) would arise from something unreal;[173] so it would not exist out of (something with) an own being;[174] (and), since this one[175] does not exist, it does not exist out of another.[176]

46 In one,[177] the four[178] do not exist; in the four, the one does not exist;[179] therefore, depending on the non-existent four great elements how would the visible (thing) exist?[180]

Impossibility of Perception or Visual Knowledge **(47-52)**

47 If it is said that, as (the visible thing) is not perceived in itself, it (can be perceived) through its attributes,[181] (we answer that) these attributes do not exist, since they are produced by causes and conditions;[182] if the visible (thing) existed, it would be illogical (that it exist) without attributes.[183]

48 If the visible (thing) were perceived, an own being would be perceived;[184] how would the non-existent visible thing be perceived through an (also) non-existent consciousness since it arises out of conditions?[185]

49 Since consciousness, which arises instantaneous, does not grasp the visible (thing) that is born (also) instantaneous,[186] how could it perceive something visible, (already) past or not (yet) arrived?[187]

50 Since colour and form are never separated,[188] (it is) not (possible to say that), being separated, they are perceived together, since it is considered that both are the visible (thing).[189]

51 The consciousness of the eye[190] does not exist in the eye,[191] does not exist in the visible (thing)[192] nor in the middle (of both);[193] to imagine it (as really arising), depending on the eye and on the visible (thing), is an error.[194]

52 If the eye does not see itself, how could it see the visible (thing)?[195] Therefore the eye and the visible do not exist *in se et per se*.[196] The remaining *āyatanas* are similar to these.[197]

Voidness of Āyatanas **(53-54)**

53[198] The eye is void of an own essence;[199] it is void of the essence of another;[200] the visible (thing) is equally void, and equally void are the remaining *āyatanas*.[201]

54 If one exists together with the contact, the other ones are void.[202] What is void does not lean upon what is not void, nor what is not void does lean upon what is void.[203]

Non-existence of Sensorial Knowledge

55 The three[204] do not exist; since there is not conjunction of natures that do not endure,[205] there is not a real contact among them,[206] therefore, perception does not exist.[207]

Unreality of Consciousness

56 Depending on an internal *āyatana*[208] and on an external one,[209] consciousness[210] arises; for this reason consciousness does not exist,[211] it is void as a mirage, a magical illusion.

Non-existence of Consciousness, of the Object and Subject of Knowledge

57 Consciousness does not exist, since it arises depending on the knowable (thing); as consciousness does not exist nor the knowable (thing), therefore, the knower does not really exist.[212]

All is Impermanent; Nothing Exists

All is impermanent[213]—impermanent or permanent, nothing exists.[214] If things existed, they would be permanent or impermanent; then can they (really) exist?[215]

Unreality of the Kleśas and of the Imagination that Produces Them (59-61)

59 Attraction, hatred and error[216] arise, born out of conditions: (something) agreeable, (something) disagreeable, (something) erroneous;[217] therefore attraction, hatred and error do not exist *in se et per se.*[218]

60 Since attraction, hatred and error exist in relation to the same thing, they are produced by imagination,[219] and imagination also does not exist really.[220]

61 The imaginable (thing) does not exist;[221] since the imaginable (thing) does not exist, how would imagination exist?[222] Because of this, as they arise out of conditions, the imaginable (thing) and the imagination are void.[223]

The Ignorance Does Not Exist nor the Other Members of Dependent Origination

62 When reality[224] is perceived, ignorance[225] born out of the four errors[226] does not exist; since it does not exist, the *saṃskāras* do not arise;[227] in the same way the remaining (members) also (do not arise).

All is Calm; All is Nirvanized

63 If a thing is born depending on another, that (thing) is born out of this one;[228] since this one does not exist, the other one does not arise;[229] existing things and non-existing things, the *saṃskṛta* and the *asaṃskṛta* are (all) calm, nirvanized.[230]

The Ignorance and the Twelve Members (64-65)

64 To consider that things born out of causes and conditions are real[231]—the Master has said that is ignorance. Because of that the twelve members arise.[232]

65 When, by seeing reality,[233] it is well known that things are void, (then) ignorance does not arise; that is the cessation of ignorance;[234] for this reason the twelve members also cease.[235]

Unreality of the Saṃskāras

66 The *saṃskāras*[236] are similar to the *gandharvas'* city,[237] to a magical illusion, to a mirage, to a bubble, to water's foam; they are similar to a dream, to the circle of light produced by a torch.[238]

Non-existence of Things and No-things

67 Things with an own being do not exist at all;[239] here[240] no-things also do not exist;[241] things and no-things, born out of causes and conditions, are void.

Dependent Origination = Voidness

68 Since all things are void of an own being, the incomparable *Tathāgata* has taught the Dependent Origination of all things.[242]

Supreme Truth = Dependent Origination. Validity of the Relative Truth (69-71)

69 The supreme truth is only that.[243] Buddha, the *Bhagavant*, holding to the relative truth, considered all the diverse things in a correct way.[244]

70 The teaching proper of the world has not been abolished;[245] in reality, a teaching of the Doctrine never existed at all;[246] by not understanding what the *Tathāgata* has said, (ignorant persons) become afraid of this principle free from (all) mental creation.[247]

71 Depending on this, that does arise[248]—this principle relative

to the world is not denied.[249] What arises in dependence lacks an own being, how could it exist?[250] (All what precedes) is perfectly evident.[251]

Means to Obtain Nirvāṇa

72 The man, who has faith, consecrates himself to the search of truth, does not cling to the teaching of any doctrine, adheres, according to logic, to that principle,[252] having abandoned being and non-being,[253] becomes calm.[254]

73 Knowing the conditionality of (all) this,[255] with the cessation of the mental creations, which constitute the net of the false doctrines,[256] and the abandonment of attraction, error and hatred,[257] one proceeds, pure, towards *nirvāṇa*.

NOTES

1. *Buddhist Text Information*, 18, p. 9.
2. The third translator, designated by the word *Khu*, would be 'the lotsāba (translator) from Khu', i.e. Mdo-sde ḥbar (Sūtrajvāla?), *Buddhist Text Information*, 18, p. 9, and *Cumulative Index*, 14-18, p. 10a.
3. Cf. *Buddhist Text Information, Cumulative Index*, 14-18, pp. 8b, 9a and 10a; Naudou, *Les Bouddhistes Kaśmīriens*, pp. 165, 171, 175, 183, 188 and 189.
4. We consider that Bhavya (?), the author of *Madhyamakaratnapradīpa*, is a late author, posterior to Candrakīrti. Cf. Ruegg, *The Literature*, pp. 66, 106 and 116, and C. Dragonetti, 'On Śuddhamati's Pratītyasamutpādahṛdayakārikā'.
5. Cf. Naudou, *Les Bouddhistes Kaśmīriens*, pp. 182-83.
6. *Hōbōgirin*, fascicule 2, p. 174 ('Busshin').
7. Cf. Hiuan Tsang, *Siddhi*, *Taisho* XXXI, 1585, p. 37a, 11.8-22 (=pp. 421-23, translation of L. de la Vallée Poussin), Asaṅga, *Mahāyānasaṃgraha*, chapter 2, paragraph 14 (ed. and trans. of Lamotte); Vasubandhu, *Trisvabhāva* 35.
8. Naudou, *Les Boddhistes Kaśmīriens*, pp. 86 and ff.
9. Cf. note 1.
10. As Ruegg, *The Literature*, p. 21, note 45, says, the differences among the three recensions, that we have of the *kārikās* (two of them contained in the commentaries of Nāgārjuna, *Svavṛtti*, and of Candrakīrti, *Vṛtti*), create several problems of historical and philological nature. It constitutes another problem, as the same Ruegg expresses, to determine whether Candrakīrti knew the commentary attributed to Nāgārjuna and whether he considered it to be authentic. Object of study would also be the comparison between the interpretations, that are presented by the

commentaries of Nāgārjuna and Candrakīrti.

11. See F. Tola, C. Dragonetti, 'Nagārjuna's Conception of Voidness'.
12. sñad: commentary of 3831 and 3827, cf. 5231; *kārikā* of 3831: sñan.
13. skyes: commentary of 3831, 3827 and 5231; *kārikā* of 3831: skye.
14. min: 3827, cf. commentary of 3831; *kārikā* of 3831: yin.
15. mi: commentary of 3831, 3827 and 5231; *kārikā* of 3831: min.
16. yin: commentary of 3831 and 3827; *kārikā* of 3831: min.
17. des gźan: commentary of 3831, cf. 3827; *kārikā* of 3831: de bźin.
18. mi: commentary of 3831, 5231; *kārikā* of 3831: min.
19. ḥgog na chad: our correction, cf. commentary of 3831; *kārikā* of 3831: ḥgog cha daṅ.
20. ltar na rtag: 3827 and 5231; *kārikā* of 3831; ltar brtag pa.
21. gcig laḥaṅ: 5231 *kārikā* and commentary, cf. 3827; *kārikā* of 3831: gcig paḥaṅ.
22. med pa: commentary of 3831 and *kārikā* and commentary of 5231; *kārikā* of 3831: med las.
23. sten: *kārikā* of 5231, cf. 5227 and commentaries of 3831 and 5231; *kārikā* of 3831: ston.
24. źi: commentary of 3831; *kārikā* of 3831: śiṅ.
25. ḥgaḥ: commentaries of 3831 and 5231; *kārikā* of 3831: ḥgag.
26. dṅos rnams kyi: commentaries of 3831 and 5231; *kārikā* of 3831: dṅos rnams kyis.
27. brtag: according to the commentary of 3831 and 3827; *kārikā* of 3831: ḥphags. We think that the Sanskrit text has the word '*udita*', from *VAD*: 'to say, to proclaim, to declare, to teach', and that the Tibetan translator understood it as coming from *ud I*: 'to arise' and therefore translated it by *ḥphags* which means *udgata=udita*: 'arisen'.
28. The Buddhas have referred to the categories of the empirical reality as if they existed, only in order to be able to communicate with other beings and teach the true doctrine, but in truth these categories do not exist. Other forms of translating the last *pāda* would be: '*(yet), from the point of view of True Reality, (the Buddhas) do not (speak at all)*' and '*(yet the Buddhas) do not (speak about the categories of empirical reality) from the point of view of True Reality*'.
29. All is conditioned according to the analysis of reality that Nāgārjuna carries on.
30. What is not a substance (i.e. the conditioned, composed, relative thing) does not really exist. This is a fundamental principle of Nāgārjuna.
31. Because, if the things designated by words existed, they had to be substances or non-substances, whose existence has been denied.
32. I.e.: extinguished *ab aeterno*. Reference to the identity of *saṃsāra* and *nirvāṇa*. See below note 101.
33. Insubstantial, non-existent *in se et per se*.
34. Nowhere do we find the own being of any thing, neither in its parts nor in the totality of these parts.
35. Then we must conclude that this own being does not exist, since it is not found anywhere.

36. What already exists, and consequently has already been born, cannot be born again.
37. Something non-existent cannot be the subject of a birth, since to be born is an action which requires the real existence of a subject which realizes it.
38. We cannot imagine the existence of anything provided with contradictory qualities.
39. The categories of permanence and destruction presuppose the category of birth.
40. The previous *kārikā* treated about the impossibility to be born; this one treats about the impossibility to be produced. The argumentation in both is the same. What is being born participates, so to say, of *being* (something of it is already arisen) and of non-being (something of it is not yet completely arisen), and this precisely is contradictory in itself.
41. It must be understood: *before* the cause.
42. We would have a cause provided with an effect that would have preceded it. This is the case of the heat of a determinate fire which would exist before that fire arises. This is contrary to the concept of cause.
43. It is not possible to say that something is a 'cause', that it exists as a cause, before something that is its specific effect has not arisen. It is not possible to say that a determinate fire is the cause of heat until the heat caused by that fire has not come into existence. This is the case of the effect that arises *after* the cause.
44. The first *pāda* considers the hypothesis that the effect *is* (already) *existent* (*yod*) when the cause arises. The second *pāda* considers the hypothesis that the effect *is* (still) *non-existent* when the cause arises. The third *pāda* contains a new hypothesis, which denies the two previous ones: the effect *is not existent* (*yod min*) and *is not non-existent* (*med pa min*). Nāgārjuna refutes this hypothesis expressing that it has a contradiction in itself, because a thing (in this case: the effect) cannot have at the same time the two contradictory attributes of *not existing* and *not non-existent*.
45. The first hypothesis (*yod*) places the effect in the past in relation to cause or (what is the same) the cause in the future in relation to the effect. The second hypothesis (*med*) places the effect in the future with relation to the cause or (what is the same) the cause in the past with relation to effect. The third hypothesis (*yod pa min, med pa min*) considers the effect and the cause simultaneous, that is to say places both in the present in relation of each one with the other. All these hypotheses have been denied. The last *pāda* affirms that the cause cannot exist either in the future (after the effect: first hypothesis), not in the past (before the effect: second hypothesis), not in the present (simultaneously with the effect: third hypothesis).
46. All things belong either to the category of 'unity' or to the category of 'multiplicity', they have as attribute unity or multiplicity. But these attributes, being relative, depending one on the other, are not entities possessing an own being, real. What the *kārikā* says in regard to unity and multiplicity can be applied to any attribute (low-high, long-short etc.). Then it can concluded that things do not possess essential characteristics,

provided with an own being, really existent.

47. The twelve members are: *avidyā* (ignorance), *saṃskāras* (subliminal impressions), *vijñāna* (consciousness), *nāmarūpa* (individuality), *ṣaḍāyatana* (the six senses and their correspondent objects), *sparśa* (contact of the senses with their correspondent objects), *vedanā* (sensation), *tṛṣṇā* (thirst, desire), *upādāna* (attachment), *bhava* (existence), *jāti* (birth), *jāramaraṇaśokādi* (old age and death, suffering, etc.).
48. *Pratītyasamutpāda.*
49. Lineal conception of *Pratītyasamutpāda,* which begins with ignorance and ends with suffering. It is an explanation of the origin of suffering.
50. Man is only a series of instantaneous consciousness. The instantaneous *dharmas* (elements of existence), which are the twelve members of the *Pratītyasamutpāda,* would have to exist either all of them inside one single consciousness or each of them in a different consciousness. If all of them exist inside one single consciousness, the entire process of the *Pratītyasamutpāda* would be instantaneous, it would arise and disappear in a single instant. This would be absurd and would mean the effective non-existence of the *Pratītyasamutpāda.* If each of these twelve members exists in a different consciousness, the process of the *Pratītyasamutpāda* would take place in several conciousnesses. But, as each consciousness is instantaneous, the member which exists in it would also be instantaneous, because of this reason (and of course because of its own instantaneous nature). A relation of causality could not be established between a member-cause, which as soon as it is born disappears, and the member which is its effect, which equally as soon as it is born disappears. Moreover, either if they are in one single consciousness or in several consciousnesses, anyhow a relation of causality could not be established among the twelve members of the *Pratītyasamutpāda,* since it has been proved in *kārikā* 6 that cause is impossible to be. This cancels the notion of *pratītyasamutpāda.*
51. The three first *pādas* could be translated in the following way: *Impermanence is not permanence; non-substance is not a substance; impurity is not purity; suffering is not happiness.* So do Yamaguchi and Uriūtsu translate. We think that our translation is the only one that allows to draw the conclusion expressed in the last *pāda.* The text of the *kārikās* (3827) corroborates our translation.
52. The four errors are mentioned by Patañjali, *Yogasūtras* II, 5. They consist in considering what is impermanent, impure, painful, unreal as permanent, pure, pleasant and real. These four errors constitute also for Patañjali the *avidyā.*
53. Since what is impermanent, permanent etc. does not exist, the four errors, which consist in their mutual confusion, do not exist either. This conclusion is not possible, if we translate the text as Yamaguchi and Uriūtsu do.
54. The four errors mentioned in the previous *kārikā.*
55. The *saṃskāras* are the second of the 12 members of the Dependent Origination and as such they are a direct effect of ignorance. See note 47.
56. Of the Dependent Origination.

57. The reciprocal causality of the ignorance and the *saṃskāras* makes them conditioned and therefore (as the following *pāda* says) lacking an own being, unreal, non-existent *in se et per se*. In the series of the 12 members of the *Pratītyasamutpāda*, the ignorance is the cause of the *saṃskāras*. Consequently the *kārikā* says that without ignorance the *saṃskāras* do not arise. But, in order that ignorance may be considered as a cause, it is necessary that which is its effect be arisen, according to the argumentation of *kārikā* 6: anything, in order to be a cause and to exist as such, requires the existence of its effect; without its effect it cannot be considered a cause nor exist as such.

58. Anything that does not possess an own being, cannot produce any other thing, since what does not possess an own being is unreal, does not exist and therefore cannot give birth to anything else. For instance, a car does not exist as a car, it is only a conglomerate of parts (wheels, seats, etc.); therefore, as a car which is really non-existent, it cannot produce anything else.

59. It refers to the 12 members of the *Pratītyasamutpāda*.

60. The father as the *cause* is not identical with the son as the *effect* and vice versa.

61. Although they are different, the son, as the effect, cannot exist without the father who is his cause; and, at his own turn the father, as the cause, cannot exist without the son, who is his effect. (See note 43 of *kārikā* 6). Both are in this way mutually conditioned.

62. *Kārikā* 6 has denied the possibility of the cause (the father) being simultaneous with the effect (the son).

63. In the same way as the father and the son, the members of the Dependent Origination are not identical among themselves, they cannot exist one without the other (See note 57 of *kārikā* 11) and they do not exist simultaneously (See note 44 of *kārikā* 6).

64. A man dreams he possesses great power and riches; the happiness, based on that power and riches, that exist only in a dream, is as unreal as the same dream. This image of the dream serves to illustrate the general principle expressed in what follows.

65. As all things in our empirical reality are conditioned, relative, dependent, any thing that arises has to arise depending on another thing, which at its own turn depends on another one and so on, without being possible to find an entity existing *in se et per se*. This general principle applies to Dependent Origination, where each member is effect of the preceding one and cause of the following one. Because of this reason it is possible to consider that this *kārikā* 14 closes the development about Dependent Origination which began in *kārikā* 8.

66. This *kārikā* presents an objection that can be adduced against the thesis of the non-existence of an own being, maintained by Nāgārjuna's school: there would be no relation among things: neither of inferiority nor of equality nor of superiority, nor of diversity nor of causality; this would imply the negation of the Dependent Origination, treated in the previous *kārikās*.

67. This *kārikā* refutes the objection of the previous *kārikā*.
68. A thing that possesses an own being cannot lose that own being, becoming a dependent thing. See Note 64 of Chapter 2 for texts in which this idea is expressed.
69. The answer is given in what follows.
70. The own being cannot cease to be; consequently things which possess an own being cannot perish. If things in our empirical reality possessed an own being, they would be eternal. This is the absurd consequence that the objection of *kārikā* 15 would produce.
71. If things do not have an own being, it is not possible to say about any thing, considered in itself, that it is 'a thing', nor about any thing, considered in relation to another thing, that it is 'another thing', because what does not possess an own being (as for instance a car; see note 58 of *kārikā* 12), is unreal, non-existent and as such nothing can be predicated about it. Nor can it be said that something that is unreal, non-existent, 'perishes'.
72. 'Non-thing' is the thing denied, as a 'non-car'. Since a 'thing' (like a car) does not exist, it is not possible to speak about its negation, 'the non-thing', because this is a concept which exists only in relation to 'thing'.
73. That is to say: concepts that correspond to nothing real; consequently it is not possible to construe upon them an argument which could reach a valid conclusion.
74. We think that in this *kārikā*, we have the exposition of the consequences which derive from the thesis of the non-existence of an own being, rather than the exposition of an objection against that thesis. The consequences are: no birth and no destruction.
75. About the impossibility of the destruction of a thing devoid of an own being see note 71 of previous *kārikā*.
76. When the pieces, that compose a car and which are the only thing (relatively) existent, are united, it is not possible to say that thereby a car is born as something existent in itself and different from the pieces that compose it. 'Car', does not designate something existent *in se et per se*; it is only a conventional denomination to designate a determinate association of pieces.
77. If the car as such does not exist, how could it be said that a birth or a destruction, which relates to the car, which exists in relation to it, takes place? See note 37 of *kārikā* 4.
78. There cannot be for the same thing at the same time existence and non-existence, which are contradictory and mutually excluding attributes.
79. The concepts of 'existent' (existence) and 'inexistent' (non-existence) are relative between themselves; without the one, the other is not able to be. A thing is existent in relation to itself considered as non-existent or after becoming non-existent. See below note 81.
80. If for one thing there existed *only* existence or non-existence, that thing would never abandon the existence (its sole possibility) and would be eternally existent or would never abandon the non-existence and would be eternally non-existent.
81. Since the concepts of existent thing (existence) and non-existent thing

(non-existence) are correlative, if one of them does not exist, the other cannot exist either. It is the principle expressed in the second *pāda* in a contrary form.

82. The first *pāda* of this *kārikā* repeats the principle expressed in the last *pāda* of the previous *kārikā*.
83. Because, if it were so, the thing would exist before itself.
84. Since, according to *kārikā* 17, it is not possible to speak about 'another thing'. Moreover, as all things are void, unreal, nothing can arise from them. See above note 58.
85. Things do not exist, since they do not arise either out of themselves or out of another. The text does not speak about two other cases, referred to in *Mūlamadhyamakakārikās* I, 3: to arise out of oneself and of another at the same time and to arise without any cause.
86. The existing things.
87. Without the existence of a thing, there cannot be the non-existence of that same thing, since existence and non-existence are correlative terms, each of which requires the other.
88. If things had existence as their own being, they would exist eternally, since the own being cannot be abandoned. See above notes 68 and 80. Moreover, if a thing possessed the attribute existence, it could never replace it by the attribute non-existence, because, if that change took place, it would happen that during an instant, however infinitisimally short it may be, both attributes would coexist, because the attribute existence cannot 'abandon' the thing before the 'arrival' of the attribute non-existence, since, if that occurred, the attributed non-existence would find a thing already non-existent. The simultaneity of the attributes existence and non-existence, however brief it may be, means the possession of two contrary attributes, which is not logically possible. So existing things cannot abandon existence and must be eternal, what means the eternity of all things, the *eternalism*.
89. If something has non-existence as its own being, it could never come to existence, since, as we have said, the own being cannot be abandoned. Besides that, something non-existent cannot be the subject of a birth. See above note 37. Finally, the change of non-existence into existence implies the same logical difficulty than the change existence into non-existence, to which we have referred in the previous note. Consequently non-existent things cannot abandon non-existence and have to be eternally non-existent, what signifies the eternal non-existence of all, the *nihilism*.
90. We understand that, after having treated about the existence and non-existence with an own being (which lead respectively to eternalism and nihilism), the author proceeds to treat about a third hypothesis: about things that exist after having not existed, about existence which follows non-existence. In this case both absurd consequences, of eternalism and nihilism, would be produced. From the non-existence of things (first stage), it would follow that they would be eternally non-existent and from the existence of things (second stage) it would follow that they would be eternally existent which is logically impossible. See notes 88 and 89. The

existence of eternalism and nihilism, which is implied by this hypothesis, cannot be accepted.

91. Because of all that has been expressed before, because of the absurd consequences which are produced by the existence, non-existence and existence and non-existence of things, these cannot be admitted, they are mere products of our imagination.

92. The first part of the *kārikā* contains an objection from the point of view of the traditional Buddhist idea that in the empirical reality all is constituted by phenomena related among themselves as causes and effects. These elements of the series, according to traditional teaching, arise to existence (as effects of other causes), produce an effect and disappear. So we have existence and non-existence, one after the other. Consequently there is no place for eternalism (only existence) or for nihilism (only non-existence).

93. The last part of the *kārikā* answers the objection of the first part, expressing that the argument of the previous *kārikā* applies also to each of the elements of the series: if any of the elements of the series existed it could not cease existing, since the substitution of the attribute existence by the attribute non-existence would imply the simultaneous existence of both, which cannot logically be admitted. So, if it existed, each element of the series would be eternal, what would imply the eternity of all. See above notes 88 and 90 of the previous *kārikā*. The position of this *kārikā* overcomes the traditional position of Buddhism in the name of Nāgārjuna's nihilism.

94. Besides the eternalism, that would be produced, if the objection of the first part of the *kārikā* is accepted, we would have another consequence, that we cannot accept: each member of the series would be eternal and consequently we would have the abrogation of the series, which implies a progression, an evolution, a transformation.

95. It was in relation to birth and perishing (*saṃsāra*) that Buddha preached his doctrine which shows the path that leads to *nirvāṇa*. Buddha acted in this way in order to be able to instruct men, using the unreal elements of the empirical reality to reveal to them the Supreme Truth or Reality. It was a propedeutic reason.

96. To be born and to perish exist from the point of view of the Relative Truth, but not from the point of view of the Supreme Truth, since from this last point of view both are void, lack an own being and consequently are unreal, non-existent. See *kārikās* 4 and 18.

97. Being born implies existence and perishing implies non-existence and both exclude themselves mutually. See above notes 88-91.

98. To perceive birth and perishing of things is only an error, because both do not exist really.

99. The first two *pādas* express the traditional Buddhist conception of *nirvāṇa*: it is the extinction of the series of reincarnations or of the empirical reality or the personal individuality etc.

100. The two last *pādas* express the Mādhyamika conception of *nirvāṇa*: that state which was never really abandoned, which is constituted by the inalterable Voidness *ab aeterno* of all, and in which either to be born or to

perish did never occur.

101. The *nirvāṇa* and the empirical reality (*saṃsāra*) are identical, since both are Voidness. All is nirvanized *ab aeterno*. If *nirvāṇa* were cessation, non-existence, i.e. if *nirvāṇa* had as its own being cessation or non-existence, the *saṃsāra* also would be cessation, non-existence, would have as its own being cessation, non-existence. The *saṃsāra* could never abandon that own being and arise to existence. See note 68. It would be nihilism. The impossibility to arise to existence on the part of empirical reality would be in contradiction with the existence of that reality which is a fact of experience.

102. The other alternative would be that *nirvāṇa* be existence, had existence as its own being. In that case, we would have the eternal existence of *saṃsāra* (identical with *nirvāṇa*), which could never abandon its own being. See above note 68. What precedes is in contradiction with the fact of the destruction of things revealed by experience.

103. The last *pāda* indicates the consequences that derive from the first three: *nirvāṇa* is neither being nor non-being, it is not born, it does not perish.

104. In order that the cessation of a determinate thing last, be maintained, it is necessary that the thing (of which it is cessation) *do not exist*, because, if the thing existed, its cessation could not be produced. But, in order that the cessation of a thing last, the existence and non-existence of that thing (as it is said in the two following *pādas*) are necessary, and that is logically impossible. So cessation cannot be produced.

105. The cessation of a thing in order to last, to be maintained, requires the existence of that thing, since that thing is its support; without that thing it would not have a support.

106. The cessation of a thing cannot last, be maintained without the non-existence of that thing, because, as we have said, while the thing exists, its cessation is impossible.

107. The characteristic of a determinate thing cannot exist without the thing of which it is characteristic: the heat of a particular fire cannot exist without that fire which is its support. And a particular thing would not exist without the attributes that characterize it: the fire, without the heat that characterizes it, would cease to exist as fire.

108. Since the characteristic depends on the thing it characterizes and vice versa, both are conditioned entities, they have not an own being, they are therefore unreal.

109. It is also impossible that the characteristic and the characterized thing, which are unreal because of being mutually conditioned, could give each other a real existence.

110. Something without firmness cannot lend firmless to another thing without firmness and vice versa.

111. The argumentation of the preceding *kārikā* applies to all the pairs of things that exist mutually conditioned. The *kārikā* enumerates several of those pairs.

112. Time is only a succession of instants which, as soon as they arise, disappear. Besides these instants there is not a time with an own being,

existing *in se et per se*, immovable, stable (*avasthita, kūṭastha*). It is a case of the problematic of the whole (the time) and the parts (the instants), considered from the Buddhist point of view. In the same way as, in relation to space, there is not a whole independent and different from its parts, so, in relation to time, there is not a time, independent and different from the instants. And, as the parts of a whole extended in the space can be divided through an abolishing analysis which never stops, so the divisions of time can at their own turn be divided *ad infinitum*. The result of this abolishing analysis, either in the case of space or in the case of time, is the non-existence of an own being, i.e. the absence of a real existence.

113. The three times exist only in mutual dependence, they are concepts totally relative, without a proper and autonomous existence, and consequently without a real existence. Moreover the mutual dependence of the three times implies their mutual coexistence and therefore the loss of their own nature as such: in order to depend on the past, the present must coexist with the past and ceases to be present.

114. Time does not exist and is not perceived independently from the instants that compose it. Its existence is only the result of an erroneous inference.

115. That is to say: they do not exist with an own being. See above note 112.

116. Time is always referred to things: a thing that has arisen and has ceased to be receives the name of 'past'; if it arises but has not been destroyed, it is said to be 'present'; if it did not yet arise to existence it is called 'future'. Time, so to say, adheres to things, exists in dependence to them; does not exist as something independent. Now for Nāgārjuna all things are void, lacking an own being, unreal. Consequently time, which depends for its existence on them, is equally void, without an own being—it does not exist.

117. In the *kārikās* 1, 4, 5, 8-14, 18, 24 and 26 the author has referred to the non-existence of birth, permanence and destruction; in *kārikā* 27 he has affirmed that the characteristic and what it characterizes does not exist.

118. All what constitutes the empirical reality.

119. The *nirvāṇa*, to which the author has referred to in *kārikās* 23-25.

120. A thing, to which destruction has not yet arrived, has no relation with destruction, has nothing to do with it.

121. A thing, after desturction arrived to it, does not exist anymore and consequently it is not able to have any kind of relation with destruction.

122. The state or situation of 'permanence' has nothing to do, does not exist for a thing that has already endured and which has ceased to endure.

123. The state or situation of 'permanence' has nothing to do, does not exist for a thing which has not begun to endure.

124. A thing cannot be born two times. See note 36 of *kārikā* 4.

125. A thing, that has not yet been born, cannot be the subject of the action of being born. See above note 37.

126. For the analysis of the Mādhyamika all that exist, conditioned or non-conditioned, falls inside the mentioned negative and opposed categories: it is neither one nor multiple, neither being nor non-being, contrary to the analysis that is normally made of empirical reality for which all falls

necessarily inside the corresponding positive categories: it is one or multiple, being or not being.

127. The present *kārikā* contains an objection that can be made to Nāgārjuna: action exists and does not perish, since that is what Buddha has taught. The following *kārikā* will make clear the meaning of Buddha's words from the perspective of Nāgārjuna's school; the action, the agent and the fruit do not exist really, they lack an own being.

128. Action subsists in its 'fruits' or deferred effects.

129. No action is exhausted in its immediate effects; it gives rise to other 'fruits' or effects in the same existence or in another existence.

130. It is the author of an action who has to experience its deferred effects.

131. Cf. above note 128.

132. Does not exist *in se et per se*, since action, to exist, depends on the person that performs it.

133. When Buddha said that action is not extinguished, what he really wanted to say is that action does not perish since it has not been born. What Buddha has said must not be taken in its explicit meaning (*nītārtha*), but in the meaning that is to be discovered (*neyārtha*). See below notes 169 and 170.

134. When there is the belief in an ego as really existing, then it is possible to think that an action exists, which is performed by that ego as its agent or author. If the existence of an ego is not admitted, when the agent or author of possible actions disappears, action disappears also.

135. The conception of an ego as really existing has no real correspondent, it is only a mental creation. It is the *nairātmya* theory taught by Buddhism since its first days.

136. The *kārikā* examines in the first place the case of the cause that produces the effect without transforming itself into that effect. If action had an own being, this own being could never abandon it; action would be consequently eternal. And also eternal would be the body produced by the action (as a cause which is not transformed into that body), since while a cause A, which produces a specific effect B, lasts, that effect has to last. On the idea that the body originates from action see below note 144.

137. The *kārikā* examines now the case of the cause that produces an effect transforming itself into that effect and disappearing consequently. Action matures, transforms itself into suffering, which is its deferred effect (through which retribution of acts is done), in the same way as the seed matures, transforms itself into the fruit. If action had an own being and were consequently eternal, it would never transform itself into suffering, as a seed which were eternal would never mature, would never transform itself into the fruit.

138. The hypothesis that action has an own being has as its absurd consequence (*prasaṅga*) the affirmation of the *eternity* of action (see above note 136), the *impossibility of suffering* as a result or maturation of action (see above note 137) and *substantiality* of action, since whatever has an own being is a substance, something existing *in se et per se*. The hypothesis of an own being for action means that action escapes from the *trilakṣaṇa* which

characterizes everything: it would be neither impermanent (*anitya*) nor painful (*duḥkha*) nor insubstantial (*anātman*); this hypothesis would destroy a basic postulate of Buddhism.

139. Reality, with an own being, *in se et per se*.
140. Nothing can arise out of something that is not a condition (or cause); such a thing cannot have an effect; nothing can come forth from it.
141. Actions and *saṃskāras* (subliminal impressions) are in mutual relation of causality: actions leave *saṃskāras*, and these, when they become reactualized produce feelings of attraction and hatred and errors and, through these ones give rise to new actions. If actions are unreal, as the *kārikā* says, the *saṃskāras* produced by them are also unreal following the principle that out of empty *dharmas* only empty *dharmas* can arise. *Gandharvas'* city: an illusory creation.
142. The cause of actions are desire, hatred, error.
143. The *saṃskāras* (subliminal impressions) arise from the impurities (desire, hatred, error) and from action which is affected by them. If there were neither impurities nor action affected by them, there would be no *saṃskāras*.
144. According to the doctrine of retribution of actions, any action produces good or bad effects in agreement with its moral value. If a life has not be sufficient for all these effects being produced, there must be reincarnation in a new body in order that these effects may be produced. In this sense the body is a consequence or an effect of actions previously performed.
145. Action, body, *saṃskāras*.
146. Since its coming forth into existence depends on causes and conditions.
147. Without action the action's agent cannot exist as such and vice versa without the action's agent, action cannot come to being. See *kārikā* 34 and note 132.
148. The fruit of the action, in order to come to be, depends on action and on the agent of action. If these do not exist, the fruit does not exist either.
149. The 'fruit' does not exist and consequently the experiencer of that inexisting 'fruit' cannot exist.
150. Action, its 'fruit', the doer of the action and the experiencer of the 'fruit' exist depending one on the other, or, what is the same, they lack an own being.
151. The true reality, the true nature of everything, universal voidness of which the emptiness of action is only an example.
152. Whatever has not an own being, does not exist really and consequently cannot be born.
153. Since the cause does not exist, its effects cannot exist either. These effects are, besides the immediate and visible ones, the *saṃskāras* (subliminal impressions) and suffering as a 'maturation' of action, as its deferred effect, manifested in a future existence.
154. Powers possessed by Buddha owing to his condition as such.
155. We could have here a reference to the *nirmāṇakāya* of the Buddhist Theory of the Three Bodies of Buddha or perhaps only a reference to the extraordinary, magical or miraculous powers possessed by the Buddhas.

Anyhow even in this last case it would be an antecedent of that theory.

156. Buddha, thanks to his extraordinary powers, manifests himself under the form of apparent bodies and through them performs actions which are also only an appearance, an illusion.
157. I.e. the body created by Buddha.
158. Unreal.
159. In the example of note 156 of previous *kārikā*: the actions performed by the apparent or fantastic creation of Buddha.
160. The apparent body of Buddha and what that body apparently performs.
161. General application to empirical reality of the example of *kārikās* 40 and 41.
162. The doer of any action corresponds to the apparent or fantastic body created by Buddha.
163. Action corresponds to the apparent or fantastic action performed by the apparent or fantastic body created by Buddha.
164. And consequently unreal, non-existent *in se et per se* as such.
165. All the empirical reality is only a mental creation, ideas—idealistic affirmation, which is a necessary consequence of the doctrine of voidness.
166. If action had an own being it would be eternal and its consequences would be eternal (see above note 136) and consequently *nirvāṇa*, which presupposes the elimination of action and its fruits, would not exist.
167. If action had an own being, it would exist *in se et per se* and consequently in order to exist it would not require the existence of an agent who would perform it.
168. See above note 148 of *kārikā* 38.
169. According to the *svavṛtti* it could be argued, against what has been said in the previous *kārikā* concerning action and its fruit, that in the *sūtras* which constitute the word of Buddha it is said (*ces pa yod*): 'Exists' (*yod*), 'Does not exist' (*med*) etc. Then how is it possible to sustain the 'non-existence' (of 'the action and its fruit')? The answer is given in this *kārikā* by saying that affirmations of the type of: 'Exists', 'Does not exist' etc. are intentional formulations by the Buddhas. See the next note. The direct meaning (*nītārtha*) of these formulations is that they affirm the *real* existence or non-existence etc.; the intentional meaning is that they affirm only the *illusory* existence or non-existence etc., i.e. *contrario sensu*, that they deny the existence and non-existence *in se et per se*.
170. It is not easy for common people to understand at once the intentional meaning of the words of Buddha. This is a reference to the *neyārta* formulations of Buddha, which must not be taken in their direct and explicit meaning (as the *nītārtha* formulations), but in their indirect and implicit one. The *intention* of Buddha was that his formulations were understood in their indirect and implicit meaning by those persons already instructed in his true doctrine. The teaching for persons not yet instructed in Buddha's true doctrine must start from the direct and explicit meaning to reach gradually the indirect and implicit meaning which as in the case of *śūnyatā* theory is not easy to understand.
171. The Tibetan text has *gzugs*, which corresonds to *rūpa*. *Rupā* designates

the objects of visual perception, which present themselves before the eye as form and colour, the visible things, the 'visible'. By *rūpa* we must understand also all 'the material', since 'the material', having form and colour, is 'the visible'. Human body belongs to the category '*rūpa*', *gzugs*. In this sense it is said that *rūpa*, *gzugs* is one of the constituent elements of man, one of the *skandhas*.

172. Water, earth, fire and air which constitute all the existing material reality.

173. The material elements are something unreal, since they are insubstantial, since they do not possess an own being, as is manifested by the abolishing analysis, proper of the Mādhyamika school, through which every thing can be divided *ad infinitum* without the possibility of finding a last support, a final limit where the analysis could stop.

174. To arise from the elements means for 'the visible' not to arise from something which has an own being.

175. The own being.

176. 'The visible' cannot arise from another thing, since this other thing would be the elements and these, as they lack an own being, are non-existent.

177. The visible thing which presents itself as form and colour.

178. The elements are the material cause of things. The *kārikā* denies two alternatives. The first one is: 'the four (elements) are not in the one (thing)'. This alternative takes into account the case of combination of the four elements. These ones combine, unify themselves in the new thing and consequently, as four, they cease to be. The four elements, as such, cannot exist in the thing.

179. The second alternative denied by the *kārikā* is 'the one (thing) is not in the four (elements)'. This alternative is the contrary of the first one. As the first one denies that the four elements are able to be in the thing, this second alternative denies the possibility of the thing being in the four elements. It must be understood that these four elements have combined, have unified themselves and that the thing, one, is in those four elements, which, as having become one, have ceased to exist as four, in the same form as in the first alternative. It is not possible to think that this alternative supposes that the thing is in the four elements, without these four elements being unified, because in that case, the thing, being in each of them, would be divided among them and each of them would produce, without the intervention of the others, a part of the thing, what is not possible.

180. Following what has been previously expressed, any thing that is an object of visual perception cannot exist, since it depends on four elements that have to be in the thing or in which the thing has to be; in any case it follows the non-existence of those elements.

181. The objection that the same author proposes is that, although the visible cannot be perceived in itself, since it is not a substance, at least its attributes can be perceived, for instance its form and colour, which are the factors that directly affect our mind.

182. The attributes, which presumably belong to all empirical things do not exist, since they are as unreal as the thing to which they inhere, because

of their lacking an own being, because of their insubstantiality. For instance, the colour of a thing does not exist *in se et per se*; it arises only when there is a series of causes and conditions, as the light rays, the human eye with its special characteristics, etc.

183. It is not possible to say that a thing does not possess form and colour, and at the same time is an object of a visual perception.

184. If something visible were really perceived, it would have an own being, since whatever does not have an own being cannot be really perceived and is only a creation of our minds. We do not really perceive a car, which does not exist truly, since it is only a conglomerate of pieces placed in a determinate way; the car that we think to perceive is a mere creation of our minds which we superimpose upon that conglomerate of pieces.

185. Neither the grasping consciousness (which depends to arise on the existence of an object and other conditions) nor the grasped object (which depends on the parts that compose it) exist *in se et per se*. So it is not possible to speak of the perception of that object by a consciousness: an empty *dharma* cannot grasp another empty *dharma*.

186. The primitive Buddhism considered the consciousness and its object as impermanent; Hīnayāna Buddhism, progressing further considered them as instantaneous, in the sense that, as soon as they appear, they disappear. An instantaneous consciousness cannot grasp an instantaneous object. The first lines of the *kārikā* treat the case of the simultaneous uprising of consciousness and its object. The simultaneous uprising means that the consciousness and the object are both in the present time each one in regard to the other one.

187. Less still can an instantaneous consciousness grasp an object, which besides being instantaneous, arose in the past (and of course disappeared) or has not yet arisen. Thus the grasping of an object by a consciousness is not possible in any of the three times.

188. It is ascertained by experience that colour and form do not exist separately, since in the perception they are always together.

189. It is not possible to argue that colour and form, although by nature are separated, nevertheless are perceived together, as a single entity, since colour and form *are* the thing; the thing is not different from them, something besides them; colour, form and visible thing, are the same. So it is not possible to say that colour and form *unite* to create the thing—which is nothing else than themselves. The implicit conclusion is that colour and form do not exist *in se et per se*, as something else, independently from 'the visible', and the visible itself constituted by colur and form has not an own being, is not real either—in the same way as any thing, being constituted by parts, has not an own being, a substantial reality.

190. Visual consciousness.

191. The visual organ, alone, without other conditions, such as the object, the light, etc., cannot produce a visual knowledge.

192. Neither the object, alone, can give rise to a visual knowledge.

193. It does not exist in something that is between the eye and the object and

that is different from both, as for instance the space which separates both or the light that unites them.

194. It is an error to think that something, that arises from a conglomerate of causes and conditions such as the eye, the object, the light, etc., could have, being conditioned, an own being.

195. See in Nāgārjuna, *Mūlamadhyamakakārikā* III, 2 and following ones, with Candrakīrti's commentary *ad locum*, an argument against Nāgārjuna's reasoning exposed in this *kārikā*: the eye can see the visible even if it does not see itself, in the same way as the fire can burn the fuel without burning itself. The argument is refuted by Nāgārjuna and Candrakīrti (*ibid.*) by saying that the parallel example of the fire is not valid, because in fact the fire cannot burn anything; neither what has already been burnt nor what has not yet been burnt nor what is being burnt.

196. The arguments to deny the (real) existence of the eye and of the visible have been exposed in the previous *kārikās*.

197. The remaining *āyatanas* are ear and sound, nose and smell, tongue and taste, body and what is object of touch, mind and ideas.

198. This *kārikā* is like a resumé of what has been expressed in *kārikās* 45-52, in relation to the eye and its object, the visible thing. And moreover it extends what has been declared before to other classes of sensorial knowledge in which other *āyatanas* intervene.

199. The eye is not a substance, which exists in and by itself; it is something constituted by parts.

200. The eye does not possess the own being of another thing, as for instance of the ear. It cannot exist as a substance, as something different of itself.

201. See above note 197.

202. Man is a series of consciousnesses. Each consciousness arises when there is a *contact* (*sparśa*) between an interior *āyatana* (an organ of senses) and an exterior *āyatana* (an object of the senses). As any *āyatana* arises owing to its contact with another *āyatana*, then any *āyatana* has to be void of an own being, since it needs, in order to arise, another *āyatana* and the contact with it. And, if a single *āyatana* (of all the *āyatanas* that are related to the series of consciousnesses which constitute the man) is void of an own being, all the other *āyatanas*, past and future, of the same series are also void of an own being. The reason of this affirmation is given in the two last *pādas*.

203. All the *āyatanas* are a part of the series which is man; all of them are connected among themselves, since they are a part of that series. If one of these *āyatanas* is void of an own being, all have to be void of an own being, because no relation, no dependence can be established between something void, and consequently unreal, and something which is not void, and vice versa.

204. The organ, the object, the consciousness.

205. There cannot be any relation among entities which as soon as they arise disappear, which have no time, so to say, to establish any relation among themselves.

206. This contact can exist only in an illusory way, but not truly.

207. Which arises in fact from the union of the organ of sense with its object. We have translated *tshor ba* of the original by 'perception'; it means also 'sensation'.
208. Any organ of sense. See above note 197.
209. Any object of an organ of sense.
210. The consciousness in the meaning of knowledge of an object through an organ of sense.
211. Consciousness does not exist in and by itself, as pure consciousness; it comes to being only when there is an organ of sense and an object and both come into contact.
212. The *kārikā* insists in the mutual relation of dependence that exists among the three elements that give rise to the cognitive act.
213. This affirmation is a traditional teaching of Buddhism.
214. Although Buddha has affirmed the impermanence of all things, in truth for Nāgārjuna nothing exists really, be it impermanent or not.
215. Nothing exists really, because, if something existed really, it would have to be either permanent or impermanent, and these forms of existence have been denied.
216. The three *Kleśas*.
217. The feelings of attraction and hatred depend on the existence of something pleasant or something unpleasant, and error depends on the existence of a false perception or of a false inference.
218. Since it arises depending on something else.
219. The same thing can produce different reactions, as for instance of pleasure or of pain. This circumstance leads to the conclusion that the condition of pleasant or unpleasant does not exist in the thing itself, because in that case it would produce always the same reaction. The condition of pleasant or unpleasant is a mere product of the mind. See Vasubandhu, *Trisvabhāva* 35-36, and our commentary, pp. 246-47. See also Introduction.
220. The affirmation expressed in the preceding *pādas* of this *kārikā* is proper of the idealistic position that pervades all the Mahāyāna and is characteristic of both Madhyamaka and Yogācāra schools. But in the last *pāda* appears a conception that is proper only of the Madhyamaka: not only there is nothing exterior to mind, but also the same mind is non-existent, unreal, empty of an own being.
221. What the mind imagines, being a mental creation, has not a real existence.
222. The imagination, the imagining mind, does not exist really, since its existence depends on the imagined object, is conditioned and as such unreal.
223. They do not possess an own being owing to their reciprocal dependence.
225. As the first of the 12 members of the Dependent Origination.
226. See *kārikās* 9 and 10.
227. They are the second of the 12 members, the birth of which depends on the ignorance. See *kārikā* 11.
228. Whatever arises in dependence has as its origin that from which it depends.
229. Cf. *imasmiṃ asati idaṃ na hoti, Udāna* I, 2.

230. What we call being and not-being, the conditioned (the empirical reality) and the un-conditioned (as the *nirvāṇa*)—nothing has abandoned ever its original condition of Voidness. The words 'calm' and 'nirvanized' express this idea.
231. The unreality of the contingent is the fundamental principle of Nāgārjuna's school.
232. See *kārikās* 8-14 and their respective notes.
233. The true nature of things.
234. Ignorance is constituted by the idea that things have an own being and consequently are real.
235. Which have ignorance as their origin.
236. The things that are composed and consequently conditioned. This term comprises all the empirical reality.
237. The example of the imaginary city and the other examples that follow, illustrate the illusory character of the empirical reality.
238. That revolves quickly.
239. Since all the empirical reality is conditioned.
240. In this world, in the empirical reality.
241. On the concept of 'no-thing' see above note 72.
242. Buddha placed in the centre of his doctrine the theory of Dependent Origination, of Universal Relativity, since this theory reveals the true nature of things: Voidness, and also since without the knowledge of the true reality there is not possibility of liberation.
243. That all things arisen in dependence are void of an own being.
244. He grasped the true nature, the true form of being of all things of this world: their emptiness of an own being.
245. All the principles and categories of the empirical reality (causality, time, existence, agent,.etc.) maintain their validity until one obtains the understanding of the true nature of things. These principles and categories are necessary for the life in this world, to manage oneself on the level of empirical reality; and moreover they are theoretically imprescindible to reach the truth—Voidness—since this one arises precisely from the abolishing analysis applied to that principles and categories.
246. From the point of view of Relative Truth there existed Buddha, who taught a doctrine leading to liberation, which consists in putting an end to reincarnations; but from the point or view of Supreme Reality (*paramārtha*) neither a Buddha nor a doctrine nor liberation from reincarnations exist.
247. The conception of *śūnyatā*, central point of the Madhyamaka philosophy produces in the common man a feeling of uneasiness and fear, because of its similarity to nothingness, since one reaches *śūnyatā* through a gradual abolishing analysis of all that belongs to empirical reality, with which man is existentially connected.
248. These words are a synthesis of the Buddhist Principle of Universal Contingency or Dependent Origination as it was taught by Buddha.
249. In the context of the Mādhyamika doctrine the principle that has been expressed in the first *pāda* has full validity since Universal Conditionality is the essence of empirical reality and at the same time the fundament of

Nāgārjuna's theory of Voidness expressed in second and third *pāda*.

250. Rhetorical question whose implicit answer is: 'it cannot exist'.
251. The affirmations contained in this *kārikā* are evident from all that has been expounded in the treatise.
252. The principle of conditionality which leads to 'emptiness'.
253. Having established himself in the Middle Path, which denies both existence and non-existence and affirms only the Voidness which is neither something nor nothing.
254. I.e. he has reached the supreme aim, the *nirvāṇa*.
255. Of the empirical reality.
256. Cf. *Brahmajālasutta* of *Dīgha Nikāya*.
257. The *kārikā* indicates the principal elements of the salvation's method taught by Buddha, its two aspects of intellectual discipline and moral discipline: to reach *nirvāṇa* it is necessary, on one side, to know the true nature of things (conditionality=voidness), which produces the elimination of all erroneous conceptions, and, on the other side, to practice the moral virtues which will give rise to an attitude of detachment and serenity.

CHAPTER 4

The *Catustava* of Nāgārjuna[1]

INTRODUCTION

Nāgārjuna's Hymns

In the Tibetan Buddhist Canon a series of hymns[2] attributed to Nāgārjuna, the founder of the Madhyamaka school of the Mahāyāna Buddhism, has been preserved.

In the *Madhyamakaśāstrastuti* of Candrakīrti[3] (seventh century A.D.) stanza 10, in the list of the eight treatises ascribed to Nāgārjuna, we find one entitled *saṃstuti* (*bstod pa* in the Tibetan translation), which is a generic term to designate the hymns (*stava, stotra*) and which J.W. de Jong translates by 'les Louanges'.[4]

G. Tucci, *Minor Buddhist Texts I* (1956), pp. 235-46, published a text which presents itself under the title of *Catuḥstavasamāsārtha*, included in a Sanskrit manuscript which he found in Tibet. As its name indicates, this text is a commentary of a work entitled *Catuḥstava* ('Four Hymns'). This commentary was composed by Amṛtākara, an author about whom nothing is known. The text contains only a part of the commentary of the *Niraupamyastava* and the complete commentaries of the *Acintyastava* and *Paramārthastava*. According to Tucci (p. 237) the hymn commented in the part that is lacking was the *Lokātītastava*, although there is nothing in the text of the commentary that has been preserved that gives support to this affirmation. Amṛtākara does not indicate about the author of the *Catuḥstava*, that he comments. As we shall see later on the three *stavas, Niraupamya, Acintya* and *Paramārtha*, and also the *Lokātīta*, were attributed to Nāgārjuna by the Tibetan Buddhist Canon, and it is possible to think that Candrakīrti attributes to Nāgārjuna the *Lokātīta* and that Prajñākaramati does the same with the *Lokātīta* and the *Acintya*. We can therefore conclude that the *Catuḥstavasamāsārtha* is a commentary of hymns that circulated under the name of Nāgārjuna, united in a whole under the title of *Catuḥstava.* Amṛtākara's commentary contains some quotations of parts of stanzas, of isolated words, taken from the hymns that he comments. A list of Amṛtākara's quotations is given later on.

There are also found in Buddhist authors quotations in Sanskrit of stanzas of the hymns ascribed to Nāgārjuna. A list of quotations from the four hymns: *Lokātīta, Niraupamya, Acintya* and *Paramārtha* is given below.

Finally, the Sanskrit text of these four hymns is available. In 1932[5] G. Tucci published the complete Sanskrit text of *Niraupamya* and *Paramārtha,* preserved is a not very old manuscript which he found in Nepal. In 1982 Chr. Lindtner published[6] the complete Sanskrit text of *Lokātīta* and *Acintya,* preserved in four manuscripts[7] which also contain the two other hymns already published by Tucci.

We must mention that there is a very faithful reconstruction from the Tibetan translation of four hymns: *Niraupamya, Lokātīta, Acintya* and *Stutyatīta,* done by P. Patel before the discovery of the Sanskrit original text by Tucci, although it was published some time after that discovery.[8]

Let us indicate that no translation of the hymns ascribed to Nāgārjuna is preserved in the Chinese Buddhist Canon, with the exception of *Dharmadhātustava.*[9]

The Catustava

Prajñākaramati (ninth century A.D.), *Pañjikā,* p. 200, 1.1, p. 229, 1.10 and p. 249, 1.1 ed. P.L. Vaidya (=p. 420, 1.1, p. 488, last line and p. 533, 1.9 ed. L. de la Vallée Poussin), quotes some isolated stanzas, attributing them expressly (*catuḥstave' pyuktam; catuḥstave' pi; catuḥstave' pyuktam*) to a work denominated Catuḥstava, *Four Hymns of Eulogy,* but without indicating the author's name.[10] The stanzas quoted by Prajñākaramati correspond to two hymns ascribed to Nāgārjuna, *Niraupamya* (7, 9) and *Lokātīta* (18-20).

Besides that, as already said, the manuscript found by Tucci in Tibet contains a commentary, *Catuḥstavasamāsārtha,* which comments the *Niraupamya,* the *Acintya* and the *Paramārtha* and which, according to Tucci, commented in its lost part the *Lokātīta.*

Lindtner indicates that the titles and order of the hymns in the four manuscripts he utilizes are without exception *Lokātīta,*

Niraupamya, Acintya and *Paramārtha;* and he has had the kindness to inform us, in a personal letter that 'none of the Mss speak of *Catuḥstava* as a whole'.

These facts can be explained in several ways:

1. There existed really an independent work composed eventually by Nāgārjuna, denominated *Catustava,* whose four hymns were translated separately into Tibetan, since in the Tibetan Buddhist Canon there is not a single work with that name.
2. There was no work as *Catustava* composed eventually by Nāgārjuna; there were only independent hymns composed by that author. By reasons we ignore, four of these hymns were united by some person under the name of *Catustava,* after they were composed by Nāgārjuna and before Prajñākaramati's and Amṛtākara's time. These authors considered as something certain that there existed a work named *Catustava* by Nāgārjuna.

We prefer the second hypothesis, because we think it is not very likely, if there really was a work *Catustava* composed eventually by Nāgārjuna, that this work should have been dismembered by their Tibetan translators and incorporated in this way into the Tibetan Buddhist Canon. The fact that these hymns circulated separately, as it is proved by the manuscript found by Tucci, in which we have only two hymns, *Niraupamya* and *Paramārtha,* and also the fact that in that manuscript and in Lindtner's manuscripts there is no indication that they formed part of a larger work—these facts corroborate our idea that these four hymns existed *originally* as separate works.

Catustava's Composition

Another difficulty caused by this work was its composition, i.e. which of the hymns attributed to Nāgārjuna composed the *Catustava,* in either of the two hypothesis we have referred to before: either if the *Catustava* is an independent treatise by Nāgārjuna or if it is a later recompilation done by some other person.

Undoubtedly, the *Lokātīta* and the *Niraupamya* are parts of the *Catustava,* because the stanzas quoted by Prajñākaramati as proceeding from the *Catustava* belong to these two hymns ascribed to Nāgārjuna.[11]

As regards the other two hymns, L. de la Vallée Poussin (1913) thought that they were the *Cittavajra* and the *Paramārtha*, and G. Tucci (1932) was of the same opinion.[12] P. Patel (1932 and 1934) considered that the two other hymns were *Stutyatīta* (*Tōhoku* 1129 = *Catalogue* 2020) and *Acintya*.

But Tucci (1956), as we have said, published a text that was composed by Amṛtākara, has *Catuḥstavasamāsārtha* as its title, and contains a part of a commentary of the *Niraupamya* and the commentaries of the *Acintya* and *Paramārtha*.

With this discovery of Tucci it could be considered that the problem about the composition of the *Catustava* was already solved: the four hymns that composed it were: *Niraupamya* (Prajñākaramati and Amṛtākara), *Acintya* and *Paramārtha* (Amṛtākara), and *Lokātīta* (Prajñākaramati).[13]

Now with Lindtner's publication, which confirms Tucci's opinion, there cannot be anymore doubt about the contents of *Catustava*.

Authorship of the Hymns of the Catustava

Of the four hymns that compose the *Catustava* only the *Lokātīta* is expressly attributed to Nāgārjuna by Candrakīrti, *Prasannapadā*, p. 171, 1.11 ed. P.L. Vaidya (= p. 413, 1.5 ed. L. de la Vallée Poussin). In this text Candrakīrti quotes stanza 4 of the *Lokātīta* attributing it to the *ācāryapāda*, 'the venerable master', by which expression we must understand *Nāgārjuna*.

Advayavajra (eleventh century A.D.), *Advayavajrasaṃgraha*, 3. *Tattvaratnāvalī*, p. 22, 1.1, quotes stanza 21 of *Niraupamya* introducing it with the words: '*nāgārjunapādair apy uktam*'.

Besides that the form in which Prajñākaramati, *Pañjikā*, p. 197, 1.26, p. 180, 1.27, and p. 275, 1.18 ed. P.L. Vaidya = p. 415, 1.1, p. 375, and p. 590 ed. L. de la Vallée Poussin, quotes the stanzas 21 of *Lokātīta* (*etad evāha*), and 18 and 40 of the *Acintya* (*yad āha; ata evāha*), seems to indicate that he is referring to Nāgārjuna as the author of those stanzas.

Another evidence in favour of the authenticity of these four hymns is the circumstance that the *Madhyamakaśāstrastuti* of Candrakīrti, to which we have already referred, in the enumeration of Nāgārjuna's works, includes also hymns under the name of *saṃstuti*.[14]

Prof. Lindtner in a personal letter informs us that the manuscripts of Tokyo and Gokhale (see note 7 of the Introduction) expressly ascribe the four hymns to Nāgārjuna.

On its side the Tibetan Buddhist Canon attributes the four hymns, *Lokātīta, Niraupamya, Acintya,* and *Paramārtha* to Nāgārjuna.

Finally we must also have in mind that the ideas expressed in these hymns in their general lines belong to the central nucleus of Nāgārjuna's thought.

All these reasons induce *prima facie* to think that the author of the four hymns is Nāgārjuna. Accordingly modern authors in general attribute these four hymns to Nāgārjuna. Cf. T.R.V. Murti, *The Central Philosophy of Buddhism*, p. 90; K. Potter, *Bibliography of Indian Philosophies*, p. 5; K. V. Ramanan, *Nāgārjuna's Philosophy*, p. 37; P.L. Vaidya, *Āryadeva*, p. 50; M. Winternitz, *A History of Indian Literature*, p. 376; É. Lamotte, *Le Traité de la Grande Vertu de Sagesse*, Tome III, Introduction, p. xliii; D.S. Ruegg, *The Literature of the Madhyamaka School*, pp. 31-32, 35, 120-21, 126, 130-31; Chr. Lindtner, *Nagarjuniana*, specially pp. 121-22; Uriūtsu Ryūshin, *Nāgārjuna Kenkyū*, p. 32, besides P. Patel and G. Tucci in their mentioned articles.

Nevertheless L. de la Vallée Poussin, 'Notes et Bibliographie Bouddhiques', p. 396 (although the title of his article is 'Les Quatre Odes de Nāgārjuna') considers that the attribution of these hymns to Nāgārjuna is not so sure as Tucci affirms[15] (in his quoted article of 1932).[16]

In spite of the title of this chapter, we are inclined to adopt the cautious position of L. de la Vallée Poussin until a more profound and careful study of the ideas expounded in this hymns allow a more precise definition on the matter.

Quotations of Stanzas of the Catustava in Other Sanskrit Texts

Many stanzas of the hymns, to which the present chapter refers, are quoted in other Sanskrit Buddhist texts, and in Tibetan translations of lost Sanskrit texts, as we have already said. Of course there are also many parallel or similar passages in other texts. Now we indicate only the number of the stanzas of each hymn that have been quoted in a complete form in other Buddhist Sanskrit texts; in the notes, that accompany the text of the hymns, we have given in the corresponding place the full references of the quotations. See also the following section that indicates the quotations from

Amṛtākara's commentary.

1. *Lokātītastava*: the Sanskrit text of 12 stanzas, of the 28 stanzas that compose this hymn, has been preserved in quotations by other Buddhist authors: stanzas 4, 8, 9, 11, 13, 18, 19, 20, 21, 22, 23, 24.

2. *Niraupamyastava*: of the 25 stanzas that compose this hymn, 7 are quoted by other Buddhist authors. They are stanzas 7, 9, 13, 18, 19, 21, 24.

3. *Acintyastava*: of the 59 stanzas of this hymn 6 are preserved in Sanskrit in quotations by other Buddhist authors. They are: 19, 29, 36, 40, 41, 42.

Quotations of the Catustava in Amṛtākara's Commentary

We indicate also in the notes that accompany the text, the quotations, found in Amṛtākara's commentary, of portions of the text of the hymns. These quotations are taken from Amṛtākara's commentary as edited by Tucci, *Minor Buddhist Texts I*, pp. 238-46. It is very important to observe that many of the words found in Amṛtākara's quotations do not appear with the morphological form they have in the respective stanzas, but with the morphological form that corresponds to them in the phrases that comment them. Amṛtākara's quotations refer to stanzas 1, 2, 20, 22, 24, 25 of *Niraupamya*; stanza 1 of *Acintya*, and stanzas 1, 2, 3, 8, 9, 10 of *Paramārtha*.

Scheme of the Exposition

We indicate the principal themes developed in the hymns in the order they appear.

Lokātīta

Kārikā 1: Homage to Buddha, who possesses the true knowledge and compassion.
Kārikās 2-4: Unreality of beings and of the elements which constitute them.
Kārikā 5: Impossibility of perception.
Kārikā 6: Interdependence and insubstantiality of sensation and of the sensible object.
Kārikā 7: Impossibility of a relation between the word and the object it designates.
Kārikās 8-9: Impossibility of the existence of action, of the agent, of the fruit of the action and of the experiencer of the fruit of action.

Kārikā 10: Unsubstantiality of knowledge and its object.
Kārikā 11: Impossibility of the essential characteristic and of the characterized object.
Kārikā 12: Nirvanization *ab aeterno* of the world.
Kārikā 13: Impossibility of origination.
Kārikās 14-16: Impossibility of destruction.
Kārikās 17-18: Unreality of origination.
Kārikā 19: Non-existence of the world.
Kārikā 20: Non-existence or unreality of transmigration.
Kārikā 21: Dependent character of suffering.
Kārikā 22: Universality of Dependent Origination=Voidness.
Kārikā 23: Aim of the teaching of Voidness.
Kārikā 24: Voidness of *dharmas*.
Kārikā 25: Unalterableness of the true reality.
Kārikās 26-27: Method to reach the true reality.
Kārikā 28: Transference of the merit obtained by means of this praise of Buddha.

Niraupamya

Kārikā 1: Homage to Buddha, who knows universal Voidness and who endeavoured for the benefit of all beings.
Kārikā 2: Universal Voidness. Buddha perceived the truth.
Kārikā 3: Non-existence of the subject and object of knowledge. Buddha knew the true nature of things.
Kārikās 4-5: Knowledge is the means to reach *nirvāṇa*.
Kārikā 6: Universal sameness. Purity of Buddha.
Kārikā 7: Voidness of Buddha's teaching.
Kārikā 8: Detachment of Buddha.
Kārikā 9: Non-existence of beings. Buddha's compassion.
Kārikā 10: All is mental creation.
Kārikā 11: Non-existence of arising and cessation of *dharmas*. Non-existence of conglomerates.
Kārikā 12: Non-existence of Buddha
Kārikā 13: Unreality of the world.
Kārikā 14: Unreality of *saṃsāra*.
Kārikā 15: The empirical reality as the root of evil and salvation.
Kārikā 16: Unreality of form. Buddha's body.
Kārikā 17: Identity of Buddha and its doctrine.
Kārikās 18-20: Apparent nature of Buddha's body.
Kārikā 21: Identity of the three Vehicles. Adequation of Buddha's

teaching to the nature of diverse men.
Kārikā 22: Buddha's body made of doctrine. Apparent nature of Buddha's nirvanization.
Kārikā 23: Ubiquity of Buddha's vision by his disciples.
Kārikā 24: Buddha's attributes.
Kārikā 25: Exaltation of Buddha. Transference of merits.

Acintya

Kārikā 1: Homage to Buddha, teacher of the Voidness of all conditioned things. Buddha's qualities.
Kārikā 2: The teaching of the unsubstantiality of *dharmas*, as proper of Mahāyāna.
Kārikās 3-4: Non-existence, Voidness and unreality of origination.
Kārikās 5-8: Conventional or illusory existence of all conditioned things.
Kārikās 9-10: Impossibility of origination.
Kārikās 11-14: Relativity and non-existence of all.
Kārikās 15-16: Denial of the existence of what has not an own being.
Kārikā 17: Sameness and nirvanization *ab aeterno* of the *dharmas*.
Kārikās 18-19: Unreality and Voidness of sensible objects.
Kārikā 20: Incapacity of senses to reach the true knowledge.
Kārikā 21: Effect of ignorance.
Kārikās 22-23: The Doctrine of the Middle Way and the consequence it has for the *dharmas*.
Kārikās 24-27: Unreality of the world and of its categories, including liberation.
Kārikā 28: Unreality of the duality of knowledge.
Kārikās 29-30: Nirvanization *ab aeterno* of all: neither origination nor cessation do really exist.
Kārikās 31-32: Non-existence of the masters, the liberation and the liberated ones.
Kārikās 33-34: Unreality of the world and of its creator.
Kārikā 35: Voidness of the world and of what it designates.
Kārikā 36: Unreal character of the mental creation, including that of Voidness.
Kārikās 37-39: Characterization of Voidness as the absolutely heterogeneous.
Kārikā 40: Identity of Dependent Origination, Voidness, the

Doctrine and Buddha.
Kārikā 41: Characterization of Voidness.
Kārikās 42-43: Universal sameness: all is Voidness.
Kārikās 44-45: The empirical and the true realities. Denominations of the latter one. Non-existence of the imagined and of the dependent.
Kārikās 46-49: Overcoming of eternalism and nihilism: all is void of an own being, illusory.
Kārikā 50: Non-existence of knowledge and of the knowable object.
Kārikās 51-52: Therapeutic value of the Doctrine of Voidness, the supreme truth.
Kārikā 53: The Doctrine as the best sacrifice.
Kārikās 54-55: Praise of Buddha as the teacher of insubstantiality, of Voidness.
Kārikās 56-57: The Voidness of the *dharmas*, as the nucleus of Buddha's teaching.
Kārikā 58: Exaltation of Buddha and of the Perfection of knowledge.
Kārikā 59: Transference of merit.

Paramārtha

Kārikā 1: Difficulty to praise Buddha, owing to Voidness, which constitutes his nature.
Kārikā 2: Form to praise Buddha.
Kārikās 3-7: Non-existence in Buddha of an own being, duality, colour, measure, situation.
Kārikā 8: Buddha reached Voidness.
Kārikās 9-10: Impossibility of any praise from the point of view of supreme truth.
Kārikā 11: Characteristics of Buddha. Transference of merits.

Cittavajra

Kārikā 1: Homage to the mind, the source of error and liberation.
Kārikā 2: Liberation is the only 'god'.
Kārikā 3: All is mind.
Kārikā 4: Mind as the creator of the illusion that is the empirical reality.
Kārikā 5: The *saṃsāra* is a mere illusion, liberation is the cessation of imagination.
Kārikā 6: Exaltation of the Mind of Illumination (*bodhicitta*).

Kārikā 7: Importance of mind.

Contents and Importance of the Hymns[17]

As is seeing by the preceding Section, in these hymns we find the exposition of the fundamental theories of the Madhyamaka school in a succinct form as is required by the nature of this kind of literature. All the enunciations of their *kārikās* present themselves related to the essential thesis of Voidness (*śūnyatā*): all is 'void', lacking an own being, insubstantial, a mere creation of mind without anything corresponding to it in reality.

On the importance of these four hymns it is enough to say that they can be considered among the best samples of the hymn's literature,[18] not only because they contain the basic theories of the great master of the Madhyamaka but also because of their concise and effective exposition of these theories. The great number of times that stanzas from these hymns have been quoted by several authors is a proof of the great appraisal in which these hymns were held.

Editions and Translations of the Catustava

Sanskrit Text: Ed. G.Tucci, in 'Two Hymns of the Catuḥstava', in *JRAS*, 1932, pp. 312-20 (*Niraupamya*) and pp. 322-24 (*Paramārtha*);

Ed. S. Sakei, in 'Ryūju ni kiserareru Sanka' ('Hymns attributed to Nāgārjuna'), *NBGN* 24, 1959, pp. 10-16 (*Niraupamya*), pp. 39-41 (*Paramārtha*).

Ed. C. Dragonetti, in '*Niraupamyastava* y *Paramārthastava*', in *Oriente-Occidente*, 1982, pp. 258-66 (*Niraupamya*), pp. 268-70 (*Paramārtha*).

Ed. Chr. Lindtner, in *Nagarjuniana*, 1982, pp. 128-38 (*Lokātīta*), and pp. 140-60 (*Acintya*).

Ed. F. Tola, C. Dragonetti, in 'Nāgārjuna's Catustava', in *JIP*, 1985, pp. 10-20 (*Lokātīta, Niraupamya, Acintya, Paramārtha*).

Sanskrit reconstruction from the Tibetan Tanslation: P. Patel, in 'Catustava', in *IHQ* 8, 1932, pp. 317-19 (*Niraupamya*), pp. 324-26 (*Lokātīta*), pp. 689-93 (*Acintya*); (pp. 701-03: *Statyatīta*).

Tibetan translation in the Bstan-ḥgyur: *Niraupamya: Tōhoku* 1119 = *Catalogue* 2011. In both editions under the title: *Dpe-med-par bstod-pa* (= Sanskrit *Niraupamyastava*); attributed to Klu-sgrub (=Nāgārjuna) and translated by Kṛṣṇa Paṇḍit and Tshul-khrims rgyal-ba.

Lokātīta: Tōhoku 1120 = *Catalogue* 2011. In both editions under the title : *Ḥjig-rten-las ḥdas-par bstod-pa* (= Sanskrit *Lokātītastava*); attributed to Klu-sgrub and translated by Kṛṣṇa Paṇḍit and Tshul-khrims rgyal-ba.

Paramārtha: Tōhoku 1122 = *Catalogue* 2014. In both editions under the title: *Don-dam-par bstod-pa* (Sanskrit *Paramārthastava*); attributed to Klu-sgrub and translated by Kṛṣṇa Paṇḍit and Tshul-khrims rgyal-ba.

Acintya: Tōhoku 1128= *Catalogue* 2019. In both editions under the title: *Bsam-gyis-mi-khyab-par bstod-pa* (= Sanskrit *Acint-yastava*); attributed to Klu-sgrub and translated, according to *Tōhoku*, by Tilaka, Pa Tshab Ñi-ma grags; *Catalogue* does not mention the name of the translator.

We give also the data regarding the Tibetan translation of the *Cittavajrastava*, which, as we have said, was considered by L. de la Vallée Poussin as the third hymn of the *Catustava* and which has been incorporated in this chapter in an *Appendix*.

Cittavajra: Tōhoku 1121 = *Catalogue* 2013. In both editions under the title: *Sems-kyi rdo-rjeḥi bstod-pa* (= Sanskrit *Cittavajrastava*); attributed to Klu-sgrub and translated, according to *Tōhoku*, by Kṛṣṇa Paṇḍit and Tshul-khrims rgyal-ba; *Catalogue* does not mention the name of the translator.

Tibetan translation in modern editions: Ed. L. de la Vallée Poussin, in 'Quatre Odes de Nāgārjuna', in *LMM* n.s., 14, 1913, pp. 1-3 (*Niraupamya*) pp. 7-10 (*Lokātīta*), pp. 16-17 (*Paramārtha*), pp. 14-15 (*Cittavajra*).

Ed. G. Tucci, in 'Two Hymns of the Catuḥstava', in *JRAS*, 1932, pp. 312-20 (*Niraupamya*) and pp. 322-24 (*Paramārtha*);

Ed. P. Patel, in 'Catustava', in *IHQ* 8, 1932, pp. 319-23 (*Niraupamya*) and pp. 326-31 (*Lokātīta*); pp. 694-701 (*Acintya*) and pp. 703-05 (*Stutyatīta*).

Ed. Chr. Lindtner, in *Nagarjunina*, 1982, pp. 128-38 (*Lokātīta*) and pp. 140-60 (*Acintya*).

English translation of the Sanskrit text: G. Tucci, in 'Two Hymns of the Catuḥstava', 1932, pp. 313-21 (*Niraupamya*) and pp. 323-25 (*Paramārtha*).

Chr. Lindtner, in *Nagarjuniana*, 1982, pp. 129-39 (*Lokātita*) and pp. 141-61 (*Acintya*).

F. Tola and C. Dragonetti, in 'Nāgārjuna's Catustava', in *JIP*, 1985, pp. 20-38 (*Lokātīta, Niraupamya, Acintya, Paramartha* from Sanskrit and in *Appendix Cittavajra* from Tibetan).

French translation of the Sanskrit text and of the Tibetan translation: L. Silburn, in *Le Bouddhisme*, 1977, pp. 201-09 (*Niraupamya* and *Paramārtha*), from Sanskrit.

L. de la Vallée Poussin, in 'Quatre Odes', in *LM* n.s., 14, 1913, pp. 4-7 (*Niraupamya*), pp. 10-14 (*Lokātīta*), pp. 17-18 (*Paramārtha*), (and pp. 15-16: *Cittavajra*), from Tibetan.

Italian translation of the Sanskrit text and of the Tibetan translation: R. Gnoli, in *Nāgārjuna*, 1961, pp. 157-79 (*Niraupamya* and *Paramārtha*, from Sanskrit; *Lokātīta* and *Acintya* from Tibetan).

Japanese translation of the Sanskrit text and of the Tibetan translation (and besides that of the Sanskrit text of Amṛtākara's commentary): S. Sakei, in 'Ryūju ni kiserareru Sanka', in *NBGN* 24, 1959, pp. 10-16 (*Niraupamya*, from Sanskrit), pp. 38-41 (*Paramārtha*, from Sanskrit), pp. 6-9 (*Lokātīta*, from Tibetan), pp. 29-33 (*Acintya*, from Tibetan).

Danish translation from the Sanskrit text: Ch. Lindtner, *Juvelkaeden og andre skrifter*, 1980 (*Niraupamya* and *Paramārtha*);

Chr. Lindtner, *Nāgārjunas Filosofiske Vaerker*, 1982, pp. 55-58 (*Lokātītastava*), pp. 58-66 (*Acintyastava*).

Spanish translation from the Sanskrit text: C. Dragonetti, '*Niraupamyastava* y *Paramārthastava*', in *Oriente Occidente*, 1982, pp. 259-67 (*Niraupamya*), pp. 269-71 (*Paramārtha*).

The Present Work

We give the Sanskrit text of the four hymns that compose the *Catustava*, reproducing Tucci's edition for *Niraupamyastava* and *Paramārthastava*, and Lindtner's edition for *Lokātītastava* and *Acintyastava*. We thank Prof. Lindtner for his kind permission to reproduce the text of his *editio princeps* of the above-mentioned two hymns in *Nagarjuniana*.

We present also an English translation of the four hymns from the Sanskrit with some simple notes.

In *Appendix* we include the text of the Tibetan translation of *Cittavajrastava* and its English translation, because L. de la Vallée Poussin and Tucci (1932) considered it to be the forth hymn of the *Catustava*.

CATUSTAVAḤ

Sanskrit Text

LOKĀTĪTASTAVAḤ

lokātīta namas tubhyaṃ viviktajñānavedine/
yas tvaṃ jagaddhitāyaiva khinnaḥ karuṇayā ciram//1//

skandhamātravinirmukto na sattvo 'stīti te matam/
sattvārthaṃ ca paraṃ khedam agamas tvaṃ mahāmune//2//

te' pi skandhās tvayā dhīman dhīmadbhyaḥ saṃprakāśitāḥ/
māyāmarīcigandharvanagarasvapnasaṃnibhāḥ//3//

hetutaḥ saṃbhavo yeṣāṃ tadabhāvān na santi ye/
kathaṃ nāma na te spaṣṭaṃ pratibimbasamā matāḥ[19]//4//

bhūtāny acakṣurgrāhyāṇi tanmayaṃ cākṣuṣaṃ katham/
rūpaṃ tvayaivaṃ bruvatā rūpagrāho nivāritaḥ//5//

vedanīyaṃ vinā nāsti vedanāto nirātmikā/
tac ca vedyaṃ svabhāvena nāstīty abhimataṃ tava//6//

saṃjñārthayor ananyatve mukhaṃ dahyeta vahninā/
anyatve' dhigamābhāvas tvayoktaṃ bhūtavādinā//7//

kartā svatantraḥ karmāpi tvayoktaṃ vyavahārataḥ/
parasparāpekṣikī tu siddhis te' bhimatānayoḥ[20]//8//

na kartāsti na bhoktāsti puṇyāpuṇyaṃ pratītyajam/
yat pratītya na taj jātaṃ proktaṃ vācaspate tvayā[21]//9//

ajñāyamānaṃ na jñeyaṃ vijñānaṃ tad vinā na ca/
tasmāt svabhāvato na sto jñānajñeye tvam ūcivān//10//

lakṣyāl lakṣaṇam anyac cet syāt tal lakṣyam alakṣaṇam/
tayor abhāvo 'nanyatve vispaṣṭaṃ kathitaṃ tvayā[22]//11//

lakṣyalakṣaṇanirmuktaṃ vāgudāhāravarjitam/
śāntaṃ jagad idaṃ dṛṣṭaṃ bhavatā jñānacakṣuṣā//12//

na sann utpadyate bhāvo nāpy asan sadasan na ca/
na svato nāpi parato na dvābhyāṃ jāyate katham[23]//13//

na sataḥ sthitiyuktasya vināśa upapadyate/
nāsato 'śvaviṣāṇena samasya śamatā katham//14//

bhāvān nārthāntaraṃ nāśo nāpy anarthāntaraṃ matam/
arthāntare bhaven nityo nāpy anarthāntare bhavet//15//

ekatve na hi bhāvasya vināśa upapadyate/
pṛthaktve na hi bhāvasya vināśa upapadyate[24]//16//

vinaṣṭāt kāraṇāt tāvat kāryotpattir na yujyate/
na cāvinaṣṭāt svapnena tulyotpattir matā tava//17//

na niruddhān nāniruddhād bījād aṅkurasaṃbhavaḥ/
māyotpādavad utpādaḥ sarva eva tvayocyate[25]//18//

atas tvayā jagad idaṃ parikalpasamudbhavam/
parijñātam asadbhūtam anutpannam na naśyati[26]//19//

nityasya saṃsṛtir nāsti naivānityasya saṃsṛtiḥ/
svapnavat saṃsṛtiḥ proktā tvayā tattvavidāṃ vara[27]//20//

svayaṃkṛtaṃ parakṛtaṃ dvābhyāṃ kṛtam ahetukam/
tārkikair iṣyate duḥkhaṃ tvayā tūktaṃ pratītyajam[28]//21//

yaḥ pratītyasamutpādaḥ śūnyatā saiva te matā/
bhāvaḥ svatantro nāstīti siṃhanādas tavātulaḥ[29]//22//

sarvasaṃkalpanāśāya śūnyatāmṛtadeśanā/
yasya tasyām api grāhas tvayāsāv avasāditaḥ[30]//23//

nirīhā vaśikāḥ śūnyā māyāvat pratyayodbhavāḥ/
sarvadharmās tvayā nātha niḥsvabhāvāḥ prakāśitāḥ[31]//24//

na tvayotpāditaṃ kiṃ cin na ca kiṃ cin nirodhitam/
yathā pūrvaṃ tathā paścāt tathatāṃ buddhavān asi//25//

aryair nisevitām enām anāgamya hi bhāvanām/
nānimittaṃ hi vijñānaṃ bhavatīha kathaṃ cana//26//

animittam anāgamya mokṣo nāsti tvam uktavān/
atas tvayā mahāyāne tat sākalyena deśitam//27//

yad avāptaṃ mayā puṇyaṃ stutvā tvāṃ stutibhājanam/
nimittabandhanāpetaṃ bhūyāt tenākhilaṃ jagat//28//

NIRAUPAMYASTAVAḤ

niraupamya[32] namas tubhyaṃ niḥsvabhāvārthavedine[33]/
yas tvaṃ dṛṣṭivipannasya lokasyāsya hitodyataḥ[34]//1//

na ca nāma tvayā[35] kiṃcid dṛṣṭaṃ[36] bauddhena cakṣuṣā[37]/
anuttarā[38] ca te nātha dṛṣṭis tattvārthadarśinī[39]//2//

na boddhā na ca boddhavyam[40] astīha paramārthataḥ/
aho paramadurbodhāṃ dharmatāṃ buddhavān asi//3//

na tvayotpāditaḥ kaścid dharmo nāpi nirodhitaḥ/
samatādarśanenaiva prāptaṃ padam[41] anuttaram//4//

na saṃsārāpakarṣeṇa tvayā nirvāṇam īpsitam/
śāntis te 'dhigatā nātha saṃsārānupalabdhitaḥ//5//

tvaṃ vivedaikarasatāṃ[42] saṃkleśavyavadānayoḥ /
dharmadhātvavinirbhedād viśuddhaś cāsi sarvataḥ //6//

nodāhṛtaṃ tvayā kiñcid ekam apy akṣaraṃ vibho/
kṛtsnaś ca vaineyajano dharmavarṣeṇa tarpitaḥ[43]//7//

na te 'sti saktiḥ skandheṣu[44] dhātuṣv āyataneṣu ca/
ākāśasamacittas tvaṃ sarvadharmeṣv aniśritaḥ//8//

sattvasaṁjñā ca te nātha sarvathā na pravartate/
duḥkhārteṣu ca sattveṣu tvam atīva kṛpātmakaḥ[45]//9//

sukhaduḥkhātmanairātmyanityānityādiṣu prabho/
iti nānāvikalpeṣu buddhis tava na sajjate/10//

na gatir nāgatiḥ kācid dharmāṇām iti te matiḥ/
na kvacid rāśibhavo 'to 'si paramārthavit//11//

sarvatrānugataś cāsi na ca jāto[46] 'si kutracit/
janmadharmaśarīrābhyām acintyas tvaṃ mahāmune//12//

ekānekatvarahitaṃ pratiśrutkopamaṃ jagat/
saṃkrāntināśāpagataṃ buddhavāṃs tvam aninditaḥ[47]//13//

śāśvatocchedarahitaṃ lakṣyalakṣaṇavarjitam/
saṃsāram avabuddhas[48] tvaṃ svapnamāyādivat prabho//14//

vāsanāmūlaparyantāḥ kleśās te 'nagha nirjitāḥ/
kleśaprakṛtitaś caiva tvayāmṛtam upārjitam//15//

alakṣaṇaṃ tvayā dhīra dṛṣṭaṃ rūpa arūpavat/
lakṣaṇojjvalagātraś[49] ca dṛśyase rūpagocare//16//

na ca rūpeṇa dṛṣṭena dṛṣṭa ity abhidhīyase/
dharme dṛṣṭe sudṛṣṭo 'si dharmatā na ca dṛśyate//17//

śauṣiryaṃ nāsti te kāye māṃsāsthirudhiraṃ na ca/
indrāyudham ivākāśe kāyaṃ darśitavān asi[50]//18//

nāmayo nāśuciḥ kāye kṣuttṛṣṇāsaṃbhavo na ca/
tvayā lokānuvṛttyarthaṃ darśitā laukikī kriyā[51]//19//

karmāvaraṇadoṣaś ca sarvathānagha nāsti te/
tvayā lokānukampārthaṃ karmaplutiḥ[52] pradarśitā//20//

dharmadhātor asambhedād yānabhedo 'sti na prabho/
yānatritayam ākhyātaṃ tvayā sattvāvatārataḥ[53]//21//

nityo[54] dhruvaḥ[55] śivaḥ kāyas tava dharmamayo jinaḥ/
vineyajanahetoś ca darśitā nirvṛtis tvayā//22//

lokadhātuṣv ameyeṣu tvadbhaktaiḥ punar īkṣase[56]/
cyutijanmābhisaṃbhodhicakranirvṛtilālasaiḥ//23//

na te 'sti manyanā [57] nātha na vikalpo[58] na ceñjanā[59]/
anābhogena te loke buddhakṛtyaṃ pravartate[60]//24//

iti sugatam[61] acintyam[62] aprameyaṃ
guṇakusumair avakīrya yan mayāptam/
kuśalam iha bhavantu tena sattvāḥ
paramagabhīramunīndradharmabhājaḥ//25//

ACINTYASTAVAḤ

pratītyajānāṃ bhāvānāṃ naiḥsvābhāvyaṃ jagāda yaḥ[63]/
taṃ namāmy asamajñānam[64] acintyam[65] anidarśanam//1//

yathā tvayā mahāyāne dharmanairātmyam ātmanā/
viditaṃ deśitaṃ tadvad dhīmadbhyaḥ karuṇāvaśāt//2//

pratyayebhyaḥ samutpannam anutpannaṃ tvayoditam/
svabhāvena na taj jātam iti śūnyaṃ prakāśitam//3//

yadvac chabdaṃ pratītyeha pratiśabdasamudbhavaḥ/
māyāmarīcivac cāpi tathā bhavasamudbhavaḥ//4//

māyāmarīcigandharvanagarapratibimbakāḥ/
yady ajātāḥ saha svapnair na syāt taddarśanādikam//5//

hetupratyayasaṃbhūtā yathaite kṛtakāḥ smṛtāḥ/
tadvat pratyayajaṃ viśvaṃ tvayoktaṃ nātha sāṃvṛtam//6//

asty etat kṛtakaṃ sarvaṃ yat kiṃcid bālalāpanam/
riktamuṣṭipratīkāśam ayathārthaprakāśitam//7//

kṛtakaṃ vastu no jātaṃ tadā kiṃ vārtamānikam/
kasya nāśād atītaṃ syād utpitsuḥ kim apekṣate//8//

svasmān na jāyate bhāvaḥ parasmān nobhayād api/
na san nāsan na sadasan kutaḥ kasyodayas tadā//9//

ajāte na svabhāvo 'sti kutaḥ svasmāt samudbhavaḥ/
svabhāvābhāvasiddhyaiva parasmād apy asaṃbhavaḥ//10//

svatve sati paratvaṃ syāt paratve svatvam iṣyate/
āpekṣikī tayoḥ siddhiḥ pārāvāram ivoditā//11//

yadā nāpekṣate kiṃ cit kutaḥ kiṃ cit tadā bhavet/
yadā nāpekṣate dīrghaṃ kuto hrasvādikaṃ tadā//12//

astitve sati nāstitvaṃ dīrghe hrasvaṃ tathā sati/
nāstitve sati cāstitvaṃ yat tasmād ubhayaṃ na sat//13//

ekatvaṃ ca tathānekam atītānāgatādi ca/
saṃkleśo vyavadānaṃ ca samyaṅmithyā svataḥ kutaḥ//14//

svata eva hi yo nāsti bhāvaḥ sarvo 'sti kas tadā/
para ity ucyate yo 'yaṃ na vinā svasvabhāvataḥ//15//

na svabhāvo 'sti bhāvānāṃ parabhāvo 'sti no yadā/
bhāvagrāhagrahāveśaḥ[66] paratantro 'sti kas tadā//16//

ādāv eva samaṃ jātāḥ svabhāvena ca nirvṛtāḥ/
anutpannāś ca tattvena tasmād dharmās tvayoditāḥ//17//

niḥsvabhāvās tvayā dhīman rūpādyāḥ saṃprakāśitāḥ/
phenabudbudamāyābhramarīcikadalīsamāḥ//18//

indriyair upalabdhaṃ yat tat tattvena bhaved yadi/
jātās tattvavido bālās tattvajñānena kiṃ tadā[67]//19//

jaḍatvam apramāṇatvam athāvyākṛtatām api/
viparītaparijñānam indriyāṇāṃ tvam ūcivān//20//

ajñānenāvṛto yena yathāvan na prapadyate/

catuṣkoṭivinirmuktās tena dharmās tvayoditāḥ/
vijñānasyāpy avijñeyā vācāṃ kim uta gocarāḥ//23//

svapnendrajālikodbhūtaṃ dvicandrodvīkṣaṇaṃ yathā/
bhūtaṃ tadvastu no bhūtaṃ[68] tathā dṛṣṭaṃ jagat tvayā//24//

utpannaś ca sthito naṣṭaḥ svapne yadvat sutas tathā/
na cotpannaḥ sthito naṣṭa ukto loko 'rthatas tvayā//25//

kāraṇāt saṃbhavo dṛṣṭo yathā svapne tathetaraḥ/
saṃbhavaḥ sarvabhāvānāṃ vibhavo 'pi matas tathā//26//

rāgādijaṃ yathā duḥkhaṃ saṃkleśasaṃsṛtī tathā/
saṃbhārapūraṇān muktiḥ svapnavad bhāṣitā tvayā//27//

jātaṃ tathaiva no jātam āgataṃ gatam ity api/
baddho muktas tathā jñānī dvayam icchen na tattvavit//28//

utpattir yasya naivāsti tasya kā nirvṛtir bhavet/
māyāgajaprakāśatvād ādiśāntatvam arthataḥ[69]//29//

utpanno 'pi na cotpanno yadvan māyāgajo mataḥ/
utpannaṃ ca tathā viśvam anutpannaṃ ca tattvataḥ//30//

ameyair aprameyānāṃ pratyekaṃ nirvṛtiḥ kṛtā/
lokanāthair hi sattvānāṃ na kaś cin mocitaś ca taiḥ//31//

te ca sattvāś ca no jātā ye nirvānti na te sphuṭam/
na kaś cin mocitaḥ kaiś cid iti proktaṃ mahāmune//32//

māyākārakṛtaṃ yadvad vastuśūnyaṃ tathetarat/
vastuśūnyaṃ jagat sarvaṃ tvayoktaṃ kārakas tathā//33//

kārako 'pi kṛto 'nyena kṛtatvaṃ nātivartate/
atha vā tatkriyā kartṛ[69a] kārakasya prasajyate//34//

nāmamātraṃ jagat sarvam ity uccair bhāṣitaṃ tvayā/
abhidhānāt pṛthagbhūtam abhidheyaṃ na vidyate//35//

kalpanāmātram ity asmāt sarvadharmāḥ prakāśitāḥ/
kalpanāpy asatī proktā yayā śūnyaṃ vikalpyate[70]//36//

bhāvābhāvadvayātītam anatītaṃ ca kutra cit/
na ca jñānaṃ na ca jñeyaṃ na cāsti na ca nāsti yat//37//

yan na caikaṃ na cānekaṃ nobhayaṃ na ca nobhayam/
anālayam athāvyaktam acintyam anidarśanam//38//

yan nodeti na ca vyeti nocchedi na ca śāśvatam/
tad ākāśapratīkāśaṃ nākṣarajñānagocaram//39//

yaḥ pratītyasamutpādaḥ śūnyatā saiva te matā/
tathāvidhaś ca saddharmas tatsamaś ca tathāgataḥ[71]//40//

tat tattvaṃ paramārtho 'pi tathatā dravyam iṣyate/
bhūtaṃ tad avisaṃvādi tadbodhād buddha ucyate[72]//41//

buddhānāṃ sattvadhātoś ca tenābhinnatvam arthataḥ/
ātmanaś ca pareṣāṃ ca samatā tena te matā[73]//42//

bhāvebhyaḥ śūnyatā nānyā na ca bhāvo 'sti tāṃ vinā/
tasmāt pratītyajā bhāvās tvayā śūnyāḥ prakāśitāḥ//43//

hetupratyayasaṃbhūtā paratantrā ca saṃvṛtiḥ/
paratantra iti proktaḥ paramārthas tv akṛtrimaḥ//44//

svabhāvaḥ prakṛtis tattvaṃ dravyaṃ vastu sad ity api/
nāsti vai kalpito bhāvo paratantras na vidyate[74]//45//

astīti kalpite bhāve samāropas tvayoditaḥ/
nāstīti kṛtakocchedād ucchedaś ca prakāśitaḥ//46//

tattvajñānena nocchedo na ca śāśvatatā matā/
vastuśūnyaṃ jagat sarvaṃ marīcipratimaṃ matam//47//

mṛgatṛṣṇājalaṃ yadvan nocchedi na ca śāśvatam/
tadvat sarvaṃ jagat proktaṃ nocchedi na ca śāśvatam//48//

dravyam utpadyate yasya tasyocchedādikaṃ bhavet/
antavān nāntavāṃś cāpi lokas tasya prasajyate//49//

jñāne sati yathā jñeyaṃ jñeye jñānaṃ tathā sati/
yatrobhayam anutpannam iti buddhaṃ tadāsti kim//50//

iti māyādidṛṣṭāntaiḥ sphuṭam uktvā bhiṣagvaraḥ/
deśayām āsa saddharmaṃ sarvadṛṣṭicikitsakam//51//

etat tat paramaṃ tattvaṃ niḥsvabhāvārthadeśanā/
bhāvagrahagṛhītānāṃ cikitseyam anuttarā//52//

dharmayājñika tenaiva dharmayajño niruttaraḥ/
abhīkṣṇam iṣṭas trailokye niṣkapāṭo nirargalaḥ//53//

vastugrāhabhayocchedī kutīrthyamṛgabhīkaraḥ/
nairātmyasiṃhanādo 'yam adbhuto naditas tvayā//54//

śūnyatādharmagambhīrā dharmabherī parāhatā/
naiḥsvābhāvyamahānādo dharmaśaṅkhaḥ prapūritaḥ//55//

dharmayautukam ākhyātaṃ buddhānāṃ śāsanāmṛtam/
nītārtham iti nirdiṣṭaṃ dharmāṇāṃ śūnyataiva hi//56//

yā tūtpādanirodhādisattvajīvādideśanā/
neyārthā ca tvayā nātha bhāṣitā saṃvṛtiś ca sā//57//

prajñāpāramitāmbhodher yo 'tyantam pāram āgataḥ/
sa puṇyaguṇaratnāḍhyas tvadguṇārṇavapāragaḥ//58//

iti stutvā jagannātham acintyam anidarśanam/
yad avāptaṃ mayā puṇyaṃ tenāstu tvatsamaṃ jagat//59//

PARAMĀRTHASTAVAḤ

kathaṃ stoṣyāmi te[75] nātham[76] anutpannam anālayam[77]/
lokopamām atikrāntaṃ vākpathātītagocaram//1//

tathāpi[78] yādṛśo vāsi tathatārtheṣu gocaraḥ/
lokaprajñaptim āgamya stoṣye 'haṃ bhaktito gurum//2//

anutpannasvabhāvena[79] utpādas te na vidyate/
na gatir nāgatir nāthāsvabhāvāya namo 'stu te//3//

na bhāvo nāpy abhāvo 'si nocchedo nāpi śāśvataḥ/
na nityo nāpy anityas tvam advayāya namo 'stu te//4//

na rakto haritamāṃjiṣṭho[80] varṇas te nopalabhyate[81]/
na pītakṛṣṇaśuklo[82] vā 'varṇāya namo 'stu te//5//

na mahān nāpi hrasvo[83] 'si na dīrghaparimaṇḍalaḥ/
apramāṇagatiṃ prāpto 'pramāṇāya namo 'stu te//6//

na dūre nāpi cāsanne nākāśe nāpi vā kṣitau/
na saṃsāre na nirvāṇe 'sthitāya namo 'stu te//7//

asthitaḥ sarvadharmeṣu dharmadhātugatiṃ gataḥ/
parāṃ gaṃbhīratāṃ prāpto gaṃbhīrāya namo 'stu te[84]//8//

evaṃ stutaḥ[85] stuto bhūyās[86] athavā kim uta stutaḥ[87]/
śūnyeṣu sarvadharmeṣu kaḥ stutaḥ kena vā stutaḥ//9//

kas tvāṃ śaknoti saṃstotum[88] utpādavyayavarjitam/
yasya nānto na madhyaṃ vā grāho grāhyaṃ na vidyate//10//

na gataṃ nāgataṃ stutvā sugataṃ gativarjitam/
tena puṇyena loko 'yaṃ vrajatāṃ saugatīṃ gatim//11//

Translation

HYMN TO HIM WHO HAS GONE BEYOND THE WORLD

1. O you who have gone beyond the world, homage to you versed in pure knowledge,[89] who have suffered pain, out of compassion, during long time, only for the benefit of all living beings.[90]

2. Your opinion is that a living being does not exist, liberated just from the *skandhas*;[91] nevertheless you have suffered extreme pain, O great *muni*,[92] for the sake of living beings.[93]

3. The *skandhas* also have been shown by you to the intelligent ones to be similar to a magical illusion, a mirage, a *gandharvas'* city,[94] a dream.

4. Why indeed are not considered openly similar to a reflected image those (*skandhas*),[95] whose birth is out of causes, and which do not exist in (the case of) the non-existence of these (causes)?[96]

5. 'Elements are not perceived through the eye; how what consists of them (could be) perceptible by the eye?'[97] by you who speak thus about *rūpa*,[98] the perception of *rūpa* has been rejected.

6. Your opinion is that sensation does not exist without the sensible (object); therefore, it is insubstantial[99] and the sensible (object) does not exist either with an own being.[100]

7. If there were identity between the word and its object, the mouth would be burnt by the (word) 'fire';[101] if there were difference, there would be non-existence of knowledge (of the object)[102]—(thus) has been said by you who speak the truth.

8. It has been said by you, (speaking) from the point of view of the empirical truth, (that) the agent is independent and

also the action; but the establishment[103] of both has been considered by you to be (only) mutually dependent.[104]

9. There is no agent, there is no experiencer;[105] merit and demerit are born in dependence; what is in dependence, that is not born—(thus) has been proclaimed by you, O Lord of words.

10. The knowable (object) does not exist when it is not known and without it knowledge does not exist either; therefore the knowable (object) and knowledge do not exist *per se*—(thus) you have said.

11. If the essential characteristic were different from the object which it characterizes, that characterized object would be without an essential characteristic;[106] if there were identity (of both), (there would be also) non-existence of both[107]—(thus) it has been clearly expressed by you.

12. This world, deprived of essential characteristics and characterized objects, devoid of utterances through words,[108] has been seen as calm[109] by you with your eye of knowledge.

13. A thing does not comes forth, either if it is (already) existent, nor if it is non-existent, nor if it is existent and non-existent, neither from itself nor from other (thing) nor from both.[110] How is it born?

14. Destruction is not possible for an existent being (essentially) united to permanence;[111] how could cessation be for a non-existent being (which is) similar to the horns of the horse.[112]

15. The being destructed cannot be considered as something different from the being existent, nor as something non-different (from it). If it (the being destructed) were different (from the being existent), it (the being existent) would be permanent. If it (the being destructed) were non-different (from the being existent), it (the being destructed) would not exist.[113]

16. For in (the case of) identity (of both), the being destructed is not possible for the being existent; for in (the case of) separateness, the being destructed is not possible for the being existent.

17 The forthcoming of an effect from an (already) destroyed cause is indeed not logical, neither it is from a not destroyed (cause).[114] The forthcoming has been considered by you (to be) similar to a dream.

18 The birth of a sprout is neither from a seed (already) destroyed nor (from a seed) not (yet) destroyed;[115] (therefore) all birth is said by you (to be) similar to the birth of a magical illusion.

19 Therefore, this world, born from imagination, has been fully understood by you to be non-existent: not (really) arisen, does not perish.[116]

20 There is neither transmigration of what is permanent, nor transmigration of what is non-permanent; transmigration has been proclaimed by you (to be) like a dream,[117] O you the best of the knowers of truth.

21 Suffering has been considered by logicians to be produced by itself, to be produced by others, to be produced by both or without cause, but it has been said by you to be born in dependence.[118]

22 Dependent Origination has been considered by you to be just Voidness.[119] 'There is not an independent being': (this is) your incomparable lion's roar.

23 The teaching about the ambrosia of Voidness is for the destruction of all mental creations, but also who holds to it has been blamed by you.[120]

24 All *dharmas*—inert, dependent,[121] void, like a magical illusion, arisen out of conditions—have been declared by you, O Master, to lack an own being.[122]

25 Nothing has been produced by you and nothing has been suppressed;[123] you have understood that reality, as it was before, so it is afterwards.[124]

26 Without entering into that meditation practised by the noble ones, consciousness devoid of characteristics is not produced in this world in any way.[125]

27 You have said (that) without entering in what is devoid of characteristics, there is no liberation;[126] therefore that[127] has been taught (by you) in its integrity in the Mahāyāna.

28 Let all living beings be liberated from the bonds of what has characteristics,[128] through the merit I have obtained[129] by praising you, receptacle of praises!

HYMN TO THE INCOMPARABLE ONE[130]

1 Homage to you, O incomparable one, who know the non-existence of an own being,[131] to you who exert yourself for the benefit of this world, gone astray by the false doctrines.

2 Nothing really has been seen by you with your *buddha*'s eye, but your supreme vision, O Lord, perceives the truth.[132]

3 According to the supreme truth there are not in this world either a knower or a knowable (object).[133] Ah!, you have known the *dharmas*' nature[134] extremely difficult to be known.

4 No *dharma* has been produced or supressed by you:[135] only with the perception of the (universal) sameness[136] the supreme state[137] has been attained (by you).

5 *Nirvāṇa* has not been aimed at by you through the elimination of the *saṃsāra;*[138] peace has been obtained by you, O Lord, through the non-perception of *saṃsāra.*[139]

6 You have known the identity of essence of purity and impurity,[140] because of the non-difference in the fundament of the *dharmas;*[141] you are completely pure.

7 Not a single syllable has been uttered by you, O Lord, but any man who has to be converted,[142] has been gladdened by the rain of your Doctrine.[143]

8 There is no attachment in you for the *skandhas, dhātus* and *āyatanas*;[144] with your mind equal to the space,[145] you are not dependent on any *dharma*.

9 Perception of living beings by you does not take place, O Lord; but, in a highest degree, you are pervaded by compassion for living beings tortured by suffering.[146]

10 Your mind is not attached, O Lord, to the various mental creations: happiness, suffering; *ātman*, non-existence of *ātman*; eternal, non eternal; etc.[147]

11 'For the *dharmas* there is no going, no coming at all'[148]—such is your idea. Nowhere there is existence of conglomerates;[149] therefore, you are the knower of supreme truth.[150]

12 Everywhere you are followed, but nowhere you have been born;[151] you are unthinkable, O great *muni*, in terms of the *dharma* birth and of the body.[152]

13 You, the irreprochable one, has known the world to be deprived of unity and multiplicity, similar to an echo, devoid of transmigration[153] and destruction.

14 You have known, O Lord, the *saṃsāra* to be deprived of eternity and annihilation, lacking characterized objects and characteristics—as a dream, as a magical illusion etc.

15 The *kleśas*,[154] up to their root, the *vāsanās*,[155] have been subdued by you, O immaculate; but the ambrosia (extracted) out of the matter constituted by the *kleśas*, has been procured (to us) by you.[156]

16 The form has been seen by you, O sage, as (something) without characteristics—as no-form; but you are seen, in the realm of form, possessing a body resplendent by its characteristics.[157]

17 It is not by seeing a form (of yours), that you are said to be seen; when the Doctrine is seen, you are well seen, but the nature of the *dharmas* is not seen.[158]

18 In your body there are not either any hollow, or flesh or

bones or blood; you have shown a body similar to Indra's arch in the sky.[159]

19 In your body there are not either illness or impurity or appearance of hunger and thirst; (but) to adequate yourself to the world a human behaviour has been shown by you.

20 For you, O immaculate, there is not absolutely the evil constituted by the obstacles that are the actions;[160] (but) out of compassion for the world, submersion (of yourself) into action has been shown by you.

21 Because of the non-difference in the fundament of the *dharmas*, there is no difference between the Vehicles,[161] O Lord, (but) the Three Vehicles have been preached by you, according to the (degree of) comprehension[162] (of the Doctrine) by the beings.

22 Your body is eternal, unalterable, fortunate, made out of Doctrine,[163] victorious; but because of men who are to be converted, extinction[164] (of yourself) has been shown by you.

23 (But) in the numberless worlds you are seen anew by your devotees[165] who desire the perfect comprehension of death and birth and (thanks to it) the extinction of the (existence's) wheel.

24 There are in you neither thought, O Lord, nor mental creation nor movement; (nevertheless) in this world, without any effort from you,[166] your *buddha*'s function is accomplished.

25 Let the beings (of this world) participate of the supreme and profound Doctrine of the Indra of *munis*, thanks to the merit that has been obtained by me, by covering, with the flowers of his qualities, the well gone, the unthinkable, the unmeasurable one![167]

HYMN TO THE UNTHINKABLE ONE

1 I pay homage to him who taught the non-existence of an own being for things born in dependence, (to him) of

unequalled knowledge, unthinkable,[168] who cannot be pointed out.[169]

2 As, in the Mahāyāna, the insubstantiality of the *dharmas* was known by you by yourself (to be), thus was it taught (by you), by compassion, to the intelligent ones.[170]

3 What has arisen from conditions has been said by you to be un-arisen;[171] that is not born with an own being, therefore it has been proclaimed to be void.[172]

4 As in this world the forthcoming of an echo (is produced) depending on a sound, and also as (are produced) a magical illusion, a mirage, so[173] is the forthcoming of existence.

5 If the magical illusion, the mirage, the *gandharvas'* city, the reflected image, together with dreams, were not born (in some way), there would not be vision etc. of them.[174]

6 In the same way as those[175] (things), arisen out of causes and conditions, are declared (to be) effected,[176] so all things born out of conditions have been said by you, O Lord, (to be) existent (only) by convention.

7 All the things effected, whatever they are, are a foolish talk, similar to an empty fist, declared to be false.[177]

8 An effected thing is not (really) born, how then (could it be a) present (thing)? Through the destruction of what could it be (a) past (thing)? What does the future[178] (time) relate to?[179]

9 A thing is not born from itself, (nor) from other (thing) neither from both; neither (it is born) having existed (before), nor not having existed (before), nor having and not having existed (before). Then from where, of what (could it be) a forthcoming?[180]

10 There is not an own being for an unborn (thing). How (could it be for it) a forthcoming from itself?[181] Because of the admission of the non-existence of an own being, there is non-production from another either.[182]

11 If there were 'the one', there would be 'the other';[183] if there

were 'the other', 'the one' could be accepted;[184] the admission of these two has been said (by you) to be mutually relative, like the obverse and reverse (of the same thing).[185]

12 When it is not related to something (else), how then could something exist?[186] When it is not related to (something) long, how then could (something) short etc. (exist)?

13 If there is existence, there is non-existence; if there is something long, similarly, (there is) something short; and if there is non-existence, (there is) existence; therefore, both[187] are not existent.[188]

14 Unity and so multiplicity, and past, future etc., defilement and purification, correct and false (opinion)—how can they exist *per se*?[189]

15 Since a thing that is *per se* does not exist, then which (thing)—whatever it be—exist? That (thing) which is called 'other', does not exist without an own being of itself.[190]

16 Since, for things, there is not an own being neither there is the being 'other', then which devotedness to the holding to the belief in things, being dependent (on non-existent things), could exist (with ground)?[191]

17 *Dharmas* have been said by you to be, from the beginning, born alike and extinguished by their own nature, and therefore, in truth non-arisen.[192]

18 Form etc. have been fully proclaimed by you, O intelligent one, to be without an own being, similar to foam, bubbles, magical illusion, clouds, mirages, the *kadalī*.[193]

19 If what is grasped by the senses existed in truth, the ignorant ones would happen to be knowers of truth. Then which would be the use of knowledge of truth?[194]

20 You have mentioned the inertness, the not being a means of knowledge, the indistinctness[195] and the wrong knowledge,[196] (as proper) of the senses.

21 It has been said by you, (after) having meditated, that the world does not properly attain the truth, because of the ignorance by which it is covered.[197]

22 'It exists'—the doctrine of eternality; 'It does not exist'—the doctrine of annihilation. Therefore, the doctrine free from the two extremes has been taught by you.[198]

23 Therefore the *dharmas* have been said by you to be free from the four alternative positions,[199] unknowable even for the consciousness, how much less objects of words?

24 Like what arises in dreams and by (the action of) a magician, (like) the vision of two moons—that is existent and non-existent—so the world has been seen by you.

25 And like a son born, existing, perishing in a dream, so also the world has been said by you not to be born, existing, perishing in reality.

26 As the forthcoming out of a cause, seen in a dream, and also the contrary (process are considered to be), so is considered to be the forthcoming of all beings—and (so) also (their) destruction.[200]

27 As well as suffering born from passion etc., and also impurities and transmigration, (so) liberation through the fulfilling of (the two) requisites[201] has been said by you to be like a dream.

28 One who cognizes (something as) 'born' and 'unborn', 'come' and 'gone', and also (somebody as) 'enchained' and 'liberated', accepts duality;[202] is not a knower of reality.

29 For what there is not arising, for that which cessation could be? Because of (its) being (like) the appearance of the elephant of the magical illusion, there is in reality (as characteristic of everything) the being extinguished *ab origine*.[203]

30 As the elephant of the magical illusion is considered to be, although (illusory) arisen, not (really) arisen, so all is (illusory) arisen, and not arisen in reality.[204]

31 The cessation of numberless beings has been realized individually by numberless protectors of the world, but (in reality) nobody has been liberated by them.[205]

32 O great *muni*, it has been proclaimed (by you) that they (the protectors of the world) and beings have not been born; that those who are extinguished (do) not (exist) certainly; (thus) no body is liberated by any body.[206]

33 As what is done by an illusion-maker is devoid of reality, so are also the others;[207] the whole world has been said by you to be devoid of reality, (and) so also the maker.

34 The maker also (if he is) made by another does not pass beyond the state of being (a thing) made;[208] or else his (own) action would result being the (thing) maker of the maker.[209]

35 It has been loudly declared by you that the whole world is only name;[210] separated from the word (that expresses it), that which is expressed does not exist.[211]

36 Therefore, all *dharmas* have been shown (by you) to be only mental creation; the mental creation itself, by which Voidness is conceived, has been proclaimed (by you) to be non-existent.[212]

37[213] (That) which is beyond both, existence and non-existence, but (which is) not passed over to any place,[214] and (which is) neither knowledge nor a knowable (object) and (which) neither is nor is not,

38 which is neither one nor not one, neither both nor not both, (which is) without base and not manifest, unthinkable, which cannot be pointed out,

39 which neither arises nor disappears, (which is) neither liable to destruction nor eternal—that, similar to the space, is not within the range of words and knowledge.[215]

40 What is Origination in Dependence, that indeed has been considered by you to be Voidness; and of the same sort[216] is the Good Doctrine, and identical to it is the *tathāgata*.

41 That[217] is regarded as the truth, the supreme reality, the suchness,[218] the substance;[219] that is the element which coincides (with all);[220] through its knowledge (*bodha*) one is called *buddha*.

42 Therefore, there is truly non-difference between the *buddhas*

and the essence of being; therefore, the sameness between oneself and the others has been approved by you.[221]

43 Voidness is not different from things and a thing does not exist without it,[222] therefore things born in dependence have been shown by you to be void.

44 The conceiling (reality)[223] is produced from causes and conditions, and is dependent[224] on something else; it has been called (by you) 'the dependent (reality)'; but the supreme reality is non-effected,[225]

45 also (it could be) called: an own being, the primary matter, the truth, the substance, entity, being;[226] an imagined thing does not exist, a dependent (thing) does not exist.[227]

46 (The affirmation:) 'It exists' in relation to an imagined thing has been said by you to be a superimposition;[228] and (the affirmation) 'It does not exist', as a consequence of the destruction of a made thing, has been shown to be annihilation.[229]

47 Through the knowledge of truth, neither annihilation nor eternity have been thought (by you to exist);[230] the whole world has been thought (by you) to be void of reality, similar to a mirage.[231]

48 As the water of a mirage is not liable to destruction nor eternal, so the whole world has been proclaimed (by you to be) neither liable to destruction nor eternal.[232]

49 For whom a substance comes forth, for him there would be destruction and so on; for him the world would result being limited or not limited.[233]

50 As, when knowledge exists, the knowable (object exists), so, when the knowable (object) exists, knowledge (exists); when it is realized that both do not arise, then what does exist?[234]

51 Thus the best of physicians,[235] having spoken clearly, by means of the analogies of the magical illusion and so on,[236] taught the Good Doctrine, healer of all wrong opinions.

52 This is the supreme truth: the teaching of the insub-

stantiality; this one is the insuperable medicine for those captured by the monster of (the false belief in) being.

53 O sacrificer of the Doctrine,[237] for this reason indeed the insuperable sacrifice of the Doctrine has been constantly offered (by you) in the three worlds without obstacles, without impediments.

54 This wonderful lion's roar, which is the insubstantiality, destructor of the fear (provoked) by the monster of (the false belief in) reality, and causing dread to the deers which are the heretic teachers, has been uttered by you.

55 The drum of the Doctrine, (drum) profound because of the doctrine of Voidness, has been beaten (by you); the trumpet of the Doctrine, loud-sounding because of (the doctrine of) insubstantiality has been blown (by you).

56 The gift of the Doctrine, the ambrosia of the teaching of the *buddhas*, has been made known; it has been declared to be of a well-established meaning, since (it is) only the Voidness of the *dharmas*.[238]

57 But the instruction about coming forth, cessation etc., being, soul etc. has been declared by you, O Lord, to be of a meaning which has to be determined, and it is (referring only to) the conceiling (reality).[239]

58 That (man) who has gone to the extreme limit of the ocean of *Prajñāpāramitā*, (that man) richly endowed with the jewels[240] of merits and good qualities,[241] has crossed over the ocean of your good qualities.

59 May the world be similar to you through that merit, that has been obtained by me (while) thus praising (you), the Lord of the world, unthinkable, who cannot be pointed out.[242]

HYMN ACCORDING TO THE SUPREME TRUTH[243]

1 How shall I praise you, the Lord who has not been born, who remains nowhere, who is beyond all comparison

proper of the world, something beyond the path of words.[244]

2 Any how—be you whatever you may be in the sense of the true reality—I, abiding by the world's conventions,[245] shall praise the Master out of devotion.[246]

3 Since there is not a forthcoming with an own being,[247] there is not forthcoming for you, either going or coming, O Lord. I pay homage to you devoid of an own being.

4 You are neither an existing being nor a non-existing being, nor (liable to) destruction nor eternal, nor permanent nor impermanent. I pay homage to you devoid of duality.

5 No colour is perceived in you, neither red nor green nor garnet nor yellow nor black nor white. I pay homage to you devoid of colour.

6 You are neither big nor small, neither long nor round; you have reached a measureless state. I pay homage to you devoid of measure.

7 (You are not) either far or near, either in the space or on earth, either in the *saṃsāra* or in the *nirvāṇa*.[248] I pay homage to you who are in no place.

8 You are not in the *dharmas*;[249] you have reached the state of the fundament of the *dharmas*;[250] you have reached the extreme profundity.[251] I pay homage to you profound.

9 Praised in this way, so may you be praised—but have you been praised in truth? Since all the *dharmas* are void, who is praised? by whom is he praised?[252]

10 Who can praise you devoid of birth and destruction, for whom there is neither end nor middle, nor perception nor perceptible object?

11 Having praised him who has neither gone nor come, the well-gone, devoid of going[253]—thanks to this merit,[254] let the world follow the path of the well-gone.

Appendix

SEMS KYI RDO RJEḤI BSTOD PA

(CITTAVAJRASTAVA)

Tibetan Text

1 gaṅ gis sems byuṅ dra ba ni/
sems ñid kyis ni bsal mdzad de/
sems kyi rmoṅs pa sel ba yi/
raṅ sems de la phyag ḥtshal lo//

2 sems can mos pa sna tshogs rnams/
tha dad lha yi dmigs pa la/
rin chen sems ni rnam grol las/
lha gźan bsgrub tu yod ma yin//

3 sems thob pa ni byaṅ chub ste/
sems ni ḥgro ba lṅa po yin/
bde daṅ sdug bsṅal mtshan ñid dag/
sems las ma gtogs cuṅ zad med//

4 ḥgro ba kun gyis[255] mthoṅ ba rnams/
cuṅ zad bsgom paḥi rnam pa yaṅ/
de kun sems kyi dra ba ru/
de ñid gsuṅ bas bstan pa yin//

5 rnam par rtog pa spaṅs paḥi sems/
rnam par rtog pas bsṅos byas paḥi/
ḥkhor ba rnam rtog tsam ñid de/
rnam rtog med pa thar pa yin//

6 de bas kun gyis ḥbad pa yis/
byaṅ chub sems la phyag byaḥo/
sems kyi rdo rje bsgom paḥi phyir/
de ni byaṅ chub mchog ces bya//

7 khams bskyed sems ni lus kyis bciṅs/
sems med khams ni bde bar ḥjug/
de phyir sems ni kun tu bsruṅ/
bde legs sems las saṅs rgyas ḥbyuṅ//

HYMN TO THE JEWEL OF THE MIND

Translation

1 Homage to one's own mind, which suppresses mind's confusion and through which, in its mind's condition, the (error's) net, produced by just the mind, is eliminated.[256]

2 Beings imagine, according to their different tendencies, different gods, but for the jewel of the mind no god can be proved (to be) besides the liberation.[257]

3 Attainment of the mind is illumination; only mind are the five destinies,[258] the essence of happiness and suffering does not exist at all outside the mind.

4 Things seen by all beings (and) even some forms of meditation,[259] they are all in the (illusory) net of the mind—so it was taught by him who preached truth.

5 For the mind which is deprived of imagination,[260] the *saṃsāra*, produced by imagination, is only imagination; when there is no imagination, it is liberation.

6 Therefore all men, with endeavour, must render homage to the mind of illumination;[261] since it produces the mind's jewel, it is called 'Supreme Illumination'.[262]

7 Mind, produced by the elements, is enchained to the body; when the mind does not exist, elements get into (a state) of calm;[263] therefore, guard well your mind; *Buddhas* arise from a calm and pure mind.[264]

Notes

1. The name of the present work can be written (1) *Catustava*, (2) *Catuḥstava*, and (3) *Catustava*, according to Pāṇini 8, 3, 36 (*s* or *ḥ*); Kātyāyana, *Vārttika ad Vyākaraṇa-mahā-bhāṣya* 8, 3, 36 (optional elision of *ḥ*); *Ṛgveda-prātiśākhya* 4, 36, p. 272, ed. Virendra Kumāra Varmā, and *Taittirīya-prātiśākhya* 9, 1 (the two last texts consider that the elision of *ḥ* is obligatory). For more references see J. Wackernagel, *Altindische Grammatik* I, p. 342 (edn. 1957). We have adopted *Catustava* following P. Patel.
2. See, for example: *Tōhoku* 1118, 1119, 1120, 1121, 1122, 1125, 1126, 1127, 1128, 1129, 1130 etc. = *Catalogue* 2010, 2011, 2012, 2013, 2014, 2017,—, 2018, 2019, 2020, 2021 etc. respectively. On the Buddhist hymns in general see Dieter Schlingloff, *Buddhistische Stotras*, pp. 8-15. On Nāgārjuna's hymns see D.S. Ruegg, *The Literature of the Madhyamaka School*, pp. 31-32 and pp. 120-22.
3. With this name J.W. de Jong designated a poem in 14 stanzas contained in a Sanskrit manuscript relatively modern, in Nepali alphabet, which G. Tucci discovered and photographs of which he gave to de Jong for its edition. J.W. de Jong edited the Sanskrit text, the Tibetan translation and his French translation of the poem in *Oriens Extremus* IX, 1 (1962), pp. 47-56. On p. 48 of this article de Jong indicates that in the manuscript, after the stanzas, there are some lines which he supposes were written by the copyist. From these lines he takes the expression *Madhyamakaśāstrastuti* to designate this poem of Candrakīrti. These stanzas were known, previously to Tucci's discovery, in their Tibetan translation, which is included at the end of the Tibetan translation of Candrakīrti's *Prasannapadā* (*Tōhoku* 3860 = *Catalogue* 5260). The manuscripts of the Sanskrit original text of the *Prasannapadā* do not contain these stanzas. See the editions of L. de la Vallée Poussin and P.L. Vaidya.
4. J.W. de Jong, 'La *Madhyamakaśāstrastuti* de Candrakīrti', p. 48.
5. G. Tucci, 'Two Hymns of the Catuḥ-stava', in *JRAS*, 1932, pp. 309-25.
6. Ch. Lindtner, *Nagarjuniana, Studies in the Writings and Philosophy of Nāgārjuna* (1982).
7. About these manuscripts see Lindtner, *Nagarjuniana*, pp. 123-24 (*Sigla*). These manuscripts are: (1) a manuscript kept in Tokyo University; (2) a manuscript from Mongolia copied by Prof. M. Tubiansky; (3) a manuscript of the Kundeling monastery copied by Prof. V.V. Gokhale, and (4) a manuscript in possession of Manavajra Vajracharya, Kathmandu.
8. P. Patel, 'Catustava', in *IHQ*, 1932, pp. 316-31 and pp. 689-705.
9. See *Taisho* 1675, Nanjio 1070, and D.S. Ruegg, 'Le Dharmadhātustava'.
10. Ch. Lindtner, *Nagarjuniana*, p. 121, note 144, indicates that there is a

reference to *Catustava* as a whole in Vairocanarakṣita's *Bodhisattvacaryāvatārapañjikā*, no. 5277, *Śa* fol. 169 a 2 and 174 b 8 (*Peking* Edition). He considers this to be 'the earliest reference to *Catuḥstava*'. However D.S. Ruegg, *The Literature*, p. 84 and p. 116, gives for Prajñākaramati the date *c.* 950-1000, and for Vairocanarakṣita the eleventh century. Vairocanarakṣita quotes stanzas 6 and 7 of the *Niraupamya*, which he introduces with the words: *bstod pa bźi pa las kyaṅ* and *de skad du bstod pa bźi pa las kyaṅ*.

11. L. de la Vallée Poussin, 'Les Quatres Odes de Nāgārjuna', in *Le Muséon*, n.s., 14, 1913, pp. 1-18, G. Tucci and P. Patel in their articles quoted in the notes 5 and 8, p. 309 and pp. 83-84 respectively, are of the same opinion.
12. Also E. Lamotte, *Le Traité de la Grande Vertu de Sagesse* III, p. xliii, considered even in 1970 that the four mentioned hymns (*Niraupamya, Lokātīta, Paramārtha* and *Cittavajra)* composed the *Catustava*. We think that in favour of the *Cittavajra* as one of the four hymns, could be the fact that it is found in the Tibetan Buddhist Canon after the other three hymns, and also the fact that the four have been translated into Tibetan by the same translator. But after Lindtner's publication this hypothesis has to be rejected.
13. D.S. Ruegg, *The Literature of the Madhyamaka School*, (1981), p. 31, although he takes into account Amṛtākara's commentary, thinks that the question about the *Catustava*'s composition is not definitively solved. But we think that with Lindtner's publication there is no more place for this doubt.
14. E. Lamotte, *Le Traité de la Grande Vertu de Sagesse*, III, *Introduction*, p. xliii, thinks that the word *saṃstuti* of the *Madhyamakaśāstrastuti* designates the *Catustava*. Unfortunately this opinion is a mere supposition. If it could be confirmed, we should have another solid argument in favour of the *Catustava*'s authenticity.
15. In general terms, the authenticity of many works attributed to Nāgārjuna in the Tibetan Buddhist Canon is doubtful. Cf. Lindtner, *Nagarjuniana*, pp. 9-18, and also Ruegg, *The Literature*, pp. 31-36, on the authenticity's question.
16. D.S. Ruegg, *The Literature of the Madhyamaka School*, p. 31 (and also p. 35) indicates some ideas which appear in the hymns and which may not be of Nāgārjuna, such as the cataphatic conception of the absolute reality, which is contrary to the apophatism characteristic of Nāgārjuna's philosophical treatises; the devotional (*bhakti*) element; some proximity to the theory of the absolute which is proper of the *tathāgatagarbha* doctrine. Let us add the presence in the *Niraupamyastava* of a reference to the Buddha's bodies which goes beyond Nāgārjuna's own conception. See note 140 of our translation of *Niraupamyastava*. Cf. also Lindtner, *Nagarjuniana*, p. 122 note 149.
17. Cf. F. Tola and C. Dragonetti, 'Nāgārjuna's Conception of 'Voidness' (*Śūnyatā*)'.
18. G. Tucci, 'Two Hymns of the Catuḥstava of Nāgārjuna', p. 310.
19. This stanza is quoted by Candrakīrti, *Prasannapadā ad* XXI, 4, p. 179,

l. 11-12 ed. Vaidya (= p. 413, 1.6-7 ed. de la Vallée Poussin) and Prajñākaramati, *Pañjikā ad* IX, 145, p. 272, 1.13-14 ed. Vaidya (= p. 583, 1.18-19 ed. de la Vallée Poussin). It would be, according to Vaidya and de la Vallée Poussin, in their editions of the *Pañjikā*, a quotation of the *Yuktiṣaṣṭikā* (a Nāgārjuna's work not preserved in Sanskrit). It is a mistake, because the Sanskrit text of the this stanza, that is quoted as referred above by Candrakīrti and Prajñākaramati, corresponds *exactly* to the original Sanskrit text and also to the Tibetan translation of the stanza 4 of *Lokātītastava*, but not to the stanza 39 of the *Yuktiṣaṣṭikā*, although it expresses a similar idea. The *Yuktiṣaṣṭikā* has been preserved in its Tibetan translation (*Tōhoku* 3825 = *Catalogue* 5225) and in its Chinese translation (*Taisho* 1575, Nanjio 1307, *Hōbōgirin, Fascicule Annexe*, p. 93). See chapter 2 of this book.

20. This stanza is quoted by Prajñākaramati, *Pañjikā ad* IX, 73, p. 224, 1.13-14 ed. Vaidya (= p. 476, 1.14-15 ed. de la Vallée Poussin).
21. This stanza is quoted by Prajñākaramati, *Pañjikā ad* IX, 73, p. 224, 1.15-16 ed. Vaidya (= p. 476, 1.16-17 ed. de la Vallée Poussin).
22. This stanza is quoted by Candrakīrti, *Prasannapadā ad* I, 3, p. 22, 1.3-4 ed. Vaidya (= p. 64, 1.5-6 ed. de la Vallée Poussin).
23. This stanza is quoted by Prajñākaramati, *Pañjikā ad* IX, 150, p. 274, 1.1-2 ed. Vaidya (= p. 587, 1.7-8 ed. de la Vallée Poussin).
24. The stanzas 15 and 16 do not appear in the Tibetan translation (*Sde-dge, Peking, Narthang* editions). This is why the Tibetan translation has only 26 stanzas.
25. This stanza is quoted by Prajñākaramati, *Pañjikā ad* IX, 108, p. 249, 1.2-3 ed. Vaidya (= p. 533, 1.9-10 ed. de la Vallée Poussin), who has in *pāda a: niruddhād vāniruddhād vā.*
26. This stanza is quoted by Prajñākaramati, *Pañjikā ad* IX, 108, p. 249, 1.4-5 ed. Vaidya (= p. 533, 1.11-12 ed. de la Vallée Poussin).
27. This stanza is quoted by Prajñākaramati, *Pañjikā ad* IX, 108, p. 249, 1.6-7 ed. Vaidya (= p. 533, 1.13-14 ed. de la Vallée Poussin).
28. This stanza is quoted by Candrakīrti, *Prasannapadā ad* I, 3, p. 18, 1.28-29 ed. Vaidya (= p. 55, 1.3-4 ed. de la Vallée Poussin) and XII, 8, p. 103, 1. 3-4 ed. Vaidya (= p. 234, l. 8-9 ed. de la Vallée Poussin).
29. This stanza is quoted by Prajñākaramati, *Pañjikā ad* IX, 34, p. 198, 1.24-25 (= p. 417, 1. 6-7 ed. de la Vallée Poussin). Cf. *Acintyastava* 40.
30. This stanza is quoted by Prajñākaramati, *Pañjikā ad* IX, 2, p. 174, 1.8-9 ed. Vaidya (= p. 359, 1.8-9 ed. de la Vallée Poussin) and *ad* IX, 33, p. 197, 1. 27-28 (= p. 415, 1.3-4 ed. de la Vallée Poussin). Vaidya has in *pāda c*, in p. 174: *yasya* (*yaś ca*) *tasyām*, and in p. 197: *yaś ca (yasya) tasyām*. Vaidya attributes the first of these two quotations of Prajñākaramati to the *Niraupamyastava*, what is without any doubt a mistake; he attributes rightly the second one to the *Lokātītastava*. Besides that Prajñākaramati has in *pāda* a, °*hānāya* instead of °*nāśāya*.
31. This stanza is quoted by Prajñākaramati, *Pañjikā ad* IX, 77, p. 229, 1.25-26, ed. Vaidya (= p. 489 ed. de la Vallée Poussin).
32. Amṛtākara: *niraupamyo. . . .*

33. Tucci's manuscript has *niḥsvabhāvavādine* which Tucci (1932, p. 312 note 1) corrects into, °*vedine*, following the *Ṭīkā* contained in his manuscript and the Tibetan translation. Tucci's correction was confirmed afterwards (1956) by Amṛtākara's commentary and now by Lindtner's manuscripts (*Nagarjuniana*, p. 121 note 147). Our reading: *niḥsvabhāvārthavedine* is supported by Amṛtākara's commentary (*niḥsvabhāvārthavedī*) and by Lindtner's manuscripts, *Nagarjuniana*, p. 121, note 147 (*niḥsvabhāvārthavedine*).
34. Amṛtākara: *yas tvaṃ dṛṣṭivipannasya lokasyāsya hitodyata (iti).*
35. Tucci's manuscript has *na ca nāsatvayā* which Tucci (1932, p. 312 note 2) corrects into *na ca nāma tvayā.*
36. Amṛtākara: *tvayā na kiṃ cid dṛṣṭaṃ. . . .*
37. Amṛtākara: *bauddhaṃ cakṣur. . . .*
38. Amṛtākara: *anuttarā.*
39. Tucci has: *tattvadarśinī.* We correct into *tattvārthadarśinī* according to Lindtner's manuscripts (*Nagarjuniana*, p. 121 note 147).
40. *Boddhavyam*: our correction (confirmed by Lindtner's manuscripts (*Nagarjuniana*, p. 121 note 147); Tucci has: *bodhavyam.*
41. *Padam*: according to Lindtner's manuscripts (*Nagarjuniana*, p. 121 note 147); Tucci has: *pādam.*
42. *Viveda*: third singular person used irregularly as second. Cf. Edgerton, *Buddhist Hybrid Sanskrit Grammar*, p. 129, paragraph 25.4.
43. This stanza is quoted by Prajñākaramati, *Pañjikā ad* IX, 36, p. 200, 1.1-2 ed. Vaidya (= p. 420, 1.1-2 ed. de la Vallée Poussin) and by Advayavajra, *Advayavajrasaṃgraha*, 3. *Tattvaratnāvalī*, p. 22, 1.8-9 ed. Shastri, who has as second line: *kṛtsnaś ca vai māyajano dharmavarṣanatarṣitaḥ.*
44. *Skandheṣu*: our correction; Tucci has: *skandeṣu.*
45. This stanza is quoted by Prajñākaramati, *Pañjikā ad* IX, 76, p. 229, 1.11-12 ed. Vaidya (= p. 489, 1.1-2 ed. de la Vallée Poussin).
46. Tucci's manuscript has *yāto*, which he corrects into *jāto.*
47. *Buddhavāṃs*: our correction; Tucci has: *buddhāvāṃs.*
    This stanza is quoted by Candrakīrti, *Prasannapadā ad* X, 16, p. 93, 1.1-2 ed. Vaidya (= p. 215, 1. 5-6 ed. de la Vallée Poussin) with some variants. Candrakīrti has:

    ekatvānyatvarahitaṃ pratiśrutkopamaṃ jagat,
    saṃkrāntim āsādya gataṃ buddhavāṃs tvam aninditaḥ.

    De la Vallée Poussin, Vaidya, in their editions, and Tucci, in 'Two Hymns', p. 36, note 2, Patel, in 'Catustava', 1932, p. 318, note 3, indicate that Candrakīrti's *pāda c* is corrupted. Tucci's manuscript gives a correct reading for this *pāda.*
48. Observe the employ of *avabuddhas* with active meaning and governing an accusative. Cf. F. Edgerton, *Buddhist Hybrid Sanskrit Grammar*, p. 169, paragraph 34.13.
49. *Lakṣaṇojjvalagātraś* : our correction; Tucci has: *lakṣaṇojvalagātraś.*
50. This stanza is quoted by (Nāgārjuna's) *Pañcakrama* IV, 2, p. 36, ed. de la Vallée Poussin.
51. This stanza is quoted also by (Nāgārjuna's) *Pañcakrama* IV, 3, p. 36, ed.

de la Vallée Poussin, who has *nāmayā nāśuci* and *lokānucyutyartham* instead of *nāmayo nāśuciḥ* and *lokānuvṛttyartham*.

52. Amṛtākara: *karmaplutiḥ*.
53. This stanza is quoted by *Subhāṣitasaṃgraha*, p. 388, 1.20-21 ed. Bendall and by Advayavajra, *Advayavajrasaṃgraha*, 3. *Tattvaratnāvalī* p. 22, 1. 2-3 ed. Shastri, who has *dhyānabhedo* instead of *yānabhedo*.
54. Amṛtākara: *nityo*. . . .
55. Amṛtākara: *dhruvaḥ*.
56. *Īkṣase*: medial form with passive value. Cf. Edgerton, *Buddhist Hybrid Sanskrit Grammar*, p. 182, paragraph, 37.16. Lindtner's manuscripts have: *Īkṣyase* (*Nagarjuniana*, p. 121 note 147), the correct passive form.
57. Amṛtākara: *manyanā*° .
58. Amṛtākara: *vikalpa*° .
59. Amṛtākara: *injanā* ° .
60. This stanza is quoted by Advayavajra, *Advayavajrasaṃgraha*, 1. *Kudṛṣṭinirghātanam*, p. 1, 1.12-13 ed. Shastri, who has *pravarttate* instead of *pravartate*.
61. Amṛtākara: *sugataḥ*.
62. Amṛtākara: *acintyaḥ*.
63. Amṛtākara: *pratītyajānāṃ bhāvānāṃ naiḥsvābhāvyaṃ jagāda ya (iti)*.
64. Amṛtākara: *asamajñānam*.
65. Amṛtākara: *acintyam*.
66. We adopt the reading *bhāvagrāha*° indicated by Lindtner in note, instead of *bhāvagraha*°.
67. This stanza is quoted by Prajñākaramati, *Pañjikā ad* IX, 5, p. 180, 1.28-29 ed. Vaidya (= p. 375 ed. de la Vallée Poussin).
68. Prof. Lindtner communicates to us in a personal letter of 11.4.1984 that Prof. de Jong suggests the following interesting emmendation for *pāda c* of stanza 24: *tad vastuto 'bhūtaṃ*. Anyhow we have preferred to follow Lindtner's text that reproduces the manuscripts' reading.
69. This stanza is quoted by Prajñākaramati, *Pañjikā ad* IX, 106, p. 246, 1.22-23 ed. Vaidya (= p. 528 ed. de la Vallée Poussin). Prajñākaramati has in *pāda d: ādiśāntam tv ayatnataḥ*.

69a. Our reading: *tatkriyā kartṛ*. Lindtner has: *tatkriyākartṛ*.

70. This stanza is quoted by Prajñākaramati, *Pañjikā ad* IX, 141, p. 267, 1.25-28 ed. Vaidya (= p. 573 ed. de la Vallée Poussin).
71. This stanza is quoted by Prajñākaramati, *Pañjikā ad* IX, 106, p. 246, 1.24-25. ed., Vaidya (= p. 528 ed. de la Vallée Poussin). Cf. *Lokātītastava* 22.
72. This stanza is quoted by Prajñākaramati, *Pañjikā ad* IX, 106, p. 246, 1.26-27 ed. Vaidya (= p. 528 ed. de la Vallée Poussin).
73. This stanza is quoted by Prajñākaramati, *Pañjikā ad* IX, 154, p. 275, 1.19-20 ed. Vaidya (= p. 590 ed. de la Vallée Poussin). Prajñākaramati has in *pāda b: yena* instead of *tena*.
74. We adopt the reading *na vidyate* indicated by Lindtner in note, instead of *tu vidyate*. See the note for the translation.
75. *Te*, Accusative form of the Buddhist Hybrid Sanskrit. See Edgerton, *Buddhist Hybrid Sanskrit Grammar*, p. 109, paragraph 20.16.

76. Amṛtākara: *kathaṃ stoṣyāmi te nātha (iti).*
77. Amṛtākara: *anutpannam anālayam.*
78. Amṛtākara: *tathāpi (iti).*
79. Amṛtākara: *anutpannasvabhāvena (iti).*
80. Lindtner's manuscripts have: *harin māñjiṣṭho* (Nagarjuniana, p. 121 note 147).
81. *Nopalabhyate*: our correction, confirmed by Lindtner's manuscripts (*Nagarjuniana*, p. 121 note 147); Tucci has: *notalabhyate.*
82. Lindtner's manuscripts have: *pītaḥ kṛṣṇaḥ śuklo* (*Nagarjuniana*, p. 121 note 147).
83. *Hrasvo* : our correction; Tucci has: *hraso.*
84. Amṛtākara: *gambhīrāya namo' stu ta (iti).*
85. Lindtner's manuscripts have: *stute* (*Nagarjuniana*, p. 121, note 147).
86. Tucci, in his edition of the hymns, 'Two Hymns', p. 324, has: *bhūyād,* but in his edition of Amṛtākara's commentary in *Minor Buddhist Texts* I, p. 245, expresses that it is an error for *bhūyās*, which is the form that appears in Amṛtākara's work, whose text reads: *evaṃ stute stuto bhūyās. . .*
87. Amṛtākara: *athavā kiṃ bata stutaḥ.*
88. Amṛtākara: *kas tvāṃ śaknoti saṃstotum.*
89. The pure knowledge is the knowledge of Voidness.
90. The *kārikā* mentions two fundamental elements of Mahāyāna Buddhism: knowledge and compassion.
91. Living beings are only conglomerates of *skandhas* (species of *dharmas*, elements of existence); they do not exist as something independent or different from them; when the *skandhas* come to an end, living beings are liberated.
92. Sage.
93. Although beings have only an illusory existence, Buddha feels compassion for them.
94. Celestial musicians. The city referred to in the *kārikā* is an illusory one, created by magic.
95. The *skandhas* or the beings that they constitute.
96. This stanza expresses clearly the idea of Nāgārjuna that conditionedness is the basis of unreality of everything. Cf. *Acintyastava* 3.
97. If the primordial elements, which constitute the things, cannot be the object of our perception, then things constituted by them cannot be perceived either.
98. With the word 'form' (*rūpa* in Sanskrit) is designated the object of visual perception.
99. If the sensible object does not exist, then, according to what has been said in previous stanza, sensation also, which is produced depending on the object, cannot exist. It has not an own being, is insubstantial because it is produced in dependence.
100. At its turn the sensible object does not exist *in se et per se* since it cannot exist without the sensation.
101. If there is identity between the word and its object, the word would produce the effects of the object. Perhaps we have in this affirmation a

criticism of the Hinduist doctrine of the identity of the symbol and what is symbolized by it. OM: the Absolute.

102. If the word and its object are different, then the object could not be known through the word, as any thing cannot be known through any other thing. Since the word and the object cannot be either identical or different, the consequence is that there is a logical impossibility for any relation between them.

103. The existence.

104. From the point of view of the empirical reality it seems that the agent and the action are independent entities, but in reality they do not exist independently one from the other. The agent does not exist while the action is not done, and the action does not exist while there is not somebody doing the action.

105. According to what has been said in previous *kārikā*, we must understand that neither the actor nor the experiencer exist *in se*, but only depending on the action and on the experience. And this kind of existence 'in dependence' is for Nāgārjuna an unreal existence, lacking an own being, Voidness. The same thing is to be said about merit and demerit, which are mentioned in this *kārikā*, and about knowledge and its object, which are mentioned in next *kārikā*: they are relative concepts, mutually dependent entities.

106. If the characteristic or essential attribute of anything (*e.g.* heat) is different, something apart from the object (fire), then the object has not in itself, as something proper to it, that characteristic, that essential attribute, without which it cannot exist. We should have a fire without heat, and as something outside, apart from it, the heat. It could not be said that heat is the essential characteristic or attribute of fire.

107. If heat (attribute) and fire (object) were the same thing, fire would be heat and heat would be fire. Neither of them would keep its own existence and identity, as heat or as fire.

108. For the vision of Buddha, who perceives the true nature of things, in the world there are not in reality characteristics nor characterized objects nor expression through words, since the world is void, i.e. unreal.

109. The world, beings and things, are nirvanized *ab aeterno*.

110. We cannot say that a thing comes to existence if it already existed before being produced. We cannot say about an non-existent thing that *it* comes to existence. And it is contradictory in itself that a thing exists and does not exist at the same time. A thing cannot be born from itself, since this corresponds to the first hypothesis. A thing cannot be born from another thing, since this corresponds to the second hypothesis. And it cannot be born from itself and another, since this affirmation is contradictory in itself.

111. It cannot be deprived of its own characteristic: being cannot cease to be, i.e. to remain, to last, to persist.

112. Nothing can be said of an non-existing thing.

113. Destruction or non-existence and existence cannot be either different or identical. If they were different, existence would be a thing and destruction another, and existence could never transform itself into destruction

and consequently it would be eternal. If they were identical, destruction would be existence, and existence, in this case also, would be eternal, since it could never become destruction, because nothing can become something different from itself. Moreover, if destruction or non-existence and existence were identical, destruction or non-existence could not occur for existence (as the following *kārikā* explains), since no change would happen to existence on the arrival to it of destruction or non-existence which is identical to it.

114. Next stanza exemplifies this idea through the relation seed-sprout.

115. The uprise of an effect can be from a cause either already destroyed or not destroyed. In the first case, nothing can come forth from something non-existent; in the second case the cause (the seed) and the effect (the sprout) would exist at the same time. The production of an effect must be either from a cause already destroyed or not. In the first case nothing can be produced from something which does not exist, and in the second case the cause (the seed) and the effect (the sprout) would coexist. Therefore, production is logically impossible.

116. This world is only a mental product; consequently it has no real birth or real end.

117. A permanent soul or ego must maintain always its own being, it cannot undergo the modifications and changes which transmigration produces; a non-permanent soul or ego will perish when life ends and cannot incarnate in another body.

118. Suffering has not an own existence; it is the effect of several factors.

119. Dependent Origination fully realized is nothing else than Voidness in its integrity.

120. Voidness, manifested by the analysis of the empirical reality, cannot be conceived as 'something', as a substance, as a positive and sacred Absolute to which one holds intellectually and emotionally.

121. F. Edgerton, *Buddhist Hybrid Sanskrit* II, *Dictionary*, indicates for the word *vaśika* of the original two meanings: (1) 'submitted to' and (2) 'empty, void'. We have translated this word by 'dependent' following the interpretation of the Tibetan translation (*gźan dbaṅ*). The idea is that *dharmas* are not autonomous, existing *in se et per se*, since they are conditioned by others, are dependent on others.

122. The real existence of the soul was denied by Primitive and Hīnayāna Buddhism; Mahāyāna denied also the real existence of *dharmas*.

123. Cf. *Niraupamyastava* 4.

124. True reality, Voidness, is unalterable, it has been always the same.

125. Only following the method taught by the Mahāyāna and practising the meditation it recommends, Voidness can be realized.

126. 'What is devoid of characteristics': Voidness, the true way of being of empirical reality. Without a complete knowledge of reality, there is no liberation.

127. The true nature of reality.

128. 'What has characteristics': the empirical reality.

129. Transference of merits.

130. Buddha, who is also the destinatary of the other three hymns of the *Catustava*.
131. Substantiality, existence *in se et per se*.
132. Thanks to his supreme intuition Buddha perceived the unreality, the non-existence as such of empirical reality and reached the true reality: the non-existence of an own being, Voidness.
133. Knower and knowable object are categories which exist only from the point of view of empirical reality or relative truth, but from the point of view of supreme truth they are non-existent, as being interdependent, mutually relative and consequently lacking an own being.
134. *Dharmatā*: the true nature of the *dharmas* is the *śūnyatā*, emptiness, the non-existence of an own being, the conditionedness, the relativity. About *dharmas* as factors or elements of existence see F. Tola and C. Dragonetti, 'La doctrina de los *dharmas* en al Budismo'.
135. As all the *dharmas* are unreal, non-existent, like all the empirical reality they create, Buddha had not the power to produce them or to make them disappear. Moreover to obtain the *summun bonum* it has not been necessary for Buddha to produce good (*kuśala*) *dharmas* nor to destroy bad (*akuśala*) *dharmas*. The knowledge of universal Voidness was enough for him.
136. All things and beings are identical among themselves, because they are all void (*samatā*'s doctrine).
137. *Nirvāṇa*.
138. The *saṃsāra*, the empirical reality, cannot be destroyed or eliminated, because according to the Mādhyamika school it does not exist truly and is only a mere illusion.
139. When the knowledge of the true nature of the *saṃsāra* is obtained, then it cannot be perceived, since it is a mere illusion which disappears with true knowledge.
140. The same idea appears in Vasubandhu, *Trisvabhāvakārikā* 10. Cf. F. Tola and C. Dragonetti, 'The Trisvabhāvakārikā of Vasubandhu'. Impurity is the empirical reality, purity is Voidness. Both are identical since the essence of the empirical reality is Voidness. Buddha, as everything else, participates in the universal Voidness.
141. The fundament of the *dharmas*, *dharmadhātu*, is Voidness.
142. The Buddhist doctrine.
143. From the point of view of supreme truth Buddha and the doctrine he taught are void, unreal, non-existent. Buddha, unreal, did not teach any doctrine. But from the point of view of relative truth, in the level of apparent existence, there has been a doctrine preached by Buddha for the benefit of all beings.
144. The *skandhas*, the *āyatanas* and the *dhātus* are the names of different classifications of the *dharmas* that constitute man. Buddha has no attachment neither for the *dharmas* that constitute his own being nor for the *dharmas* that constitute other beings.
145. I.e. void, lacking an own being as all.
146. Although Buddha knows perfectly well that all beings are unreal, anyhow

he feels compassion for the beings and their suffering even if they have only an apparent existence.

147. Everything without exception is a mere mental creation, an illusion without a true existence.

148. Beings and things of the empirical reality are only mere conglomerates of *dharmas*. These conglomerates do not exist truly; they can be analyzed into the parts that constitute them and, at their own turn, these parts into their respective parts in an abolishing analytical process which does not find an ultimate substance as their last fundament.

149. Neither coming forth nor passing away nor any movement at all.

150. Voidness, the illusory character of all.

151. In his unreal, apparent aspect, Buddha is followed by his devotees, but in truth Buddha has not been born, since birth is only a mere mental creation.

152. Birth and body are categories proper of the empirical reality; they cannot be applied to Buddha from the point of view of supreme truth.

153. *Saṃkrānti*, in the original, literally 'passage'. Cf. (Nāgārjuna), *Pratītyasamutpādahṛdayakārikā* 5, *Sālistambasūtra*, pp. 6 and 17 ed. N.A. Sastri (= pp. 50 and 60 of our translation in *Budismo Mahāyāna*).

154. *Impurities*: ignorance (*avidyā*), consciousness of one's own existence (*asmitā*), passion (*rāga*), hate (*dveṣa*), and attachment to existence (*abhiniveśa*).

155. The subliminal impressions left in the subconsciousness by any experience man has, which remain in a latent form until they are reactivated by special circumstances.

156. The nectar of the doctrine taught by Buddha has been extracted by him from the elements provided by the empirical reality. This one must be abolished in order to reach truth, but it can be abolished only through elements (mind etc.) that belong to it.

157. To see the form (the body) of Buddha, to which this *kārikā* refers, is not to see Buddha in his true essence that is Voidness. Only when the Doctrine 'is seen', Buddha is seen. We find in this tenet the identification of Buddha with his Doctrine. See *kārikā* 22 of the same hymn.

158. *Dharmas'* nature, Voidness, cannot be grasped neither by the senses nor by the mind.

159. We have in this stanza perhaps a reference to the docetic doctrine that Buddha's body was only a mere appearance, like the rainbow in the sky. C. Anesaki, 'Docetism (Buddhist)', in Hastings, *ERE* IV, pp. 835-40. Cf. *kārikās* 19, 20, 22.

160. Actions leave *karmical* residues, which require new reincarnations and therefore they are an obstacle to obtain liberation.

161. From the point of view of Mahāyāna Buddhism the vehicles that lead man to *nirvāṇa* are three: (1) the vehicle of the *Śrāvakas* (disciples) *Śrāvakayāna*; (2) the vehicle of the *Pratyekabuddhas* or *Pratyekabuddhayāna*. There is not a great difference between these two vehicles as salvific means. Both conduct to illumination (*bodhi*) and to *nirvāṇa*; the *arhant* and the *pratyekabuddha* who constitute the highest degree of spiritual development in both vehicles, respectively, look only for their personal Illumina-

tion and consequent Liberation. Both vehicles constitute the so-called Hīnayāna or 'Small Vehicle'. And (3) the vehicle of the *Bodhisattvas* or *Bodhisattvayāna*. That happens to be the Mahāyāna or 'Great Vehicle'. This last Vehicle differs from the two previous ones in its ideal of the sage, the *Bodhisattva* (or future Buddha). The *Bodhisattva* seeks his personal salvation only after long periods of self-sacrifice in which he postpones his own attainment of *nirvāṇa*, consecrating himself out of compassion to help beings to reach Illumination. It differs also in its fundamental doctrine of Voidness and in the devotional element, to which it gives emphasis. Cf. L. de la Vallée Poussin, *'Mahāyāna'*, in Hastings, *Encyclopaedia of Religion*, VIII, pp. 330-36; H. Kern, *Manual of Indian Buddhism*, pp. 60-68; D.T. Suzuki, *Outlines of Mahayana Buddhism*, pp. 8-9; W.W. Soothill, *A Dictionary of Chinese Buddhist Terms, sub 'Triyāna'* (in Chinese), p. 58 *a-b*.

162. 'According to the (degree of) comprehension': *avatārataḥ* in the original. This word could also be translated as 'according to the manifestation (on earth)', i.e. 'according to their form of incarnation'. Adopting any one of these two possible translations, the idea of the *kārikā* is that Buddha taught his Doctrine to men taking into account the degree of spiritual development with which they have appeared on earth. This teaching is adequate to the level of understanding the beings possess.

163(*a*) The reference is to the idea that the true body of the Buddha is his Doctrine as opposed to his physical body which ends with death. Hīnayāna Buddhism and Nāgārjuna accept the existence of these two bodies, the physical body and the body made out of Doctrine. Cf. 'Busshin' in *Hōbōgirin*, p. 174 *b*: *'La question du corps, ou des Corps du B., se pose, en logique comme dans la tradition, à l'occasion du Parinirvāṇa. Le B. une fois eteint, la communaté a-t-elle perdu tout, et jusqu'à sa raison d'être, ou si elle subsiste, comment s'établie la continuité? Le néant méthaphysique peut constituer une philosophie, il ne crée pas une Église. La première reponse, la plus simple et la plus pratique, c'est de substituer à la personne du fondateur la Loi qu'il a leguée; on pose en regard du B. de chair (Formel) le Corps de Loi, dharmakāya. On a ainsi, dès le debut, un groupe de deux Corps; le P.V.* (Petit Véhicule) *ne va jamais plus loin, et dans les écoles du G.V.* (Grand Véhicule) *Nāgārjuna, p. ex., ne depasse pas ce stade.* 'See also Anesaki, 'Docetism (Buddhist)', in Hastings, *ERE* IV, specially p. 838 *a-b*: 4. Nāgārjuna. Afterwards this conception of the two bodies will be replaced by the doctrine of the three bodies, which characterizes Mahāyāna Buddhism after Nāgārjuna and specially the Yogācāra school.

(*b*) It is true that in some stanzas of this hymn we find the tendency to sublimate Buddha's body, attributing to it supernatural qualities and powers, for example stanza 16: *resplendent body*; stanza 18: *lack of all the characteristics common to any body*; stanza 19: *non-existence in it of illness etc.*; stanza 23: *ubiquity*.

We must indicate also that some stanzas express the idea (which will have great importance in later Buddhology) of the adequation of Buddha to the spiritual needs of his devotees, for example stanzas 19, 20 and 22.

We must mention also the docetic position which is found in some stanzas as 18, 19, 20 and 22: Buddha's body and his activity are a mere appearance. Finally, in some stanzas of these hymns there is an absolutist presentation of Buddha, as in *Niraupamya* 8, 12, 25, and *Paramārtha* 1, 4, 5, 6, 7, 8. This fact can be understood as a mere application to Buddha of the principle of Voidness—the Absolute of Nāgārjuna's school which is neither sacred nor divine, but only heterogenous in relation to the empirical reality. Cf. F. Tola and C. Dragonetti, 'Nāgārjuna's Conception of Voidness (*śūnyatā*)'. But from a religious point of view it is possible to think that these stanzas present Buddha as a divinized and sacralized Buddha.

(*c*) Although taking into account all these elements, it is possible to affirm that in these hymns we have the initial form of the Mahāyāna's doctrine of the three bodies of Buddha, in which these elements are integrated, however it seems not possible to affirm that in these hymns that doctrine is already neatly formulated. About the three bodies see the article of *Hōbōgirin* already quoted, pp. 174-85; L. de la Vallée Poussin, 'Note sur les Corps du Bouddha'; Chizen Akanuma, 'The Triple Body of the Buddha'; D.T. Suzuki, 'Outlines of Mahayana Buddhism', pp. 242-76; M.P. Masson-Oursel, 'Les trois corps du Bouddha'; N.N. Dutt, *Mahāyāna Buddhism*, p. 141; D.T. Suzuki, *Studies in the Lankavatara Sutra*, pp. 308-38; E. Conze, *Buddhist Thought*, pp. 232-34.

164. *Nirvṛti*, in the original, can be understood as the *nirvāṇa*. The Tibetan translation has *mya ṅan ḥdas pa*. According to Nāgārjuna not only birth (see stanza 12) but also *nirvāṇa* is void.

165. Devotion (*bhakti*) for Buddhas and Bodhisattvas is one of the elements that characterize Mahāyāna Buddhism in regard to Hīnayāna. It manifests itself in these hymns, although it does not appear in the great treatises of Nāgārjuna, in which *śūnyatā*'s notion lacks completely all sacralizing and deifying aspects. On *bhakti* in Buddhism in general and in these hymns specially, see E. Lamotte, *Histoire*, pp. 476-77; Ch. Eliot, *Hinduism and Buddhism*, pp. 3-35; M. Monier-Williams, *Buddhism*, pp. 195-222; L. de la Vallée Poussin, *Boudhisme*, pp. 205-24; L. de la Vallée Poussin, 'Mahāyāna', in Hastings, *ERE* VIII, pp. 330-36; Ruegg, *The Literature of the Madhyamaka School*, pp. 31-32 and 120-21. It is interesting to observe the similar situation we find in Śaṅkara: devotion appears only in his hymns (*stotras*) but not in his philosophical treatises and it is aimed not at *Brahman*, as the Absolute, but at some of the personal or theistic manifestations of *Brahman*. It is to the Buddhas and to the Bodhisattvas that the devotees direct their devotion.

166. *Anābhogena*, in the original. We have translated it by 'without effort'; it could be translated also by 'without any intervention or participation'.

167. In this stanza we find a reference to the Mahāyāna doctrine of merit's transfer.

168. The true nature of Buddha, Voidness, lies beyond mind.

169. *Anidarśana* in the original. Buddha cannot be indicated either by words, signs, symbols or comparisons.

170. Buddha taught Voidness exactly as he discovered it to be.

171. Fundamental Principle of Mahāyāna: conditioned beings and things are

neither really born nor really destroyed. Cf. *Lokātītastava* 4.

172. Whatever has not an own being is unreal like the rope which does not exist truly since it is only a conglomerate of threads in a certain position; 'rope' therefore is only a conventional way of indicating those threads as seemingly forming another entity.

173. I.e. depending on conditions and therefore it is only a mere illusion.

174. The magical illusion, the mirage etc. have a certain form of existence, an illusory one. This form of existence is the same form of existence of the empirical reality. It is this form of existence which allows the perception of the magical illusion etc. and of the empirical reality.

175. The magical illusion etc. mentioned in the foregoing stanza.

176. *Kṛtaka,* in the original means (1) made, fabricated, effected, artificial, and (2) false. Things made by the cooperation of causes and conditions are effected and therefore lack an own being and are unreal, like the rope which is only a conglomerate of threads but not something *in se et per se*.

177. In the sense that the appearance under which it presents itself does not correspond to its true nature.

178. *Utpitsuḥ,* as a masculine cannot go with *vastu;* we understand it as signifying the future (time).

179. What is produced does not really originate, since it is conditioned; therefore it cannot exist in any of the three times.

180. See *Lokātītastava* 13.

181. What does not exist has not an own being; nothing can be produced from something that has not an own being.

182. Things that seem to exist have not an own being, therefore there is not the possibility that something be produced from them. This stanza denies the possibility of the forthcoming of anything from a cause that has not an own being.

183. All is relative; 'one' exists only in relation to 'other'.

184. In the same way 'other' exists only in relation to 'one'.

185. Everything is relative: a thing is called 'other' in relation to another, that is called this 'one'.

186. Things in our empirical reality exist only in mutual relation.

187. Existence and non-existence, short and long.

188. I.e. not really existing since they are mutually conditioned.

189. They cannot exist *in se*, since they are mutually dependent.

190. See stanza 11 of this hymn.

191. The holding to the belief in things is groundless, since it is directed to a non-existing object.

192. All *dharmas* are identical among themselves, since Voidness is the only and true essence of them all; since they have never been produced really, it is logical to say that they have been always extinguished or nirvanized.

193. A plant whose trunk is formed by layers which do not cover anything. This plant is used as a symbol for inconsistency.

194. True knowledge of reality produces necessarily liberation. If the ignorant, without an intellectual and moral progess and a personal effort, could know reality as it truly is, then he would obtain immediately liberation,

and true knowledge would be unnecessary.

195. The senses are indistinct as knowledge produced by them is neither complete nor fully determinate.
196. Senses are unable to make us know the true nature of things.
197. Reason is also unable to grasp the true reality of things, Emptiness.
198. The Middle Doctrine (*madhyamā pratipād*) avoids equally the affirmation of being and of non-being. If things existed really, they would have a being that would be their own, and they would be eternal. If things do not exist, it would be impossible to explain the empirical reality that is the object of our experience. The Middle Doctrine does not accept either the existence with an own being nor the non-existence of everything. It affirms the illusory existence of the empirical reality, its existence only as a mental creation.
199. To be, not to be, to be and not be, not to be and not not to be.
200. They are conditioned and unreal.
201. Knowledge and moral discipline.
202. To believe in the true existence of the pairs of opposites that we perceive in the empirical reality is not true knowledge, since no one of the elements that constitute those pairs is real.
203. See stanza 17 and its note.
204. All is a mere illusory creation.
205. From the point of view of relative truth (*saṃvṛtisatya*) the numberless Buddhas have helped beings to obtain *nirvāṇa*, to be liberated, but from the point of view of supreme truth there is not in truth either *nirvāṇa* nor liberation. Next stanza explains why it is so.
206. Beings are extinguished, nirvanized *ab origine*, since they have never been really born; therefore, they cannot be liberated.
207. All that in the empirical reality is not a product of magic.
208. If the maker is also made, he is an effected being and consequently he is unreal.
209. One cannot be a maker without doing the action; therefore, the consequence is that it is the action which makes the maker.
210. Only conventional denominations. 'Car' is only a name to designate in a conventional way the totality of pieces that constitute the car. The car does not exist as such, *in se et per se*; only the pieces exist, and the pieces also are a conventional name to designate the elements that constitute them.
211. What is designated by the word has not a real existence, it exists only as a word.
212. Mind belongs also to the empirical reality and as such is also unreal.
213. This *kārikā* and the two next ones from a whole. They refer to the true reality, to Voidness.
214. Since existence and non-existence in reality 'do not exist'. Existence and non-existence do not exist really; neither does exist something beyond them.
215. It is only an object of the intuitive knowledge, which is produced during deep concentration.
216. Origination in Dependence and Voidness are the same and Buddhist

Doctrine is nothing else than the teaching of both and it is also void.

217. I.e. Voidness, that has been described in stanzas 37-39 and referred to in stanza 40.
218. The unalterable essence of something, its unalterable being so and not of another manner.
219. The 'substance' in the sense of 'that which is common to all', to which all is reduced when it is submitted to the abolishing analysis of Nāgārjuna's school.
220. In that all is Voidness.
221. Since Voidness is only the true nature of the empirical reality, all the beings and things are identical among themselves.
222. Voidness is not something different from the things; it constitutes their own nature; and things do not exist as something different from Voidness.
223. The empirical reality, a mere mental creation, which conceals the true form of being of things, Voidness.
224. Does not exist autonomously, it depends, in order to exist, on the mind that conceives it.
225. This *kārikā* opposes the true reality to the concealing or empirical reality. We have here the theory of the two truths which is fundamental in Nāgārjuna's school.
226. According to the grammatical construction the two first *pādas* of *kārikā* 45 must be joined to the last *pāda* of previous *kārikā*. The cataphatic description of true reality (*paramārtha*) is really surprising in the context of Mādhyamika school. For this reason we have added 'is called' in order to indicate that, since it does not depend on causes and conditions, the supreme reality could be considered an 'own being etc.' from the non-rigorous point of view of empirical conventions.
227. The last *pāda* of this stanza reads in Lindtner's text as follows: *paratantras tu vidyate* according to the Tokyo's and Gokhale's manuscripts. It seem strange that Nāgārjuna or any Mādhyamika philosopher could affirm that *dependent things*, produced out of causes and conditions, *exists*, what is against his most firm principles. So we have preferred to adopt the reading *na vidyate*, which is, as Lindtner says, p. 124, 'a *varia lectio* in the Sanskrit Ms (s) now presumably lost, but inferable from a recension of the Tibetan translation'.

    In the *kārikās* 44 and 45 we have the concepts of *paramārtha* (true reality), *paratantra* (dependent entity) and *kalpita* (imagined thing), which make us think on the theory of the three natures of the Yogācāra school. See F. Tola and C. Dragonetti, 'The Trisvabhāva of Vasubandhu'.
228. The attribution of some nature or some attributes to something which does not possess them.
229. What is produced has not an own being since it depends on causes, and what has not an own being does not really exist and consequently it cannot be really destroyed. In our empirical reality where nothing exists *in se et per se* birth and destruction are equally inadmissible.
230. If things possessed existence or non-existence as their own being, we would have *always* being or not being, since they could never abandon

their own being. We would have the doctrine of eternalism or nihilism.

231. In the second part of the *kārikā* is expressed the theory of Nāgārjuna that there is neither being nor non-being, only Voidness, unreality.

232. It is absurd to say about something, which is merely imagined, as the water of mirage or the world, that it ceases to be or that it eternally subsists. It is the illusion, which gives rise to the mirage's water or to the world, that can arise, remain or cease.

233. The person who considers the existence of beings and things with an own being can think about the possibility of the world being limited or non-limited in time; this possibility does not exist for the person who knows that the world is void and, as such, unreal.

234. If knowledge and its object (as the Mādhyamaka affirms) are non-existent, illusory as being mutually dependent, then nothing exists.

235. It is common in Buddhism the image of Buddha as the great physician and of his doctrine as the 'unsurpassable medicine' as is said in the following *kārikā*.

236. Reference to the classic examples of the Mādhyamaka school to illustrate the illusory, insubstantial character of all.

237. See *Dīgha Nikāya* I, 5, where it is found the idea that the best 'sacrifice' is the teaching of Buddha's doctrine.

238. The theory of Voidness is the central point of Buddha's doctrine and it is not necessary to recur to hermeneutic or interpretation to establish it or to grasp it.

239. The texts, in which Buddha refers to the indicated themes, must not be taken in their immediate meaning, but must be submitted to hermeneutic analysis in order to establish and grasp the true meaning which they express. When Buddha speaks birth etc., he is referring to them from the point of view of empirical reality or relative truth, without attributing to them a real existence.

240. The reference to jewels is because the ocean is considered by Indian tradition as the receptacle of great treasures.

241. On reaching the Perfection of knowledge he has realized Buddha's model.

242. Reference to the doctrine of transference of merit.

243. The title of this hymn, *Paramārthastava,* is translated by Tucci as: 'The Hymn to the Supreme Reality', and by de la Vallée Poussin as: 'Louange véritable' (from the Tibetan: *don dam par bstod*). We prefer to translate it as 'Hymn according to the Supreme truth', because it is an eulogy of Buddha from the point of view of the absolute truth.

244. Buddha is void, and consequently we cannot apply to him any of the characteristics of empirical reality that cannot be either applied to Voidness. This is the central idea of the whole hymn.

245. I.e. submitting myself to the uses and conventions which are a part of empirical reality.

246. See above note 165 of the translation of *Niraupamyastava*.

247. *Anutpannasvabhāvena*: literally 'owing to the non-produced own being'.

248. There is no difference between *saṃsāra* and *nirvāṇa* from the point of view of supreme truth, both are void, non-existent, do not constitute a 'place'

in which somebody can remain.

249. Buddha does not belong to the realm of empirical reality constituted by the totality of the *dharmas*.

250. The *dharmadhātu*, fundament of the *dharmas*, is Voidness, the ultimate essence of all, including Buddha.

251. The deepest 'level' of reality, Voidness.

252. Since all is unreal, non-existent, as being void, there is neither the person who praises nor the person who is praised, including Buddha.

253. Buddha, who traditionally is designated by the epithet of '*sugata*': 'well gone', from the point of view of supreme truth, is beyond movement including 'coming' to this world and 'going' from it.

254. New reference to the doctrine of transference of merit.

255. Gyis: *Peking*; *Sde-dge*: kyi.

256. Although the mind belongs to the empirical reality, it is the only means to produce liberation from empirical reality.

257. Liberation of course is not a deity and only metaphorically can it be called a god.

258. The five realms in which man can be reincarnated.

259. In some forms of meditation there is still some activity of the mind, like the perception of some natural or supernatural reality, or they require some material or imaginative support.

260. Imagining activity of the mind.

261. The mind which seeks illumination (*bodhicitta*).

262. The consciousness, thanks to which or in which illumination ('the jewel of the mind') is produced, is called 'Supreme Illumination'.

263. When mind ceases to function, i.e. to give rise to its mental creations, ceases also the apparent existence of the elements, which build up the body and also the empirical reality. They return to that state of original calm, to that state of nirvanization from which in truth they have never gone out.

264. Buddha's condition is obtained through the mind when its activity has ceased and it has liberated itself not only from emotional life but also from duality which is implied by the cognitive processes.

Bibliography

Advayavajra, *Advayavajrasaṃgraha*, edited by M.H. Shastri, Baroda: Oriental Institute, 1927 (Gaekwad's Oriental Series).

Ames, W.L., 'The Notion of *Svabhāva* in the Thought of Candrakīrti', in *Journal of Indian Philosophy*, vol. 10, no. 2, June 1982, pp. 161-77.

Amṛtākara, *Catuḥstavasamāsārtha*, in Tucci G., *Minor Buddhist Texts* I, pp. 233-46.

Anesaki, *M.*, 'Docetism (Buddhist)', in *ERE*, vol. IV, pp. 835-40.

Āryadeva, *Cittavisuddhiprakaraṇa*. Sanskrit and Tibetan Texts. Edited by P.B. Patel, Visva-Bharati, 1949.

Asaṅga, *Mahāyānasaṃgraha*: É. Lamottee, *La Somme du Grand Véhicule d'Asaṅga* (*Mahāyānasaṃgraha*), vol. I, II (ed. and trans.) Université de Louvain, Institut Orientaliste, Louvain-la-neuve, 1973.

Bareau, A., Schubring, W., von Fürer-Haimendorf, Chr., *Die Religionen Indiens III, Buddhismus-Jinismus-Primitivvölker*, Stuttgart, W. Kohlhammer Verlag, 1964.

Bhattacharya (Chakravarti), Bhaswati, 'The Concept of Existence and Nāgārjuna's Doctrine of Shūnyatā', in *Journal of Indian Philosophy*, vol. 7, no. 4, December 1979, pp. 335-44.

Bhattacharya, V., *The Āgamashāstra of Gaudapāda*, Calcutta, University of Calcutta, 1943.

Bstan-ḥgyur (*a*) *Sde-dge* ed.: *Sde dge Tibetan Tripiṭaka Bstan Ḥgyur preserved at the Faculty of Letters, University of Tokyo*, Tokyo: Tibetan Text Research Association—Sekai Seiten Kankō Kyōkai (The World Sacred Text Publication Society), 1977.
(*b*) *Peking* edn.: *Eiin Pekinhan Chibetto Daizōkyō* (*The Tibetan Tripiṭaka*), *Peking* Edition, compiled and edited by D.T. Suzuki and S. Yamaguchi, Tōkyo-Kyōto: Suzuki Research Foundation, 1955-61.

Buddhist Text Information, editor: Richard A. Gard, The Institute for Advanced Studies of World Religions, Melville Memorial Library, State University of New York at Stony Brook, USA,

December 1977 ss. *Cumulative Index*: it appears yearly.

'Busshin', in *Hōbōgirin* II, 1930, pp. 174b-185a.

Bu-ston, *History of Buddhism* (*Chos-ḥbyung*), Part I, *The Jewelry of Scripture*. Translated from Tibetan by E. Obermiller, Heidelberg, O. Harrassowitz, 1931 (Materialien zur Kunde des Buddhismus 18. Heft) (Reprint Series 5: Suzuki Research Foundation).

Candrakīrti, *Madhyamakaśāstrastuti*, in J.W. de Jong, 'La Madhyamakaśāstrastuti de Candrakīrti', in *Oriens Extremus, Zeitschrift für Sprache, Kunst und Kultur der Länder des Fernen Ostens*, Jahr 9, Februar 1962, Cuad. 1, pp. 47-56 (= J.W. de Jong, *Buddhist Studies*, edited by G. Schopen, Berkeley: Asian Humanities Press—Lancaster-Miller Publications, 1979, pp. 541-50).

——, *Madhyamakāvatāra*: *Madhyamakāvatāra par Candrakīrti*. Traduction tibétaine publiée par L. de la Vallée Poussin, Osnabrück, Biblio Verlag, 1970, and '*Madhyamakāvatāra*. Introduction au Traité du Milieu de L'Ācārya Candrakīrti avec la commentarie de l'auteur, traduit d'aprés la version tibétaine par L. de la Vallée Poussin,' *Le Muséon*, vol. VIII (1907), pp. 249-317, vol. IX (1910), pp. 271-358, vol. XII (1911), pp. 235-328.

——, *Prasannapadā*, in *Madhyamakaśāstra of Nāgārjuna, with the Commentary: Prasannapadā by Candrakīrti*, edited by P.L. Vaidya, Darbhanga, The Mithila Institute, 1960 (Buddhist Sanskrit Texts No. 10) and in *Madhyamakavṛttiḥ, Mūlamadhyamakakārikās* (*Mādhyamikasūtras*) *de Nāgārjuna, avec le Prasannapadā, Commentaire de Candrakīrti*, publiée par L. de la Vallée Poussin, Osnabrück, Biblio Verlag, 1970 (Neudruck der Ausgabe 1903-1913).

Catalogue of Indian (*Buddhist*) *Texts in Tibetan translation, Kanjur & Tanjur* (*alphabetically rearranged*) *vol. I Texts* (*Indian titles*) *in Tanjur*, A. Chattopadhyaya in collaboration with M. Gangopadhyaya, D. Chattopadhyaya, Calcutta, Indo-Tibetan Studies, 1972.

Catalogue: *The Tibetan Tripiṭaka, Peking Edition—Kept in the Library of the Otani University, Kyoto*. Reprinted under the Supervision of the Otani University, Kyoto. Edited by D.T. Suzuki, *Catalogue & Index*, Tokyo: Suzuki Research Foundation, 1962.

Conze, E., *Buddhist Thought in India: Three Phases of Buddhist Philosophy*, London: G. Allen & Unwin, 1962.

——, *Thirty Years of Buddhist Studies*, London: O. Cassirer, 1967.

Crittenden, Ch., 'Everyday Reality as Fiction: A Mādhyamika Interpretation', in *Journal of Indian Philosophy*, vol. IX, no. 4, December 1981, pp. 323-33.

Chakravarti, S., 'The Mādhyamika *Catuśkoti* or Tetralemma', in *Journal of Indian Philosophy*, vol. VIII, no. 3, September 1980, pp. 303-06.

——, The Philosophy of Non-involvement of the Mādhyamikas', in *Journal of Indian Philosophy* vol. X, no. 4, December 1982, pp. 397-403.

Chatterjee, A.K., *The Yogācāra Idealism*, Delhi, Motilal Banarsidass, 1975.

Chatterjee, Sastri, H., *The Philosophy of Nāgārjuna, as Contained in the Ratnāvalī*, Part I, Calcutta: Saraswat Library, 1977.

Chizen, A., 'The Triple Body of the Buddha', in *The Eastern Buddhist*, May-June, July-August, 1922, pp. 1-29.

Daijō Butten ('Literature of Mahāyāna Buddhism'), 14, Tokyo, 1975.

Dasgupta, S., *A History of Indian Philosophy*, III, Cambridge, University Press, 1961.

——, *A History of Indian Philosophy*, Volume I, Cambridge, Cambridge Univesity Press, 1963.

——, *Indian Idealism*, Cambridge, University Press, 1962.

de Jong, J.W., *Cinq Chapitres de la Prasannapadā*, Introduction, Paris: P. Geuthner, 1949.

——, 'Emptiness', in *Journal of Indian Philosophy*, vol. II, no. 1, December 1972, pp. 7-15.

——, 'La Madhyamakaśāstrastuti de Candrakīrti', in *Oriens Extremus*, 9, 1, February 1962, pp. 47-56.

——, 'Le problème de l'absolu dans l'école Madhyamaka', in *Revue Philosophique de la France et de l'étranger* CXL, 1950, pp. 323-47.

——, 'The Problem of the Absolute in the Madhyamaka School', in *Journal of Indian Philosophy*, vol. II, no. 1, December 1972, pp. 1-6.

de la Vallée Poussin, L., 'Bodhisattva', in *ERE* vol. II, pp. 739-53.

——, *Bouddhisme, Opinions sur l'Histoire de la Dogmatique*, Paris: G. Beauchesne, 1925 (Études sur l'Histoire des Religions 2).

——, 'Buddhica', in *Harvard Journal of Asian Studies* III, pp. 146-58.

——, 'Les Quatre Odes de Nāgārjuna', in *Le Muséon*, nouvelle série 14, Paris, 1913, pp. 1-18.

——, 'Madhyamaka', in *Mélanges Chinois et Bouddhiques* 2, 1932-33, pp. 1-146.

——, 'Mahāyāna', in *ERE*, vol. VIII, pp. 330a-336b.

——, 'Note et Bibliographie Bouddhiques', in *Mélanges Chinois et Bouddhiques*, 1932, pp. 379-424.

——, 'Note sur les Corps du Bouddha', in *Le Muséon*, 1913, pp. 257-90.

——, *Vijñaptimātratāsiddhi, La Siddhi de Hiuan-Tsang,* traduite et annotée par..., Tome I (1928), Tome II (1929), Paris, Paul Geuthner.

della Santina, P., 'The Division of the Mādhyamika System into the Prāsaṅgika and Svātantrika Schools', in *The Journal of Religious Studies*, vol. VII, no. 2, Autumn 1979, Punjabi University, Patiala (India), pp. 40-49.

Dīgha Nikāya I, General Editor Bhikkhu J. Kashyap, Bihar: Pāli Publication Board, Bihar Government, 1958 (Nālandā-Devanāgarī-Pāli-Series).

Dragonetti, C., *Dhammapada, El camino del dharma*, Buenos Aires, Sudamericana, 1967.

——, *Udāna. La Palabra de Buda*, Barcelona, Barral Editores, 1971.

——, *Catustava de Nāgārjuna*, I, Buenos Aires, Centro de Investigaciones Filosóficas, 1978 (Textos sánscritos, tibetanos y chinos del Budismo Mahāyāna).

——, 'Niraupamyastava y Paramārthastava: dos Himnos del *Catustava* de Nāgārjuna conservados en sánscrito', in *Oriente-Occidente*, Año III, Número 2, 1982, pp. 249-87.

——, 'On Śuddhamati's Pratītyasamutpādahṛdayakārikā and on Bodhicittavivaraṇa', in *Wiener Zeitschrift für die Kunde Sūdasiens und Archiv für indische Philosophie*, 1986.

Dutt, N., *Mahāyāna Buddhism*, Delhi: Motilal Banarsidass, 1977.

——, 'The Place of the Āryasatyas and Pratītyasamutpāda in Hīnayāna and Mahāyāna', in *Annals of the Bhandarkar Oriental Research Institute*, Poona, vol. XI, January 1930, Part II, pp. 101-27.

Edgerton, F., *Buddhist Hybrid Sanskrit*, vols. I: *Grammar*, II: *Dictionary*, New Haven-London: Yale University Press-Oxford University Press, 1953.

Eliot, Ch., *Hinduism and Buddhism. An Historical Sketch*, vol. II, London: Routledge & Kegan Paul, 1962.

ERE (J. Hastings, *Encyclopaedia of Religion and Ethics*), Edinburgh:

T. & T. Clark, 1964.

Faddegon, B., *The Vaiśeṣika-System, Described with the Help of the Oldest Texts*, Wiesbaden, Martin Sändig, 1969.

Fatone, V., *El Budismo 'nihilista', en Obras Completas* II, Buenos Aires: Sudamericana, 1972, pp. 16-156. There is an English translation of this work, published in Delhi by Motilal Banarsidass.

Fenner, P.G., 'A Reconstruction of the *Madhyamakāvatāra*'s Analysis of Person', in *The Journal of the International Association of Buddhist Studies*, vol. VI, no. 2, 1983, pp. 17-34.

Frauwallner, E., 'Dignāga, sein Werk und seine Entwicklung', in *Wiener Zeitschrift für die Kunde Süd-und Ost-Asiens und Archiv für indische Philosohie* 3, 1959, pp. 83-164. (=E. Frauwallner, *Kleine Schriften*, pp. 759-841).

——, *Die Philosophie des Buddhismus*, Berlin: Akademie Verlag, 1969.

Gangopadhyaya, M., *Indian Atomism: History and Sources*, Calcutta, K.P. Bagchi & Company, 1980.

Gnoli, R., *Nāgārjuna, Le stanze del Cammino di Mezzo*, (Madhyamaka kārikā), Torino, Boringhieri, 1979.

Gokhale, V.V., 'Encore: the Pratītyasamutpādahṛdayakārikā of Nāgājuna', (in collaboration with M.G. Dhadphale) in *Princ. V.S. Apte Commemoration Volume*, ed. by M.G. Dhadphale, D.E. Society, Fergusson College, Poona, 1978.

Gómez Rodríguez, L.O., 'Consideraciones en torno al Absoluto de los Budistas', in *Estudios de Asia y África*, vol. X, no. 2, 1975, pp. 97-154.

Haribhadra, *Āloka* in *Abhisamayālaṃkārāloka*, ed. U. Wogihara, Tokyo, 1932-35; and in *Aṣṭasāhasrikā*, ed. P.L. Vaidya, Darbhanga, The Mithila Institute, 1960.

Hastings, J., *Encyclopaedia of Religion and Ethics*, Edinburgh, T.& T. Clark, 1964.

Hattori, M., 'Dignāga ni okeru kashō to Jitsuzai' ('Opinion of Dignāga on *samvṛti-sat* and *paramārtha-sat*'), in *F.A.S.* Zen Institute, Kyoto, pp. 16-28.

——, *Dignāga, On Perception, being the Pratyakṣapariccheda* of *Dignāga's Prāmaṇasamuccaya from the Sanskrit fragments and the Tibetan versions*, Translated and Annotated by. . ., Cambridge, Mass., Harvard University Press, 1968.

Hiuan Tsang, *Vijñaptimātratāsiddhi, La Siddhi de Hiuan-Tsang,* traduite et annotée par L. de la Vallée Poussin, Paris, P. Geuthner, 1928.

Hōbōgirin: *Hōbōgirin. Dictionnaire Encyclopédique du Bouddhisme d'après les sources chinoises et japonaises*, publié sous le haut patronage de L'Académie Impériale du Japon et sous la direction de S. Lévi et. J. Takakusu, rédacteur en chef P. Demiéville, *Deuxième Fascicule*, Tōkyō: Maison Franco-Japonaise, 1930. *Fascicule Annexe*: Tables du *Taishō Issaikyō*, Tōkyō: Maison Franco-Japonaise, 1931. *Répertoire du Canon Bouddhique Sino-japonais. Édition de Taishō*, compilé par P. Demiéville, H. Durt, A. Seidel, *Fascicule Annexe du Hōbōgirin*, Deuxième Édition révisée et augmentée, Paris-Tōkyō: Maison Franco-Japonaise, 1978.

Huntington, C.W., Jr., 'The System of the Two Truths in the Prasannapadā and the Madhyamakāvatāra: A Study in Mādhyamika Soteriology', in *Journal of Indian Philosophy*, vol. XI, no. 1, March 1983, pp. 77-106.

Ichimura, S., 'A Study of the Mādhyamika Method of Refutation, Especially of its Affinity to that of *Kathāvatthu*', in *The Journal of the International Association of Buddhist Studies*, vol. III, no. 1, 1980, pp. 7-15.

——, 'A Study on the Mādhyamika Method of Refutation and its Influence on Buddhist Logic', in *The Journal of the International Association of Buddhist Studies*, vol. IV, no. 1, 1981, pp. 87-95.

——, 'A New Approach to the Intra-Mādhyamika Confrontation over the Svātantrika and Prāsaṅgika Methods of Refutation', in *The Journal of the International Association of Buddhist Studies*, vol. V, no. 2, 1982, pp. 41-52.

IHQ= Indian Historical Quarterly.

Jacobi, H., 'Atomic Theory (Indian)', in Hastings *Encyclopaedia of Religion and Ethics*, vol. II, pp. 199-202.

Jñānaśrīmitra, *Sākārasaṃgrahasūtra*, in *Jñānaśrīmitranibandhāvalī*, edited by Anantalal Thakkur, Patna, Tibetan Sanskrit Works Series, 1959.

Jones, E.W., 'Buddhist Theories of Existents: The Systems of Two Truths', in *Mahāyāna Buddhist Meditation: Theory and Practice*, ed. by Minoru Kiyota, ass. by Elvin W. Jones, Honolulu: The University Press of Hawaii, 1978, pp. 3-45.

JRAS=Journal of the Royal Asiatic Society.

Kajiyama, Y., 'Later Mādhyamikas on Epistemology and Meditation', in *Mahāyāna Buddhist Meditation. Theory and Practice*, ed. by Minoru Kiyota, ass. by Elvin W. Jones, Honolulu: The University Press of Hawaii, 1978, pp. 114-43.

——, 'The Atomic Theory of Vasubandhu, the Author of the Abhidharmakośa', in *Indogaku Bukkyo Kenkyu* 38, 1971, pp. 1001-06.

Katyāyāna, *Vārttika*, see Patañjali, *Vyākaraṇa-mahā-bhāṣya*.

Keith, A.B., *Indian Logic and Atomism: An Exposition of the Nyāya and Vaiśeṣika System*, New York, Greenwood Press, Publishers, 1968.

Koseki, A.K., "'Later Mādhyamika' in China: Some Current Perspectives on the History of Chinese *Prajñāpāramitā* Thought", in *The Journal of the International Association of Buddhist Studies*, vol. V, no. 2, 1982.

Kitayama, J., *Metaphysik des Buddhismus, Versuch einer philosophischen Interpretation der Lehre Vasubandhus und seiner Schule*, San Francisco, Chinese Materials Centre, Inc., 1976 (reprint of the edition of Stuttgart-Berlin, Verlag von W. Kohlhammer, 1934).

Kunjunni Raja, K., *New Catalogus Catalogorum. An Alphabetical Register of Sanskrit and Allied Works and Authors*, vol. IX, Madras, University of Madras, 1977.

Lai, W., 'Chou Yung vs. Shang Jung (on *Shūnyatā*); The *Pen-mo Yu-wu* Controversy in Fifth-Century China', in *The Journal of the International Association of Buddhist Studies*, vol. I, no. 2, 1979, pp. 23-44.

——, " 'Non-duality of the Two Truths in Sinitic Mādhyamika: Origin of the 'Third Truth'", in *The Journal of the International Association of Buddhist Studies*, vol. II, no. 2, 1979, pp. 45-65.

Lalou, M., *Répertoire du Tanjur d'après le Catalogue de P. Cordier*, Paris, Bibliothèque Nationale, 1933.

Lamotte, É., *Histoire du Bouddhisme Indien. Des Origines à l'ère Śaka*. Louvain: Publications Universitaires—Université de Louvain, Institut Orientaliste, 1958 (Bibliothèque du *Muséon*, vol. 43).

——, *L'enseignement de Vimalakīrti*, Introduction, Louvain: Institut Orientaliste de Louvain, 1976, Tome IV, pp. 1995-2042.

——, *Le Traité de la Grande Vertu de Sagesse de Nāgārjuna (Mahāprajñāparamitāshāstra) avec une nouvelle Introduction*, Tome III, Chapitres 31, 42, Louvain: Université de Louvain-Institut

Orientaliste, 1970 (Publications de l'Institut Orientaliste de Louvain 2).

Lancaster, L., ed., *Prajñāpāramitā and Related Systems: Studies in Honor of Edward Conze*, Ass. Ed. Luis O. Gómez, Korea: Berkeley Buddhist Studies Series, 1977.

Lindtner, Chr., 'Candrakīrti's Pañcaskandhaprakaraṇa. I. Tibetan Text', in *Acta Orientalia* XL, Copenhagen, Munskgaard, 1979, pp. 77-145.

——, *Juvelkaeden og andre skrifter*, Kobenhavn, Sankt Ansgars Forlag (Visdoms Bogerne), 1980.

——, *Nāgārjunas Filosofiske Vaerker, Nāgārjunīyam Madhyamakashāstram*, Kobenhavn, Akademisk Forlag, 1982.

——, *Nagarjuniana. Studies in the Writings and philosophy of Nāgārjuna*, Copenhagen: Akademisk Forlag, 1982 (Indiske Studier IV). Review-Article by P. Williams, in *Journal of Indian Philosophy*, vol. XII, no. 1, March 1984, pp. 73-104.

LM = Le Muséon.

Mandana Miśra, *Brahmasiddhi, Brahmakhaṇḍa*, translated by T. Vetter, Wien, Österreichische Akademie der Wissenschaften, 1969.

——, *Brahmasiddhi*, with the commentary of Shaṅkhapāni, edition by S. Kuppuswami Sastri, Delhi, Sri Satguru Publications, 1984.

Masson-Oursel, P., 'L'atomisme indien', in *Revue Philosophique (de la France et de l'étranger)*, Paris, 99, 1925, pp. 342-68.

——, 'Les trois corps du Bouddha', in *Journal Asiatique*, 1913, pp. 581-618.

Masuda, J., *Der individualistische Idealismus der Yogācāra-Schule. Versuch einer genetischen Darstellung*, Heidelberg, O. Harrassowitz, 1926. (Materialien zur Kunde des Buddhismus, Herausgegeben von M. Walleser, 10. Heft).

Matilal, B.K., *Epistemology, Logic and Grammar in Indian Philosophical Analysis*, The Hague: Mouton, 1971, pp. 146-67.

May, J., *Candrakīrti Prasannapadā Madhyamakavṛtti*, Introduction, Paris: Maisonneuve, 1959.

——, 'Chugan' (Mādhyamika), in *Hōbōgirin* V, 1979, pp. 470-93.

——, 'Kant et le Madhyamaka: A propos d'un livre récent', in *Indo-Iranian Journal* 3, 1959, pp. 102-11.

——, 'La Philosophie buddhique de la vacuité', in *Studia Philosophica* (Basle) 18, 1958, pp. 123-37.

——, 'On Mādhyamika Philosophy', in *Journal of Indian Philosophy*, vol. VI, no. 3, November 1978, pp. 233-41.

Monier-Williams, M., *Buddhism in its Connexion with Brāhmanism and Hindūism, and in its Contrast with Christianity*, Varanasi, India: The Chowkhamba Sanskrit Series Office, 1964 (The Chowkhamba Sanskrit Studies, vol. XLV).

Murti, T.R.V., *The Central Philosophy of Buddhism. A Study of the Mādhyamika System*, London, George Allen and Unwin Ltd., 1960.

Naḍapāda (Nāropā), *Sekoddeśaṭīkā*, being a commentary of the Sekoddeśa Section of the Kālācakra Tantra. The Sanskrit Text edited by Mario E. Carelli, Baroda, Oriental Institute, 1941.

Nagao, G., 'From Mādhyamika to Yogācāra, an Analysis of MMK, XXIV and MV, I. 1-2', in *The Journal of the International Association of Buddhist Studies*, vol. II no. 1, 1979, pp. 29-43.

——, "'What Remains' in Śūnyatā: A Yogācāra Interpretation of Emptiness", in *Mahāyāna Buddhist Meditation. Theory and Practice*, ed. por Minoru Kiyota, ass. by Elvin W. Jones, Honolulu: The University Press of Hawaii, 1978, pp. 66-82.

Nāgārjuna, *Madhyamakaśāstra, with the Commentary: Prasannapadā by Candrakīrti*, edited by P.L. Vaidya, Darbhanga: Mithila Institute, 1960 (Buddhist Sanskrit Texts no. 10).

——, *Mūlamadhyamakakārikās (Mādhyamikasūtras) de. . . , avec la Prasannapadā, commentaire de Candrakīrti*, publ. par L. de la Vallée Poussin, St. Pétersbourg: 1903-13 (Académie des Sciences) (Bibliotheca Buddhica, IV) reprint: Osnabrück: Biblio Verlag, 1970.

(——), *Pañcakrama*, par L. de la Vallée Poussin, Gand-Louvain: Recueil de Travaux publiés par la Faculté de Philosophie et Lettres de l'Université de Gand, 1896 (Études et Textes Tantriques).

(——), *Pratītyasamutpādahṛdayakārikā*, see Gokhale, V.V.

——, *Yuktiṣaṣṭikā*, see Tola, F. and Dragonetti, C., '*The Yuktiṣaṣṭikākārikā* of Nāgārjuna'.

Nagasawa, J., 'Kanyaku nihon Taisho chibetto Yaku Shuryō Ron Chū Wa Yaku', in *Chizan Gakuho* No. 4, 19, pp. 46-56.

Nanjio, B., *A Catalogue of the Chinese Translation of the Buddhist Tripiṭaka. The Sacred Canon of the Buddhists in China and Japan*, San Francisco (USA), Chinese Materials Centre, Inc., 1975 (Reprint: edition of Oxford, 1983).

Naudou, J., *Les Bouddhistes Kashmīriens au Moyen Age*, Paris, Presses Universitaires de France, 1968.

NBGN=Nihon

Nihon Bukkyō Gakkai Nenpō (Journal of the Nippon Buddhist Research Association).

Nyāyasūtras: Nyāyadarśanam, with Vātsyāyana's *Bhāṣya,* Uddyotakara's *Vārttika,* Vācaspati Miśra's *Tātparyaṭīkā* and Viśvanātha's *Vṛtti,* vol. I y II, Kyoto, Rinsen Book Co., 1982.

Panikkar, R., "The 'Crisis' of Mādhyamika and Indian Philosophy', in *Philosophy East and West,* vol. XVI, nos. 3 and 4, July-Oct., 1966.

Pāṇini, *The Ashtādhyāyī of...,* Edited and translated into English by Śriśa Candra Vasu, Delhi: Motilal Banarsidass, 1962.

Patañjali, *Vyākaraṇa-mahābhāṣya,* ed. Haryāṇā-sāhitya-samsthāna, 1962.

Patel, P., 'Catustava', in *Indian Historical Quarterly* 8, 1932, pp. 316-31, 689-705.

——, 'Catustava', in *Indian Historical Quarterly* 10, 1934, pp. 82-89.

Peking ed. see *Bstan-ḥgyur.*

Potter, K.H., *Bibliography of Indian Philosophies,* Delhi: Motilal Banarsidass, 1970 (American Institute of Indian Studies).

——, *Encyclopedia of Indian Philosophies. Bibliography,* compiled by..., Delhi, Motilal Banarsidass, 1983.

Prajñākaramati, *Pañjikā,* in *Bodhicaryāvatāra of Śāntideva, with the Commentary Pañjikā of Prajñākaramati,* Edited by P.L. Vaidya, Darbhanga, The Mithila Institute, 1960 (Buddhist Sanskrit Texts no. 12) and in *Bibliotheca Indica* 150, Calcutta, 1901-14, edited by L. de la Vallée Poussin.

——, *Pañjikā* in *Bodhicaryāvatāra, with the Commentary of Prajñākaramati.* Edited with Intr. by L. de la Vallée Poussin, Calcutta: Asiatic Society, 1904-14 (*Bibliotheca Indica,* nos. 983. 1031, 1090, 1126, 1139, 1305, 1399).

Pratītyasamutpādahṛdayakārikā, See Gokhale, V.V.

Quiles, I., 'El absoluto budista como 'vacío' (śūnya), según Nagarjuna', in *Stromata* 22, 1966, pp. 3-24.

Raju, P.T., *Idealistic Thought of India, Vedānta and Buddhism in the Light of Western Idealism,* New York, Johnson Reprint Corporation, 1973.

Ramanan, K.V., *Nāgārjuna's Philosophy, As presented in the*

Mahāprajñāpāramitā-Śāstra, Delhi, Motilal Banarsidass, 1975.

Ratnakīrti, *Nibandhāvaliḥ*, ed. A. Thakur, Patna, Kashi Prasad Jayaswal Research Institute, 1975.

Répertoire, See Hōbōgirin.

Riepe Dale, *The Naturalistic Tradition in Indian Thought*, Delhi, Motilal Banarsidass, 1964.

Rigvedaprātiśākhya, ed. Vīrendra Kumāra Varmā, Varanasi: The Banaras Hindu University Sanskrit Series, 1970.

Robinson, R.H., *Early Mādhyamika in India and China*, Madison: Wisconsin University, 1967.

——, 'Some Logical Aspects of Nāgārjuna's System', in *Philosophy East and West* 6, 1957, pp. 291-308.

Rosenberg, O., *Die Probleme der buddhistische Philosophie*, San Francisco (USA), Chinese Materials Centre, 1976.

Ruegg, D.S., 'Le Dharmadhātustava', in *Études Tibétaines dediées à la mémoire de Marcelle Lalou*, Paris, 1971, pp. 448-72.

——, 'Mathematical and Linguistic Models in Indian Thought: The case of *śūnyatā*', in *Wiener Zeitschrift für die Kunde Südasiens und Archiv für indische Philosophie*, her. von G. Oberhammer, Band XXII, 1978, pp. 171-81.

——, *The Literature of the Madhyamaka School of Philosophy in India*, Wiesbaden: Otto Harrassowitz, 1981 (*A History of Indian literature*, ed. by Jan Gonda, vol. VII, Fasc. 1).

——, 'The Uses of the Four Positions of the *Catuśkoti* and the Problem of the Description of Reality in Mahāyāna Buddhism', in *Journal of Indian Philosophy*, vol. V, Nos. 1-2, Sept.-Dec., 1977, pp. 1-71.

Sakei, D., 'Ryūju ni kiserareru Sanka—toku ni Shi San ni tsuite', ('Hymns attributed to Nāgārjuna—specially concerning with the Four Hymns'), in *Nihon Bukkyō Gakkai Nenpō* ('Journal of the Nippon Buddhist Research Association'), no. 24, 1959, pp. 1-44.

Śālistambasūtra, in *Ārya Śālistamba Sūtra, Pratītyasamutpādavibhaṅganirdeśa Sūtra and Pratītyasamutpādagātha Sūtra, edited with Tibetan versions, notes and introduction, etc.* by N. Aiyaswami Śastri, Adyar: Adyar Library, 1950.

Samdhong Rinpoche ed. and Mani, C., ass. ed., *Madhyamika Dialectic and the Philosophy of Nagarjuna, with an Introduction by T.R.V. Murti*, Sarnath (India): A Tibetan Institute Publication, 1977 (The Dalai Lama Tibetan Indology Studies, Vol. 1).

Śaṅkara, *Brahmasūtṛabhāṣya*, edition by Anantakṛṣṇa Śāstrī, Bombay, Nirṇaya Sāgar Press, 1938.

Śaṅkara's *Upadeśasāhasrī*, edition by S. Mayeda, Tokyo, Hokuseido Press, 1973.

Śāntideva, *Bodhicharyāvatāra*, see Prajñākaramati.

Schäffer, Phil., *Yuktiṣaṣṭikā, Die 60 Sätze des Negativismus, nach der chinesischen Version übersetzt*, Heidelberg, Materialien zur Kunde des Buddhismus-3. Heft, 1923.

Schayer, St., *Ausgewählte Kapitel aus der Prasannapadā*, Kraków: Polska Akademja Uniejetności, Prace Komisji Orjentalistyacznej, no. 14, 1931.

——, 'Das Māhāyanistische Absolutum nach der Lehre der Mādhyamikas', in *Orientalischer Literaturzeitung*, XXXVIII/ 7, Julio, 1935, pp. 401-15.

Schlingloff, D., *Buddhistische Stotras aus ostturkistanischen Sanskrit texten*, Berlin: Akademie Verlag, 1955.

Sde-dge edition, see: *Bstan-ḥgyur*.

Sekoddeśaṭīkā, *See*: Naḍapāda (Nāropā).

Sampā Dorje, *see: Śūnyatāsaptatiḥ*.

Siderits, M., 'The Madhyamaka Critique of Epistemology. I', in *Journal of Indian Philosophy*, vol. VIII, no. 4, Dec. 1980, pp. 307-35.

——, 'The Madhyamaka Critique of Epistemology. II', in *Journal of Indian Philosophy*, vol. IX, no. 2, June 1981, pp. 121-60.

Silburn, L., *Le Bouddhisme*, Paris, 1977.

Sprung, M., 'Non-Cognitive Language in Mādhyamika Buddhism', in *Buddhist Thought and Asian Civilisation. Essays in Honor of Herbert V. Guenther*, ed. by Leslie S. Kawamura and Keith Scott, Emeryville, California: Dharma Publishing, 1977.

Stcherbatsky, Th., 'Die drei Richtungen in der Philosophie des Buddhismus', in *Rocznik Orjentalistyczny*, 10, 1934, pp. 1-37.

——, *Madhyānta Vibhaṅga*, Introduction, Calcutta: Indian Studies, 1971.

——, *The Conception of Buddhist Nirvāṇa*, The Hague: Mouton & Co., 1965.

Sthiramati, *Madhyānta-vibhāga-śāstra, Containing the Kārikās of Maitreya, Bhāṣya of Vasubandhu and Ṭīkā by...*, Critical edition by R. Pandeya, Delhi, Motilal Banarsidass, 1971.

Streng, F.J., *Emptiness. Study in Religious Meaning*, Nashville, New York: Abingdon Press, 1967.

Śūnyatāsaptatiḥ, ed. Sempā Dorje, Sarnath, Central Institute of Higher Studies, 1985.

Suzuki, D.T., *Outlines of Mahayana Buddhism*, New York: Schocken Books, 1973.

——, *Studies in the Lankavatara Sutra, One of the most important texts of Mahayana Buddhism, in which almost all its principal tenets are presented, including the teaching of Zen*, London and Boston: Routledge & Kegan Paul, 1972.

Subhāṣitasaṃgraha. An anthology of extracts from Buddhist works compiled by an unknown author, to illustrate the doctrines of scholastic and of mystic (Tantric) Buddhism. Edited by C. Bendall, *Le Muséon*, nouvelle série, IV, 1903,pp. 375-402; V, 1904, pp. 5-46 and 245-74.

Sweet, M., '*Bodhicaryāvatāra* 9:2 as a Focus for Tibetan Interpretations of the Two Truths in the Prāsaṅgikā Mādhyamika', in *The Journal of the International Association of Buddhist Studies*, vol. II, no. 2, 1979, pp. 79-89.

Taishō: Taishō Shinshu Daizōkyō (The Tripiṭaka in Chinese). Revised, collated, added and rearranged, together with the original Treatises by Chinese, Korean and Japanese Authors, edited by J. Takakusu, K. Watanabe, First Edn. 1925, Reprint: Tokyo, The Taisho Shinshu Daizokyo Kanko Kai, 1960 ff.

Taittirīya-prātiśākhya with the Bhāṣya Padakramasadana of Māhiṣeya, Critical edition with appendices by V. Venkatarama Sharma, New Delhi: Panini Vaidika Granthamala 4, 1982.

Takakusu, J., *The Essentials of Buddhist Thought*, London: Routledge & Kegan Paul, 1963.

Thomas, F.W. and Ui, H., 'The Hand Treatise', a work of Āryadeva', in *Journal of the Royal Asiatic Society* 1918 (April), Vols. I & II, pp. 267-310.

Thurman, R.A., 'Transcendence and the Sacred in the Mahāyāna Middle Way', in *The Journal of Religious Studies*, vol. VIII, no. 1, Spring 1980, pp. 32-50.

Tōhoku: A Complete Catalogue of the Tibetan Buddhist Canons (Bkaḥ-ḥgyur and Bstan-ḥgyur), edited by H. Ui, M. Suzuki, Y. Kanakura, T. Tada, Sendai, Japan: Tōhoku Imperial University-Saitō Gratitude Foundation, 1934.

Tola, F. and Dragonetti, C., 'La doctrina del vacío en la escuela *Madhyamaka* y el *Hastavālanāmprakaraṇa*', in *Revista Latinoamericana de Filosofía*, vol. III, no. 2, Julio 1977, (Buenos

Aires, Argentina), pp. 159-75.

——, 'La doctrina de los *dharmas* en el Budismo', in *Boletín de la Asociación Española de Orientalistas*, Año XIII, 1977, Madrid, pp. 105-32 (pp. 91-121 F. Tola y C. Dragonetti, *Yoga y Mística de la India*.

——, *Yoga y Mística de la India*, Buenos Aires, Editorial Kier, 1978.

——, 'Saṃsāra, anāditva y nirvāṇa', in *Boletín de la Asociación Española de Orientalistas* Año XV, Madrid, 1979, pp. 95-114.

——, *El Budismo Mahāyāna. Estudios y Textos*, Buenos Aires, Kier, 1980.

——, 'The Hastavālanāmaprakaraṇavṛtti' in *The Journal of Religious Studies*, vol. VII, Spring 1980, no. 1, Punjabi University, Patiala, India, pp. 18-31.

——, '*Anāditva* or beginninglessness in Indian Philosophy', in *Annals of the Bhandarkar Oriental Research Institute*, vol. LXI, Parts I-IV, Poona, 1981, pp. 1-20.

——, "Nāgārjuna's Conception of 'Voidness' (Śūnyatā)", in *Journal of Indian Philosophy*, vol. IX, no. 3, sept. 1981, Dordrecht/ Boston, pp. 273-82.

——, '*Yuktiṣaṣṭikākārikā*. Las sesenta estrofas de la argumentación de Nāgārjuna', in *Boletín de la Asociación Española de Orientalistas*, Año XIX, Madrid, 1983, pp. 5-38.

——, 'The Trisvabhāvakārikā of Vasubandhu', in *Journal of Indian Philosophy*, vol. XI, no. 3, Sept. 1983, pp. 225-66.

——, 'The *Yuktiṣaṣṭikākārikā* of Nāgārjuna', in *The Journal of the International Association of Buddhist Studies*, vol. VI, no. 2, 1983, pp. 94-123.

——, 'Review on *Nagarjuniana. Studies in the Writings and Philosophy of Nāgārjuna* by Chr. Lindtner. Akademisk Forlag: Cophenhagen, 1982, pp. 327 (Indiske Studies IV), in *The Journal of the International Association of Buddhist Studies*, vol. VIII, no. 1, 1985, pp. 115-17.

——, "'La *Hastavālanāmaprakaraṇavṛtti*' de Āryadeva", in *Boletín de la Asociación Española de Orientalistas*, Año XXI, Madrid, 1985, pp. 137-55.

——, 'Nāgārjuna's Catustava', in *Journal of Indian Philosophy*, vol. XIII, 1985, no. 1, pp. 1-54.

——, *El Idealismo Budista*, México, Premiá, 1987.

Tosaki, Hiromasa, *Bukkyō Ninshikiron no Kenkyū*, I, Tokyo, Daitō Shuppansha, 1979.

Tucci, G., *Minor Buddhist Texts*, Part I, Roma: Istituto Italiano per il Medio ed Estremo Oriente, 1956 (Serie Orientale Roma, vol. IX).

——, 'Studi Mahāyānici', in *Rivista degli Studi Orientali (Roma)*, 10, 1923-24, pp. 521-90.

——, 'The Two Hymns of the Catuḥstava of Nāgārjuna', in *Journal of the Royal Asiatic Society of Great Britain and Ireland*, London: 1932, pp. 309-25.

Tuxen, P., 'In What Sense can We Call the Teachings of Nāgārjuna Negativism?', in *Journal of Oriental Research* 11, Madras, 1937, pp. 231-42.

Ui, H., *Jinna Chosaku no Kenkyū*, Tokyo, 1958.

——, *The Vaisheshika Philosophy, according to the Dashapādārthashāstra, Chinese Text with Introduction, Translation and Notes*, Varanasi, India, Chowkhamba Sanskrit Series Office, 1962 (The Sanskrit Series Studies, vol. XXII).

Uriūtsu Ryūshin, *Nāgārjuna Kenkyū ('A Study of Nāgārjuna')*, Tokyo, Shunjū-sha, 1985.

——, 'Nāgārjuna Kenkyū (1)' ('Studies on Nāgārjuna'), in *Meijō Daigaku Jimbun Kiyō* ('Bulletin of Humanities of Meijō College'), No. 14, 1973, pp. 23-40.

——, 'Nāgārjuna Kenkyū(2)', ('Studies on Nāgārjuna, 2'), in *Kyōto Joshi Daigaku Jimbun Ronsō* ('Collection of Treatises of Humanities of Women's University of Kyōto'), No. 23, 1974, pp. 134-60.

Vaidya, P.L., *Études sur Āryadeva et son Catuḥśataka*, Chapitres 8-16, Paris: Paul Geuthner, 1923.

Vasubandhu, *Trisvabhāvakārikā, see* Tola, F. and Dragonetti, C., 'The Trisvabhāvakārikā of Vasubandhu'.

Venkata Ramanan, K., *Nāgārjuna's Philosophy: As Presented in the Mahā-Prajñāpāramitā-Śāstra*, Delhi, Motilal Banarsidass, 1975.

Vetter, T., 'Die Lehre Nāgārjunas in the Mūla-madhyamakakārikās', in *Epiphanie des Heils*, Wien, 1982, pp. 87-108.

Vṛtti=Candrakīrti, Rigs pa drug cu paḥi ḥgrel pa (*Yuktiṣaṣṭikāvṛtti*), in *Sde-dge* edition: *Tibetan Tripiṭaka, Bstan Ḥgyur*, (*Dbu Ma*) 8 (*Ya*), Tokyo, 1978, No. 3864, (Ya. 1 b^1—30 b^6) and in *Peking* edition: vol. 98, No. 5265, pp. 169-83.

Wackernagel, J., *Altindische Grammatik*, Göttingen; Vandenhoeck & Ruprecht, 1957.

Warder, A.K., *Indian Buddhism*, Delhi, Motilal Banarsidass, 1970.

Wayman, A., 'Contributions to the Mādhyamika School of Buddhism', in *Journal of the American Oriental Society*, vol. 89, No. 1, 1969, pp. 141-52.

Williams, P.M., 'Some Aspects of Language and Construction in the Madhyamaka', in *Journal of Indian Philosophy*, vol. VIII, No. 1, March 1980, pp. 1-45.

Winternitz, M., *History of Indian Literature*, vol. II, *Buddhist Literature and Jaina Literature*, New Delhi, Oriental Books Reprint Corporation, 1972.

Yamaguchi, S., 'Ryūju ronshi no shichijū kūshō ge', ('The Seventy Stanzas on Voidness of Master Nāgārjuna'), in *Bukkyō Gaku Bunshū* ('Collection of Studies on Buddhism'), Tōkyō, 1972, vol. I, pp. 5-117.

——, 'Ryūju Ronshi no shichijū kūshō ge' ('The Seventy Stanzas on Voidness of Master Nāgārjuna'), in *Bukkyō Kenkyū* ('Studies on Buddhism'), Tōkyō, 1923-24, vol. V, Nos. 1, 3, 4; vol. VI, No. 1.

——, *Otani Gakuhō* ('Otani Bulletin'), vol. VII, No. 3, Kyōto, 1925, pp. 66-119.

——, *Chūgan Bukkyō Ronkō* ('Studies on Madhyamaka Buddhism'), Tōkyō-Kyōto, 1944; reprint. Tōkyo, 1965, pp. 29-109.

Yamakami, S., *Systems of Buddhistic Thought*, Calcutta: University of Calcutta, 1912, pp. 186-209.